MARIAN GOODMAN GALLERY

NEW YORK   24 WEST 57TH STREET NEW YORK NY 10019

John Baldessari   Movie Scripts / Art

THROUGH 22 NOVEMBER

LONDON   5–8 LOWER JOHN STREET LONDON W1F 9DY

Gerhard Richter

THROUGH 20 DECEMBER

PARIS   79 RUE DU TEMPLE 75003 PARIS

Giovanni Anselmo

THROUGH 20 DECEMBER

WWW.MARIANGOODMAN.COM

BERLINDE DE BRUYCKERE

27 NOVEMBER 2014 – 10 JANUARY 2015

23 SAVILE ROW
LONDON W1S 2ET
WWW.HAUSERWIRTH.COM

MET TERE HUID I, 2013   WAX, EPOXY, IRON, CLOTH, POLYESTER, ROPE   96×59×33 CM / 37 3/4×13×23 1/4 INCHES   PHOTO: MIRJAM DEVRIENDT

HAUSER & WIRTH
HAUSER & WIRTH SOMERSET

PIPILOTTI RIST

LONDON
WORRY WILL VANISH
27 NOVEMBER 2014 – 10 JANUARY 2015

SOMERSET
STAY STAMINA STAY
29 NOVEMBER 2014 – 22 FEBRUARY 2015

MERCY GARDEN RETOUR SKIN, 2014   AUDIO VIDEO INSTALLATION (VIDEO STILL, DETAIL)

SAINT LAURENT

JAMES EDWARD BAGSHAW

PARIS

Dior
FINE JEWELRY

CHER DIOR COLLECTION
Yellow gold, white gold, pink gold, diamonds, garnets,
rubies, tanzanite, sapphires and Paraiba tourmalines.

www.gladstonegallery.com

GLADSTONE GALLERY

ELIZABETH PEYTON
"DARK INCANDESCENCE"
NOVEMBER 18, 2014—JANUARY, 2015
12 RUE DU GRAND CERF
BRUSSELS

AHMED ALSOUDANI
NOVEMBER 14—DECEMBER 20, 2014
515 WEST 24TH STREET
NEW YORK

R. H. QUAYTMAN
"O TÓPICO, CHAPTER 27"
OCTOBER 31—DECEMBER 20, 2014
530 WEST 21ST STREET
NEW YORK

NOVEMBER
• DECEMBER
2014

35

James Hoff, *Blaster*, 2014

Courtesy
the artist and Pan

1

FRONT

——

COVER
Ella Kruglyanskaya, *The Trench*,
2013. Courtesy: the artist,
Gavin Brown's enterprise, New York,
and Kendall Koppe, Glasgow.
See: 'What's So Funny?' p. 106

frieze is printed in the UK and
published eight times a year by Frieze
Publishing Ltd. Unsolicited material
cannot be returned, though all
correspondence receives attention.
The views expressed in *frieze* are
not necessarily those of the publishers.

© 2014 issn No. 0962 0672.
Unauthorized reproduction of any
material strictly a no-no.

Exhibitions Europe

PETER DOIG
23 November 2014 – 22 March 2015
Fondation Beyeler, Basel

STAN DOUGLAS
7 November 2014 – 15 February 2015
The Fruitmarket Gallery, Edinburgh

ELMGREEN & DRAGSET: BIOGRAPHY
until 4 January 2015
Statens Museum for Kunst, Copenhagen

GRAYSON PERRY: WHO ARE YOU?
until 15 March 2015
National Portrait Gallery, London

CONRAD SHAWCROSS: TIMEPIECE
until 26 November 2014
Berwaldhallen, Stockholm

Exhibitions North & Central America

JULES DE BALINCOURT: FOCUS
15 November 2014 – 25 January 2015
Fort Worth Museum Of Art, Texas

YAYOI KUSAMA: INFINITE OBSESSION
until 18 January 2015
Museo Tamayo Arte Contemporaneo Internacional, Mexico City

WANGECHI MUTU: A FANTASTIC JOURNEY
until 7 December 2014
Mary and Leigh Block Museum of Art, Evanston, Illinois

CHRIS OFILI: NIGHT & DAY
until 1 February 2015
The New Museum, New York

ADRIANA VAREJÃO
19 November 2014 – 5 April 2015
The Institute of Contemporary Art, Boston

STEPHEN WILLATS: MAN FROM THE 21ST CENTURY
27 November 2014 – 22 March 2015
Museo Tamayo Arte Contemporaneo Internacional, Mexico City

Victoria Miro

victoria-miro.com

16 Wharf Road · London N1 7RW
14 St George Street · London W1S 1FE

2
MIDDLE
___

3
BACK
___

106

Vittorio Brodmann
Dropping poorly, 2014

Courtesy
the artist and Galerie Gregor
Staiger, Zurich

ROBERT GOBER
THE HEART IS NOT A METAPHOR

NOW ON VIEW

MoMA

THE MUSEUM OF MODERN ART
11 West 53 Street
MoMA.org

Hyundai Card

The exhibition is made possible by Hyundai Card.

Major support is provided by the Henry Luce Foundation, Maja Oeri and Hans Bodenmann, and Marie-Josée and Henry Kravis.

Additional funding is provided by Chara Schreyer, The Junior Associates of The Museum of Modern Art, Mr. and Mrs. Joseph Vandermolen, Ann and Mel Schaffer, and the MoMA Annual Exhibition Fund.

Robert Gober. *Untitled.* 1980–81. Oil on wood panel. Collection the artist. © 2014 Robert Gober. Photo: Ron Amstutz, courtesy Matthew Marks Gallery

As I write these words one warm September day at my desk in south-east England, the actor Shia LaBeouf is running 144 laps around the perimeter of the Stedelijk Museum, Amsterdam. Entitled *#METAMARATHON* (2014), this performance work is his contribution to 'Metamodernism – The Return of History', a 12-hour symposium that 'seeks to draw a cognitive map of our present in order to grasp the changing contours of our everyday lives'. Like the speakers in the auditorium – among them the anti-Cassandra of late capitalism, Francis Fukuyama, *frieze* co-editor Jörg Heiser and the artist Cally Spooner – I can't hear LaBeouf's grunts and footfalls, but nevertheless I find myself wondering what motivated the star of *Transformers III: Dark of the Moon* (2011) to stage his jog. Perhaps he simply took one look at Jay Z's Marina Abramović-inspired rap epic *Picasso Baby: A Performance Art Film* (2013) or, indeed, James Franco's various forays into contemporary art and thought: 'Well, that's got to be a whole lot better than standing in front of a green screen and pretending to emote at an anthropomorphic robot truck.'

Followers of the Dutch art scene might note that LaBeouf's performance bears a striking resemblance to Guido van der Werve's film *Nummer dertien, emotional poverty, Effugio C, You're always only half a day away* (2010–11), in which the artist runs approximately two and a half marathons around the perimeter of his house over the course of 12 hours. This is a work about endurance – not only that of its maker, but also that of his audience, who are asked to watch him

complete his feat in real time, without any of the compensatory pleasures afforded by seeing a Hollywood A-lister break a sweat. I'm a great admirer of Van der Werve, but even I couldn't hold out for more than a fraction of *Nummer dertien*. Then again, I felt much the same about LaBeouf's turn in *Indiana Jones and the Kingdom of the Crystal Skull* (2008). I check Twitter for news of *#METAMARATHON*. One user opines: '#ShiaLaBeouf so sexy in his purple spandex!' Another asks 'What Have U done 4 Situationism lately?' and links to a video of the actor warming up. In Amsterdam, LaBeouf continues to pound the pavement, accompanied by the artists Luke Turner and Nastja Säde Rönkkö, and a handful of fans. Perhaps he is thinking about the title of his 2010 film, *Wall Street: Money Never Sleeps*. Perhaps he is thinking about Guy Debord.

Before news of *#METAMA-RATHON* appeared in my social media feed this morning, I had planned to spend the day writing about the attention we pay to works of art, in what the novelist Adam Thirlwell (by neat coincidence another speaker at the 'Metamodernism' symposium) has called 'the distracted era'. I would have kicked off with a passage from Sir Kenneth's Clark's publication *Looking at Pictures* (1960), in which he asks: 'How many people can look at a picture for even long enough to peel an orange and eat it?' – a question that summons up the pleasing image of the tweedily patrician art historian, museum director and broadcaster settling down in front of a Nicolas Poussin or a Piero

della Francesca, with nothing to divert him save for a brimming bowl of fruit. Next, I would point to how the sheer volume of contemporary art production, not to mention the professional and social pressure on those who show, sell, collect, teach or write about it to demonstrate something close to omniscience, often makes the Clarkean minimum difficult to achieve. From there (perhaps via a study made by the Metropolitan Museum of Art, New York, claiming that gallery-goers spend on average 32.5 seconds looking at a single work, and a rather predictable broadside against anybody who thinks a biennial or art fair is the perfect spot to put their iPad's camera through its paces), I would segue into a paragraph on Karl Ove Knausgård's extraordinary sequence of six autobiographical novels, *Min Kamp* (My Struggle, 2009–11), in which distraction is both the enemy and the motor of the writer's achievement. Returning to visual art, I'd wonder if cohabiting with a work makes it more or less visible. It would seem appropriate, here, to mention Gilda Williams's witty new guidebook *How to Write About Contemporary Art* (2014), which is discussed by Orit Gat elsewhere in this issue.[1] Williams notes that Walter Benjamin's famous riff on Paul Klee's ink drawing *Angelus Novus* (1920), in his *Theses on the Philosophy of History* (1940), is more of a dazzling hallucinatory fantasy than an accurate description. Contra-Benjamin, Klee's image contains nothing in the way of 'a single catastrophe which keeps piling wreckage on wreckage' nor any evidence of a 'storm [...] blowing in from

Paradise', only what Williams rightly calls a 'modest fellow' with wings. Benjamin owned *Angelus Novus*, and presumably looked at it a great deal. A surfeit of attention – a surfeit of oranges peeled and eaten – might, it seems, distract us from what is actually there.

I was going to write about all of the above, but then I heard about *#METAMARATHON*. I check Twitter again. Somebody has posted a picture captioned: 'Francis Fukuyama a bemused bystander'. So I guess the author of *The End of History and the Last Man* (1992) has finished delivering his lecture and is watching the actor punish the tarmac. The account @Stedelijk informs its followers that 'Shia LaBeouf had a special meeting with performance artist Ulay!' before the event, and that there are 'Around 130 lapse [sic] to go'. In the first volume of *Min Kamp*, published in English as *A Death in the Family* (2009), Knausgård writes: 'The only thing I have learned from life is to endure it, never to question it, and to burn up the longing generated by this in writing. Where this ideal has come from I have no idea, and as I now see it before me, in black and white, it almost seems perverse.' Shia LaBeouf runs on.

1 Protocol dictates that I should mention Williams cites me in her book. It's not much more than a footnote focusing on a curatorial project (the answer to *How to Write About Contemporary Art* is not 'like Tom Morton'), so a footnote seems the right place to flag it up.

Tom Morton is a writer and curator, and a contributing editor of frieze. *His exhibition 'Panda Sex' opens at State of Concept, Athens, Greece, on 29 November.*

The Art of Distraction

Tom Morton

Movie stars, late capitalism and fragmented attention spans

frieze

Editors
Dan Fox
Jörg Heiser
Jennifer Higgie

Associate Editor
Christy Lange

Managing Editor
Rosalind Furness

Reviews Editor
Amy Sherlock

Assistant Editor
Paul Teasdale

Editorial Assistant
Paul Clinton

Art Director
Sonya Dyakova

Designer
Lorenz Klingebiel

Design Assistant
Amélie Bonhomme

Publishing Trainee
Laura Castagnini

Contributing Editors
Kirsty Bell, Barbara Casavecchia,
Colin Chinnery, Jonathan Griffin,
Shanay Jhaveri, Quinn Latimer,
Silas Martí, Tom Morton, Vivian Sky
Rehberg, Polly Staple, Robert Storr,
Sam Thorne, Jan Verwoert, Jochen Volz,
Carol Yinghua Lu

Publishing Directors
Amanda Sharp
Matthew Slotover

Publisher
Anna Starling

Commercial Director
Charlotte Robinson

Associate Publisher
Melissa Goldberg

Publishing Consultant
Mareike Dittmer

Advertising Representatives
Adair Lentini
Maria Bernal

Advertising Production Co-ordinator
Carianne Whitworth

Production Assistant
Asuka Sawa

Marketing & Circulation Manager
Sarah Hillier

Marketing Managers
Antoinette Tostivint
Rozzy Middleton

Head of Public Relations
Belinda Bowring

Public Relations Assistant
Nora Foster

Financial Director
Paul Rakkar

Financial Controller
Tim Guy

Berlin Intern
Weiland Rambke

—

To Advertise in *frieze*:
UK, Ireland, Australasia, Greece, Italy,
Portugal & Spain
Melissa Goldberg
melissa.goldberg@frieze.com
Carianne Whitworth
carianne.whitworth@frieze.com
tel +44 20 3372 6101

Rest of Europe, Middle East & Africa
Mareike Dittmer *mareike@frieze.com*
Maria Bernal *maria.bernal@frieze.com*
tel +49 30 2362 6504

USA, Canada, Central & South America
Adair Lentini *adair.lentini@frieze.com*
tel +1 212 463 7466

—

London office
1 Montclare Street, London E2 7EU, UK
tel +44 20 3372 6111 *info@frieze.com*

Berlin office
Zehdenicker Strasse 28, 10119 Berlin,
Germany tel +49 30 2362 6506
berlin@frieze.com

New York office
41 Union Square West, Suite 1623, New York,
NY 10003, USA tel +1 212 463 7461

Monika Aichele
Stormy Days,
2014

Issue 17 of *frieze d/e* focuses
on photography, with
profiles on **Peter Piller** and
Michael Schmidt as well as
a think piece by art historian
Susanne von Falkenhausen
on the role of images in
the age of digital circulation.
Elsewhere in the issue,
we have monographs on **Ellen
Gronemeyer** and **Jan Peter
Hammer** as well as reviews
of shows from Germany,
Austria and Switzerland.
frieze-magazin.de

VIDEO
We explore '**Network
Fatigue**' and intimacy in
artistic collaboration, and
we visit the Stedelijk's
Metamodernism symposium.
video.frieze.com

BLOG
Dan Kidner on the **London
Film Festival** and *Carol
Yinghua Lu* discusses the
Chinese art world's response
to the Hong Kong protests.
blog.frieze.com

FRIEZE SOCIAL MEDIA
Follow us to see what *frieze*
editors around the world have
been looking at:

f *frieze* and *frieze d/e*

⊙ frieze_magazine

▾ @frieze_magazine
@frieze_de

SUBSCRIBE
Subscribe to *frieze* and save
up to 40% off the cover price,
have it delivered to your door
and receive free access to
our full web archive (including
subscriber-only content).
Subscriptions from just £37.
shopcc.frieze.com

MELVIN EDWARDS

26 NOVEMBER 2014 – 17 JANUARY 2015

STEPHEN FRIEDMAN GALLERY

25-28 Old Burlington Street London W1S 3AN

stephenfriedman.com

O.T.T.

Is too much information ever enough?

Lynne Tillman

Daily, people receive warnings and pronouncements from all platforms. Threats are posed, facts cited, conspiracies exposed. Depending upon your P.O.V., some statements will be valid, dubious or just plain lies. Generally, beliefs exist unquestioned, though belief itself should be tested by absolutism, dogmatism and hyperbole.

Grand claims rarely escape flimsiness, worse, ludicrousness. But here's one: Oscar Wilde, king of the ludic, was one such grandee escape artist; so too was playwright, director and actor Charles Ludlam (founder, in 1967, of The Ridiculous Theatrical Company). In *Secret Lives of the Sexists* (1982), Ludlam played a feminist at a consciousness-raising session, who happily tells her group: 'And *I* have orgasms in my face.' Ludlam hilariously enacted a fierce facial orgasm. These wits, self-conscious parodists, Ludlam and Wilde, queried high seriousness with high ridicule, asking: What is *The Importance of Being Earnest*?

Theodor Adorno wrote: 'Today only exaggeration per se can be the medium for truth.' Likely, he was recalling the hideous effectiveness of Nazi propaganda, fostered by Joseph Goebbels. Now, sweeping pronouncements do provoke attention. TV's talking heads – whatever their politics – bark like scared dogs, to alarm their faithful. These speakers exaggerate with affect, vocal emphases and gestures called 'colour'. Repetition, which Goebbels relied on because it worked, still works. Seen that way, Gertrude Stein's 'Rose is a rose is a rose is a rose' shows that naming the world of things is more worrying.

In the arts, exaggeration appears as, 'So-and-so is the most important artist,' or 'X is the greatest writer of the 20th century.' A person I admire told me they thought Samuel Beckett was, and I thought,

quite ordinarily: Franz Kafka? Virginia Woolf? But I said aloud, 'Why does it matter?'

Remember the game: Which ten books would you take to a desert island? What a question. People create weird problems for themselves. People also easily count to ten and hold ten names in memory. But to hold one thought in mind that contradicts another valid and powerful one, that's a more unusual, even dangerous proposition. It makes political decisions and ethical judgments achingly complex. Reducing choice – about websites, movies, books, blogs, etc. – is functional, because of the plethora of stuff. Also, holding principles, which appears worthy, reduces choice: acting on principle, you don't have to think.

People want order in their lives and declare stuff worthless. That rejectamenta often comes on an end-of-the-year list. I don't make those lists, but do imagine, at year's end, a different life, forever called a simple life, which no one leads. In mine, I live near the ocean and, every morning, I walk to a boardwalk or sit at a café and see, in the distance, the ever-tantalizing horizon. Soon I might try to see in front of me, like the ocean, my bookshelves. Each book sits, spine out, so I can find it at a glance. Content, I imaginatively move to my desk, where everything has its place (a wonderful image, 'everything has its place'). I'm told visualizing helps, but the ability to form a picture, in an 'image-glutted' culture, comes too easily.

I read my diary of the year, but it isn't a real diary, just a Filofax where I've written what I need to do, which events to attend and occasional notes. Many crossings-out and black 'x's darken the pages: I often don't do what I'm meant to do. Sometimes, in disgust, I use white-out to neaten the page. The wet white stuff sticks to another page. What a mess, trying to create order.

In a way, the differences between blogs and diaries represent our shifting time and changing sensibilities. Diaries keep secret thoughts, but secrets are disappearing, revamped by reality TV and online self-exposure. Many tell everything and have instant opinions. Our new society doesn't seem to cherish secrets, or maybe believes that transparency is truth, and secrets are wrong. Or maybe we don't know why a secret should exist at all.

The realms of personal and social overlap, slices of a giant Venn diagram called an individual: the lines blur constantly. Philosophical questions ask of secrets to explain themselves. They have been part of the currency of social relations forever, it seems, so what are the ethics of secrets? Or, a test question:

compare secrets with gossip. Social regulators, self-surveillance, the spy within, the spy without. To me, this is fascinating mental fodder.

It's fascinating but alarming, the amount of spying and surveillance my government does. And how unsurprising the exposure was, how normal it all seems, already.

Lynne Tillman lives in New York, USA. Her most recent collection of essays, What Would Lynne Tillman Do?, *was published in April. She is currently at work on a new novel,* Men and Apparitions.

Leandro Katz
Charles Ludlam, 1970

Courtesy
the artist and Henrique Faria,
New York and Buenos Aires

SPRÜTH MAGERS BERLIN LONDON

ORANIENBURGER STRASSE 18   D-10178 BERLIN   P+49(0)30 2888 4030   F+49(0)30 2888 40352

THOMAS SCHEIBITZ
RADIOPICTURES
SEPTEMBER – NOVEMBER 2014

THOMAS DEMAND
DAILIES 2008 – 2014
SEPTEMBER – NOVEMBER 2014

ARTE POVERA AND 'MULTIPLI', TORINO 1970 – 1975
CURATED BY ELENA RE
SEPTEMBER – JANUARY 2015

LOUISE LAWLER
NO DRONES
NOVEMBER – JANUARY 2015

ROBERT ELFGEN
I WISH MY PICTURES
NOVEMBER – JANUARY 2015

SPRÜTH MAGERS BERLIN LONDON

7A GRAFTON STREET LONDON, W1S 4EJ UNITED KINGDOM P+44(0)20 7408 1613 F+44(0)20 7499 4531

ANDRO WEKUA
SOME PHEASANTS IN SINGULARITY
OCTOBER – NOVEMBER 2014

JOSEPH KOSUTH
'AMNESIA'
A SURVEY OF NEON WORKS 1965 – 2012
NOVEMBER – FEBRUARY 2015

ANALIA SABAN
FEBRUARY – MARCH 2015

Abderrahmane Sissako
Timbuktu, 2014

In May this year, during a press conference at the Cannes Film Festival for his Palme d'Or-shortlisted film *Timbuktu* (2014), Mauritanian-born director Abderrahmane Sissako broke down and cried. *Timbuktu*, Sissako's fourth feature since *La Vie sur Terre* (Life on Earth, 1998), is a spare and elegiac film. It tells the story of a close-knit Tuareg cattle-herding family who – after a fatal dispute between the family patriarch, Kidane, and a fisherman who kills his cow called 'GPS' – get drawn into a wider cataclysm. In 2012, Al Qaeda-linked jihadists took over vast swathes of Northern Mali and introduced a brutal form of Islam intolerant of Mali's mystical, ascetic and deeply musical Sufi traditions. People were lashed; video games, music and football were banned; and, in Timbuktu, an intellectual and spiritual capital for Islam in Africa, they destroyed parts of a 15th-century mosque and mausoleums of revered holy men.

During the Cannes press conference, Sissako, who lives in Paris, remarked that the events in Mali had flown under the radar of the international press. 'We remain increasingly indifferent in the face of horror,' he stated. In many respects, *Timbuktu* is an act

of idiosyncratic witnessing, one in which Sissako's brand of political reportage is modulated by his allusive approach to visual storytelling. Sissako is not the first African filmmaker to tackle Islam: Ousmane Sembène, the Senegalese director who Sissako unsuccessfully solicited to appear in his third feature, *Bamako* (2006), did the same in his controversial film *Ceddo* (1977). 'However much assistance may be given to Africa by the Arab countries, Africans are quite clear among themselves that Islam is an imposed religion,' stated Sembène in 1978. He regarded Catholicism with similar disdain.

Timbuktu is far less strident. Sissako's foreign jihadists are fallible, prone to lust and vanity. 'In every being there is a complexity, there is the good and the bad,' remarked Sissako in Cannes. 'A jihadist is someone we can see ourselves in.' Arguably, religion is not the main subject of *Timbuktu*; the film is a celebration of Mali's remarkably tolerant culture. Born in 1961 in the market town of Kiffa, Sissako grew up with his engineer father in Bamako, Mali's ancient riverside capital. He was 19 when he returned to Mauritania to live with his mother in Nouakchott, an unromantic coastal city founded in 1957.

Sissako's return forms the subject of his second feature, *Heremakono* (Waiting for Happiness, 2002), a study of alienation, exile and intergenerational friendship brilliantly performed by amateurs. The film's action is bracketed by the arrival and departure of bookish Abdallah, whose existential malaise is evident throughout. 'I had lost my bearings,' Sissako told philosopher and essayist Kwame Anthony Appiah in a 2003 interview. Cut off from his friends and his language, Sissako killed time by playing table tennis and reading literature at a Russian cultural centre. He also became 'more observant' of his surroundings and 'developed a keener sense of the importance of body language'. *Timbuktu* bears this out. The scene in which Kidane confronts the fisherman is observed through one long uninterrupted shot. A scuffle ensues, followed by a gunshot. For over half a minute, nothing happens in the off-yellow liquid landscape; only birds chirp. Suddenly, Kidane stands up. The future is open to him: he flees.

Mood is important in Sissako's elliptical films, image too. Since graduating from Moscow's prestigious Gerasimov Institute

of Cinematography, Sissako has collaborated with important cinematographers, notably Georgi Rerberg, who worked on Andrei Tarkovsky's *Stalker* (1979). *Heremakono* was shot by Jacques Besse, who also worked on *La petite vendeuse de soleil* (The Little Girl Who Sold the Sun, 1999), Senegalese auteur Djibril Diop Mambéty's melancholy yet triumphant final film. His latest feature was shot by Sofian El Fani, the cameraman on Tunisian director Abdellatif Kechiche's 2013 Palme d'Or-winning film *Blue Is the Warmest Colour*. The connections are revealing – and validate a remark Sembène made at a hotel in Ouagadougou when the pair first met in 1991. Sissako was showing his student film at the local film festival. Returning to his hotel after an all-night bender, he was spotted by the older director at breakfast. 'I'm sure this guy will go very far,' quipped Sembène, having mistaken Sissako's early-morning breakfast appearance for professional brio. But he was right.

Sean O'Toole is a writer and co-editor of CityScapes, *a critical journal for urban enquiry. He lives in Cape Town, South Africa.*

Sean O'Toole

Being Observant

The films of Abderrahmane Sissako

Richard Serra

Vertical and Horizontal Reversals

November 7 - December 20, 2014

David Zwirner

537 West 20th Street
New York, NY 10011
212 517 8677
davidzwirner.com

Productive Anguish

Kaelen Wilson-Goldie

How to survive exile

On a quiet Sunday afternoon in September, Samer Saem Eldahr – a 25-year-old artist from the Syrian city of Aleppo – was sitting in a flat with no furniture, sketching out three possible visions for the future. In the first, he would make a fourth album under the name Hello Psychaleppo, further developing the syncretic style of electro-*shaabi* music he had pioneered that elides trip-hop, gritty dance music and *tarab*. In the second, he would study traditional Bedouin music until he could compose his own, updated for the digital age. In the third, he would delve into the prevalence of birds in Arabic culture, drawing on the region's heritage to create something new.

Eldahr studied painting in a strict academic setting, but he has been messing around with music since he was a child. At five, his older brother introduced him to Iron Maiden and AC/DC. At 12, he learned classical Arabic music. When he heard Dr. Dre for the first time, he became a rapper, briefly, and later played in bands, doing vocals, on guitar, whatever he could.

But, in terms of shaping a life around work, Eldahr stuck to painting. When the uprising in Syria erupted into the Battle of Aleppo two years ago, his parents dispatched him to Beirut. At home, no galleries were open and the situation across Syria was becoming too devastating to describe. What was meant to be a quick trip turned into a record deal, a marriage and an indefinite stay. Eldahr exhibited his paintings, made two albums and began

performing live in Beirut, Cairo and Paris.

Surrounded by three electric guitars, an *oud*, two MacBooks, a Marshall amp and a keyboard, Eldahr explained to me in the briefest of terms that he left Syria for his safety, but also for his career – which seemed like a shorthand way of saying the possibility of any kind of future at all. As it happened, I visited Eldahr just a few weeks after meeting Khaled Malas, a 33-year-old architect who had devised an ingenious project for Rem Koolhaas's architecture biennale in Venice. 'Excavating the Sky' (2014) is both a collection of stories covering 100 years of flight from Syria and a 'displaced Syrian pavilion': a renegade project consisting of a 120-metre-deep well in an undisclosed location in Syria which supplies potable water to a community of 15,000 people who are both out of government control and unmoved by militant Islamic rule. Describing the work, Malas uses the words resistance, alchemy and hope.

A few months prior to speaking with Malas, I had met Charif Kiwan, a filmmaker in his 40s who is the spokesman for Abounaddara, an anonymous collective that posts a new (often brilliant, often bracing) video online every Friday, chronicling the details of daily life in Syria through three and a half years of open revolt.

That these three men, who represent three different examples of artists in exile, have made the best work I've seen or heard

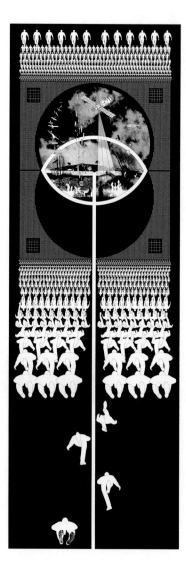

Khaled Malas
Drawing of a Well (from 'Excavating the Sky'), 2014

this year speaks to the cruel inheritance of the Syrian conflict, which, for all its horrors, has enriched Lebanon's cultural life. Relations between the two countries are gruesomely complex. Few exceptional thinkers have found common ground: the late filmmaker Omar Amiralay, the intellectual Yassin al-Haj Saleh, and the journalist Samir Kassir, who was assassinated in 2005, and probably lost his life for appealing to the Syrian opposition (the case is one of many that remain unsolved). The Lebanese have not been uniformly welcoming to the million-plus refugees in their midst.

In a lecture, later printed in the essay collection *Representations of the Intellectual* (1994), Edward Said described exile as 'productive anguish'. In another lecture, posthumously anthologized in *Between Parentheses* (2011), Roberto Bolaño considered exile, at its best, synonymous with courage. The responses of both writers are apt in relation to Syria, given the rage and violence they captured and conveyed. Said was nostalgic. Bolaño was romantic. Eldahr, Malas and Kiwan are, above all, determined to continue creating and responding. Eldahr told me brightly that, for all the uncertainty of his situation, he was never bored. To make new work and imagine sharing it was more than an affirmation of the future. It was the most basic, mind-blowing thrill of being alive.

Kaelen Wilson-Goldie is a writer who lives in Beirut, Lebanon.

Neo Rauch
At the Well
November 6 - December 20, 2014

David Zwirner
533 West 19th Street
New York, NY 10011
212 727 2070
davidzwirner.com

Franz West

November 6 - December 13, 2014

David Zwirner

537 West 20th Street
New York, NY 10011
212 517 8677
davidzwirner.com

Christopher Williams

November 6 - December 20, 2014

David Zwirner

525 West 19th Street
New York, NY 10011
212 727 2070
davidzwirner.com

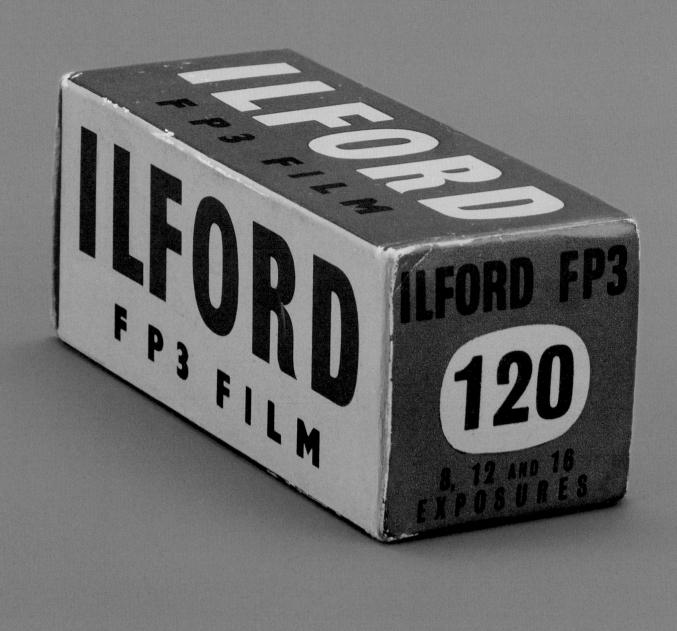

MORGAN FISHER
MAUREEN PALEY. 21 HERALD STREET, LONDON E2 6JT +44 (0)20 7729 4112 INFO@MAUREENPALEY.COM WWW.MAUREENPALEY.COM

PAST PRESENT. PRESENT PAST.

24 NOVEMBER 2014 – 20 JANUARY 2015

When I was a child, my French grandfather would take me to the park at Saint-Cloud in Paris to visit the 'standard metre', a metal bar kept at a constant temperature in a vault buried deep under the hill. It was a source of great amusement to us that the British had tricked the French into ratifying the British meridian at Greenwich via the promise of recognizing the metal metre as a standard (which they still haven't done more than 200 years later). I am still amazed by the vastness of the project of standardizing units and measures using handmade objects in velvet-lined cases.

I have often travelled to visit particular sites and buildings, initially inspired by my parents' apparently limitless enthusiasm for cultural destinations. At some point in the late 1970s, we visited the Maeght Foundation in Saint-Paul de Vence. I became obsessed with Alexander Calder's *Circus* (1926–31), which I saw there; much later, I paid homage to the work again at the Whitney Museum of American Art after they acquired it. Something about how it was made from bits of leftover crap is fascinating; every character hinted at a recognizable form, which came to life when made to perform by Calder's bear-like hands. *Circus* is endless and fantastic; Calder carried it around the world in two battered suitcases and never really considered it an artwork, and yet he worked on it for much of his life. It affected me in ways that the French puppet theatre, Théâtre de Guignol, never did.

On visits to Paris, our grandmother (who did not live with nor talk to the grandfather mentioned above) would hypnotize us with tales of her youth in Alexandria aided by the mysterious objects that populated the exquisite Bauhaus interior of her home. Her best friend, the photographer Denise Colomb, used to tell us how she'd managed to convince Antonin Artaud to have his first portrait taken, and that compassionate image formed my first encounter with him.

One of my innumerable 'aunts', who kept a Pablo Picasso in her cupboard, also lived in Saint-Cloud. One day, at a neighbour's house-warming party, a giraffe's head suddenly appeared, framed through the first-floor windows above a billowing silk curtain. For some strange reason, the new neighbours had hired it to celebrate their even stranger house: the swimming pool was on the roof, its columns went in different directions and the curtains billowed outside the building. The next time I saw those curtains was in a book, when I was at architecture school; only then did I realize that they belonged to the Villa dall'Ava, one of Rem Koolhaas's first domestic builds. I was studying at the Architectural Association School in London, where the architects Alison and Peter Smithson were, at the time, something of a cult. The Smithsons had, in fact, banned curtains from their Economist Plaza in London, so as not to interfere with the building's lines. The significance of curtains struck me again during trips to the Middle East, when I'd often be stuck on the women's side of the fabric divide while visiting mosques. Those curtains always seemed somewhat tokenistic, hanging loosely and carelessly, never actually blocking the view, and yet defining boundaries.

While studying, I quickly realized I was much more committed to the conversations that the theorist Mark Cousins and the architect Cedric Price had in the bar than to designing buildings myself. My first London years were heavily influenced by daytime cinema visits and late nights. I was mesmerized by the mysterious associative fragments of Chris Marker's *Sans Soleil* (1983), Andrei Tarkovsky's *The Sacrifice* (1986), Pier Paolo Pasolini's *Teorema* (1968), Luchino Visconti's *La Terra Trema* (The Earth Trembles, 1948), and the clock scene in Wong Kar Wai's *Days of Being Wild* (1990). I was reading bits of Artaud, Georges Bataille, Walter Benjamin, Beatriz Colomina, Luigi Pirandello and Manfredo Tafuri, dancing to Broken Beat, listening to Steve Reich's *Music for Pieces of Wood* (1995), attempting to decipher Henri Michaux's squiggles and navigating London using the techniques I had learned from the Situationist International. As a result of all of this, I never designed a single building and

Céline Condorelli

Life in Fragments

Conversations, buildings, books and films

Rem Koolhaas
Villa dall'Ava, Paris,
1991

Courtesy: OMA; photograph: Peter Aaron/OTTO

One summer, I went to see Malmö's Eastern Cemetery, in southern Sweden, and fell in love with the fittings of the Flower Kiosk, designed by Sigurd Lewerentz.

made myself unemployable in that field forever. Full of questions about how to position myself, I visited the film director Jean-Marie Straub, who gave me precious advice: walk around a place three times and find the strategic point from which you can see something without destroying its mystery. 'There is nothing', he said, 'but topography.'

It was at the Architectural Association that I met Dominic Cullinan; I don't remember how I ended up being shown around the houses that he built with his friend Ivan Harbour, from the leftovers of building sites using a lot of goodwill, on what was then known as 'crack alley' in Dalston, east London. The buildings were designed around an exuberant concrete staircase, a double helix cast *in situ* like some sort of homemade baroque device, functioning separately for each house and yet beautifully complicating the properties' boundaries.

I once dragged a friend hundreds of kilometres on a detour across America to go to Marfa, Texas, but it's Donald Judd's car that has stuck with me. He owned a jeep, which he adapted to his particular needs with a monstrous brushed-steel box containing cooking and storage facilities. That same year, I slept in a car several nights in a row (I was 20 and couldn't even legally drink in the US), on a trip to track down Louis Khan's villas around Philadelphia. I used Khan's enormous monograph as a guidebook and, through sheer luck or perseverance, managed to get invited inside all of the properties. I was enchanted by an element in one particular house: a bench inserted into a window wall that allowed you to sit both in the corner of the building and seemingly in the garden. I have never forgotten how tenderly people spoke of living in Khan's buildings. It was something I encountered again in the Kimbell Art Museum in Fort Worth, Texas, which he also designed: the shop's cashier almost made me cry describing

how much she loved sitting beneath the concealed skylight that washed sunlight down the concrete walls. I was won over by this intimacy with the things that surround a life, and how they depend on their relationships to other things (which is true of all things, but with furniture and objects it becomes intentional, as Louise Lawler's photographs have shown me). Of course, I had known this through the almost talismanic power of certain objects, present or missing, that related to my scattered family and its complicated history. However, I still didn't really trust the notion of the 'genius creator'.

Then, one summer, I went to see Malmö's Eastern Cemetery, in southern Sweden, and fell in love with the fittings of the Flower Kiosk, which was designed by Sigurd Lewerentz. Not much more than a shell, it wears everything related to use on its concrete skin: electric wires and lighting fold out like line drawings on the ceiling and walls, doorframes are attached directly onto surfaces and windows are glass panels fixed onto openings. This revealed a path for me that seemed worth following, between necessity and delight.

There is something apparently passive about functional objects, as if they are always waiting and wanting, and yet they structure gestures and form possible approaches. I am grateful to Martha Rosler's video *Semiotics of the Kitchen* (1975) for exposing domestic objects as instruments of normalization, and for her refusal to be determined by them. But it is always hard to clarify in what way our habits form our environment, or whether it is existing conditions that, in fact, shape our actions. The elements of the built environment are always prepositions: they speak with, in, on, by, of – like the work of artists such as Mierle Laderman Ukeles and Rita McBride.

I have always been biased towards the fragment, the elements of larger wholes. In *Saint Jerome in his Study*

(c. 1475), by Antonello da Messina, it is the unrealizable (as I discovered during several attempts to reconstruct it) architectural dias on which the saint sits at his desk that I keep lingering on, both as material and conceptual form – it organizes the painting and the architecture of the interior, but it also delimits the figure of the intellectual, surrounded by 'cats and books' (as Georges Perec might have it) in solitary contemplation. Through this painting, I learned that the domestication of space happens by means of its being inscribed (here, both the inscription of the book and of the furniture). It is the part, the segment, that allows space to be habitable, which is not communicated as knowledge but as the possibility for life.

Perhaps this explains my particular affection for Roland Barthes's *A Lover's Discourse: Fragments* (1977), which was given to me by the filmmaker Eyal Sivan at exactly the right moment. In it, I found a voice, a tone and a position which undoes that most cruel of intellectual fallacies: analytical distance. The book explicitly foregrounds its construction and, in this way, exposes its own ambiguity, its fundamentally biased and deceptive angle and the fact that – just like art – any work is always part of the world it attempts to address.

Céline Condorelli lives in London, UK. In 2014, she had solo exhibitions at the Chisenhale Gallery, London, and GfZK, Leipzig, Germany, and her work has been included in shows at MuHKA, Antwerp, Belgium; Van Abbemuseum, Eindhoven, the Netherlands; Beirut Art Center, Lebanon; and 21er Haus, Vienna, Austria. Her solo show at Hangar Bicocca, Milan, Italy, opens 10 December and runs until May 2015.

Sigurd Lewerentz
Flower Kiosk at the Eastern
Cemetery, Malmö

HOWARD HODGKIN

Indian Waves

November 28, 2014 – January 31, 2015

GAGOSIAN GALLERY

17–19 Davies Street
London W1K 3DE
+44 207 493 3020
www.gagosian.com

Turbulent Waters, 1990–91, hand-painted gouache on intaglio impressed Khadi paper, 71 × 93 cm

Andy Warhol

1950s Drawings

November 20 – December 20, 2014

Anton Kern Gallery

Art Basel Miami Beach

Booth C03

December 4 – 7, 2014

Anton Kern Gallery   532 West 20th Street   New York NY 10011   T: 212.367.9663   F: 212.367.8135   antonkerngallery.com

Rare Minds

The dark, unsettling feminism of Jacqueline Rose

In times of crisis, what is the political efficacy of dwelling in shadows? Of remaining with the fine line that separates doubt from certainty, sanity from mental oblivion? Jacqueline Rose's work has always tarried with the ambiguous. Her *Sexuality in the Field of Vision* (1986) provided a highly influential and admirably clear account of the fraught theoretical and political entanglement between psychoanalysis and feminism. While in *The Haunting of Sylvia Plath* (1991) she fathomed the ambiguity of literary identity, writing: 'Plath hovers between the furthest poles of positive and negative appraisal; she hovers in the space of what is most extreme, most violent, about appraisal, valuation, about moral and literary assessment as such.' Rose has also written on Palestinian struggles and Israeli violence. In 2007, in response to the common charge of being a 'self-hating Jew', she claimed: 'I hate neither myself nor Israel when I criticize the policies of the state. I hate what the Israeli government is doing, and has been doing for a very long time, to the Palestinians and to itself.' With *Albertine* (2002), Rose published a book of fiction imagined from the standpoint of Marcel Proust's captive; and she has examined children's fiction in *The Case of Peter Pan or the Impossibility of Children's Fiction* (1984).

The stylistic paradox of Rose's *oeuvre* as a whole is played out in the enjoyable tension between a crystalline lucidity, clear political conviction and a deeper desire to adhere to what is most difficult, most unsettling, most recalcitrant. Rose remains that rare mind: as at home in academic prose as in fiction, public intellectual debate or, especially, in the gaps that usually – and unfortunately – separate these spheres from one another. She is, above all, an essayist who seeks not to tidy away but to expose 'the overlooked, the rejected, the unseen', as she puts it in her new book, *Women in Dark Times* (2014).

Charlotte Salomon
Leben? oder Theater? (Life? Or Theatre?, detail), 1940–42

Courtesy
Collection Jewish Historical Museum, Amsterdam;
© Charlotte Salomon Foundation, Charlotte Salomon®

Nina Power

Rosa Luxemburg
addressing a meeting in
Stuttgart, 1907

Rose's latest work, at first glance, contains a rather bizarre collection of themes – some historical, some artistic, some political. There is a chapter each on three 'stars', as she calls them: Rosa Luxemburg, the artist Charlotte Salomon and Marilyn Monroe; a section on the so-called 'honour killings' of Shafilea Ahmed and Heshu Yones in the UK, and Fadime Sahindal in Sweden; and a final section, entitled 'Living', that discusses three contemporary female artists: Yael Bartana, Thérèse Oulton and Esther Shalev-Gerz. It is a book clearly written from the standpoint of magisterial self-confidence, not only in the material but also in the not initially obvious connections between these figures.

What binds these stories together is a kind of conceptual, two-component glue: firstly, Rose's urgent declaration that we

are in dire need of 'a scandalous feminism', which embraces 'without inhibition the most painful, outrageous aspects of the human heart, giving them their place at the very core of the world that feminism wants to create', and, secondly, that these are all stories that refuse victimhood at the very point at which oppression and death are most intertwined.

That all of Rose's three 'stars' are murdered or pushed towards death (Luxemburg was shot alongside Karl Liebknecht by the Freikorps in 1919, Salomon – five months pregnant – died in Auschwitz, and Monroe's death is still shrouded in mystery) does not make them, for her, 'victims'. Instead, they are 'truth-tellers who lay bare the ugly secrets of the consensus'. In Luxemburg's case, this is achieved through revolutionary enthusiasm. Rose quotes

her prison letter that contains the line: 'To be a human being is the main thing above all else […] And that means to be firm and clear and cheerful, yes cheerful in spite of everything and anything because howling is the business of the weak.' In Salomon's case, truth is laid bare through 'painting against terror', as Rose writes in regard to Salomon's epic *Leben? oder Theater?* (Life? Or Theatre?, 1940–42), which consists of over 700 gouaches that intertwine text, images and musical scores. Salomon's 'counter-fascist ethic' is her 'hymn to freedom', not only against the rising Nazi threat but also against the many suicides of family members, including her mother and grandmother, and her own fear of madness. Rose is at her strongest in the Salomon chapter, weaving together art criticism with political history, biography with detailed analysis of individual sections of the work. She notes, for example, that there is no black in any of Salomon's paintings, so that the painted darkness forms a continuum with colour, rather than setting up opposites: 'The most sombre moments are in visual continuum with the rest of her life.'

The chapter on honour killings might appear to be something of a leap, were it not for the fact that, as Rose points out, the

same question applies: 'How to think of women as subjected but not – solely – the victims of their lives?' Directly confronting the horror of these killings, as well as the opportunistic use made of them by racist media narratives, Rose seeks to go to the heart of the difficulties inherent in explaining and punishing these kinds of murders: 'The problem goes deeper [than the law],' she writes, and 'into the darkest sexual recesses of the mind where – historical evidence suggests – neither love nor reason has ever found it easy to follow.' Rose's part-etymological, part-political discussion of the concepts of 'shame', 'honour' and 'purity' in a variety of languages does much to move the discussion on and away from reactionary tropes of 'moderate' and 'extremist' Islam and purely 'cultural' non-explanations.

The final section on the three contemporary artists Bartana, Oulton and Shalev-Gerz, is both an original contribution to art-historical scholarship and an opportunity to reiterate the claims Rose has been making throughout the book. Indeed, often she will repeat a phrase from one of her 'stars' at various junctures – for example Monroe's perhaps surprising claim that: 'Everyone has violence in them. I am violent.' – as if unable and unwilling simply to have done with the idea at hand. That these notions circulate around violence, a lack of innocence, ambiguity, madness, emotional existence and creativity testifies not only to Rose's long-term psychoanalytically inflected passions, but also to the complexity of the world as it really is, and not how we might optimistically want it to be. Rose's dark, unsettling feminism does not turn away from injustice but cuts into its deepest, most troubling core.

Nina Power is a senior lecturer in philosophy at Roehampton University, London, UK, and the author of One Dimensional Woman *(2009).*

Rose urgently declares that we need 'a scandalous feminism' which embraces 'the most painful, outrageous aspects of the human heart'.

Art & Language
Nobody Spoke

LISSON GALLERY

14 November 2014 — 17 January 2015
52 Bell Street, London
lissongallery.com

Prada Classic #4

Prada: A cosmos on its own
composed of heavenly bodies
set in a complex orbit.
A universe of contradictions
and endless elaborations —
noble causes and base temptations —
where idealism meets vanity,
intelligence meets passion,
fashion meets fiction.
Welcome to the Pradasphere,
Prada Classic #4.

prada.com

PRADA

NOVEMBER 22, 2014 TO JANUARY 24, 2015
ALEX HUBBARD
MAAG AREAL

NOVEMBER 22, 2014 TO JANUARY 24, 2015
CANDIDA HÖFER
LÖWENBRÄU AREAL

NOVEMBER 22, 2014 TO JANUARY 24, 2015
JUSTIN MATHERLY
OSCAR MURILLO
DAVID OSTROWSKI
TOBIAS PILS
LÖWENBRÄU AREAL

GALERIE EVA PRESENHUBER

MAAG AREAL
ZAHNRADSTR. 21, CH-8005 ZURICH
TEL: +41 (0) 43 444 70 50 / FAX: +41 (0) 43 444 70 60
OPENING HOURS: TUE-FRI 10-6, SAT 11-5

LÖWENBRÄU AREAL
LIMMATSTR. 270, CH-8005 ZURICH
TEL: +41 (0) 44 515 78 50 / FAX: +41 (0) 43 444 70 60
OPENING HOURS: TUE-FRI 11-6, SAT 11-5

WWW.PRESENHUBER.COM

Stuxnet No. 1
2014

All images courtesy
the artist and Callicoon Fine
Arts, New York

Music

Andy Battaglia

James Hoff's music goes viral

To infect, contaminate and corrupt – the language of the virus is unstinting and severe. Viruses attack or bind or otherwise besiege their targets, which stand little chance of going unharmed. Even as a metaphor, the virus screams of wreckage and ruination: it has destruction written into its code; it is an exterminating agent.

New York-based artist and musician James Hoff sees the virus as something less frightful. *Blaster* (2014), Hoff's latest LP for the enterprising electronic music label PAN, is a radical incursion into, and a tribute of sorts to, the culture of dance music. Dance music demands innovation, or at least likes to think it does, and Hoff's work serves as both a challenge and an offering to a movement anxious for mutation by whatever means. The album begins with a blast of noise, a static-slathered howl. Thirty seconds is a long spell to endure with sound operating at such extremes. But then beats begin, reminiscent of the so-called 'glitch' aesthetic of machines on the fritz, but more frenetic and fully formed. Fans of the heady intelligent dance music (IDM) of the late 1990s and early 2000s will hear much to appreciate, but *Blaster* is less fussy and preoccupied with the mastery of craft; rather, it's conceptual and curious in terms of its execution.

There's no extracting the concept from the commodity in any of Hoff's many strands of work. The seven main tracks of *Blaster* were all created by subjecting samples to computer viruses. From hackers and shadowy online archives – most of them 'found surreptitiously', in his words – Hoff has amassed a store of operational viruses with names such as Stuxnet, ILOVEYOU and Anna Kournikova. (He is particularly fond of the 'Morris Worm' for its evocation, for him at least, of the artist Robert Morris.) Using Hex Editor software, Hoff distills his sound files down to their arcane source codes and positions the letters and numbers of virus codes at various junctures throughout – a sort of subtextual punctuation of destruction.

Dance music demands innovation and Hoff's work serves as both a challenge and an offering to a movement anxious for mutation by whatever means.

But 'destruction' puts too fine a point on music that proves, if not pleasurable, at least very enticing for the strangeness of its effects. On *Blaster*, rhythms move and progress with a recognizable suggestion of dance music, even as they splay apart and explode. Dance floors at the most hardline techno clubs in Berlin could be made to move with certain of its patterns, but then, just as the movement starts to coalesce, it might fall into states of utter confusion.

The same effect finds form in another of Hoff's viral sound works, a free downloadable collection of mangled telephone ringtones assembled under the title *I Just Called to Say ILOVEYOU* (2013). Using stock ringtone sounds from Apple's hack-averse iPhone, he infected all the old familiars (the 'marimba', for instance, or the vintage one that sounds like a telephone bell) so that they detonate into brusque ruptures of digital noise. Take a call in a public place on a phone with one of Hoff's ringtones installed, and you'll be stared at with wide eyes.

Hoff's viral experiments are not confined to sound. He has applied a similar process to painting, in a series of striking works that strive to further abstract the notion of abstraction itself. The earliest of them, from his 'Concept' series, which he began last year, enlist a rudimentary virus known as Concept that feasted on software for Microsoft Word. 'Everyone kept calling me a conceptual painter,' Hoff says, 'so I decided to make what I considered a conceptual painting.' His 'Stuxnet' series (2013–ongoing), numbering around a dozen paintings so far, uses the more imposing virus of the same name to transform monochromatic images into fields of streaking colour, with an effect pitched peculiarly between hi-tech spectacle and Gerhard Richter-esque meditation.

This process also figured in *Morris Worm No. 1* (2013), an architectural intervention for which Hoff removed pieces of a wall at Kunsthall Oslo. Coordinates for the cutting were arrived at by infecting the source code of a photograph of the wall with Hoff's beloved Morris Worm, and then carving into the wall according to the corrupted result.

In addition to the virus works and related syndrome paintings (spare abstractions labelled with maladies like *Alien Hand Syndrome, Shrinking Penis Syndrome* and *Photographing the Ruins of Detroit Syndrome*, all 2013), Hoff is also a poet and a champion of the artist book – an interest he maintains with his publishing project Primary Information. The imprint, which Hoff co-directs with Miriam Katzeff, has reproduced the fabled 1970s run of *Avalanche* magazine and issued books by Carl Andre, Destroy All Monsters, Genesis P-Orridge, Dan Graham, Florian Hecker, Lee Lozano, Aram Saroyan and others.

Books are versatile instruments for Hoff, who recently made a new volume of his own: *Everybody's Pixelated*, published in an edition of 250 by Printed Matter. The book is two things at once: firstly, a facsimile of a formative 1937 study of the art of doodling by Russell M. Arandel, called *Everybody's Pixillated*, and secondly, what Hoff himself calls 'a carrying device' for a covert digital memory card hidden in the back, stuck beneath the price tag and filled with three gigabytes of text that hackers use for cracking passwords online.

The idea of the carrying device circulates within Hoff's many different modes of work, which centre on parasites in search of a home. All media are hosts, in the end, and the end is only the beginning of the next phase of transformation.

Andy Battaglia is a writer based in New York, USA. His work has appeared in The Wall Street Journal, The Paris Review *and* The National, *among others.*

James Hoff's solo exhibition at Callicoon Fine Arts, New York, runs from 2 November to 21 December 2014.

Morris Worm No. 1, 2013, installation view at Kunsthall Oslo

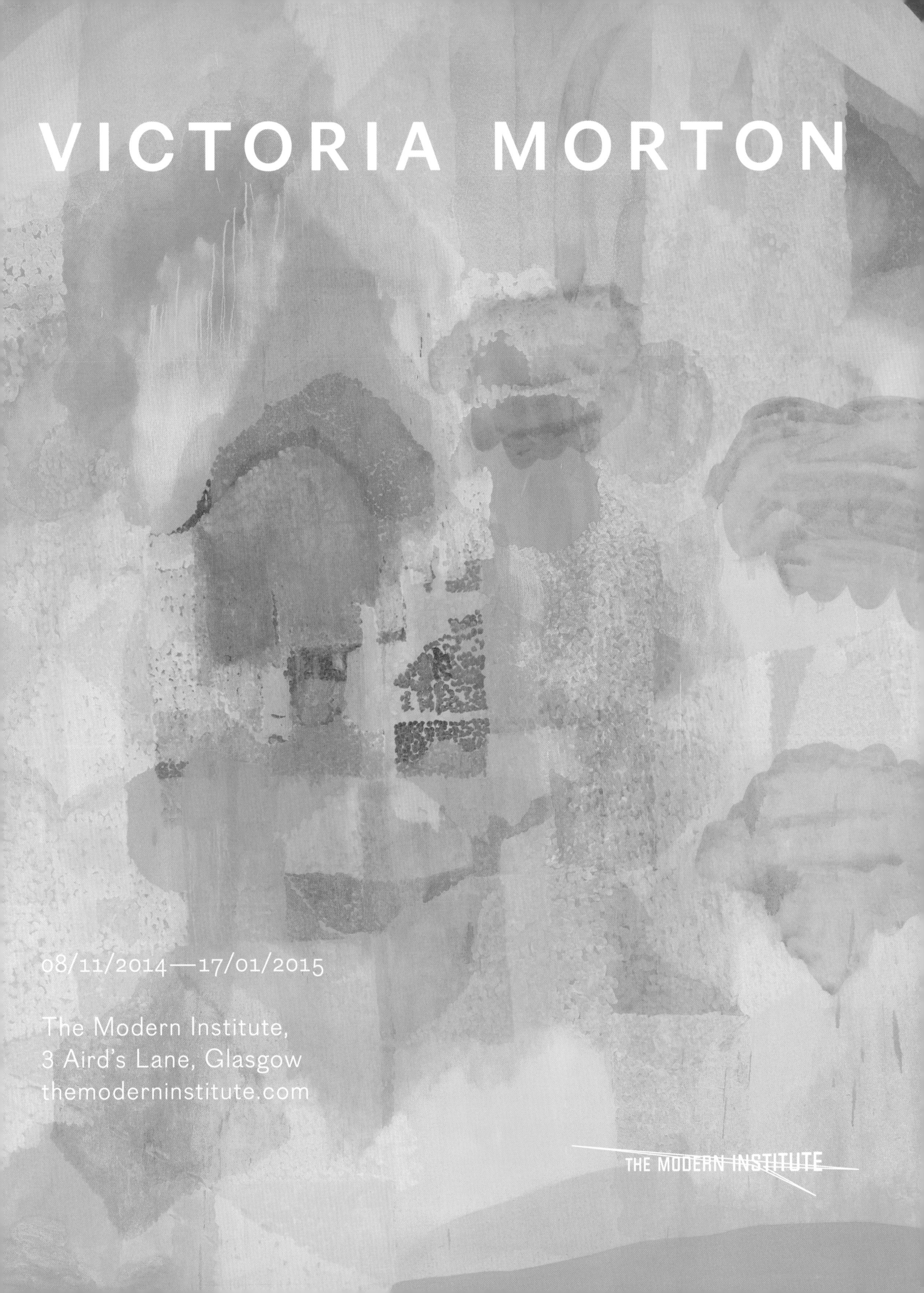

VICTORIA MORTON

08/11/2014—17/01/2015

The Modern Institute,
3 Aird's Lane, Glasgow
themoderninstitute.com

THE MODERN INSTITUTE

LIZA LOU

ixube

OCTOBER – NOVEMBER 2014
PARIS MARAIS, 7 RUE DEBELLEYME
ROPAC.NET

GALERIE THADDAEUS ROPAC

PARIS MARAIS   PARIS PANTIN   SALZBURG

STURTEVANT

RELOADED

NOVEMBER 2014 – JANUARY 2015
PARIS MARAIS, 7 RUE DEBELLEYME
ROPAC.NET

GALERIE THADDAEUS ROPAC

PARIS MARAIS, PARIS PANTIN, SALZBURG

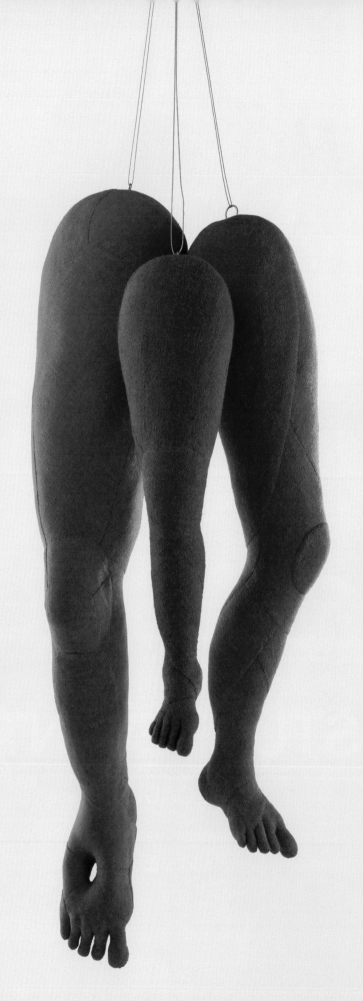

Legs 2001 fabric 76 x 34 x 22 1/2 in 193 x 86.4 x 57.2 cm ©The Easton Foundation / Licensed by VAGA

LOUISE BOURGEOIS SUSPENSION

CHEIM & READ 10/30/14–1/10/15

Museum Guide

Frederick Wiseman's new documentary about
London's National Gallery

Nick Pinkerton

Frederick Wiseman
National Gallery,
2014

When I think of depictions of art museums in cinema, scenes of rapt visitors aren't what first comes to mind. There is the breakneck tour of the Louvre in Jean-Luc Godard's *Bande à part* (Band of Outsiders, 1964); the pursuit through a Berlin museum in Alfred Hitchcock's 1966 *Torn Curtain* (heavily borrowed from in Wes Anderson's *The Grand Budapest Hotel* this year); the art gallery as a cruising ground in Brian De Palma's 1980 *Dressed to Kill* (the interior is the Philadelphia Museum of Art, the exterior New York's Metropolitan Museum); and the continuous Steadicam shot that blows through the State Hermitage Museum in Alexander Sokurov's *Russian Ark* (2002).

If these examples suggest that the moving image is somehow inimical to the still canvas, I urge you to see Frederick Wiseman's documentary *National Gallery* (2014). Realized thanks to an unprecedented level of access to the London institution, Wiseman's film documents activity in every strata of the museum, from board-room to classroom, director to gallery guide, conservator to care-taker. Introducing *National Gallery* at this year's Toronto International Film Festival, Wiseman laid out the numbers. Shot over the course of three months in 2012, the resulting 170 hours of footage was edited down to three hours. To this, I'll add another figure: *National Gallery* is the 39th documentary produced by Wiseman, whose *oeuvre* may be said to constitute a museum unto itself. To wander the rooms of this museum is to view a remarkable variety of Western democratic institutions in action – or, just as often, in deadlock – as seen over a nearly 50-year period by a curious and patient observer.

Wiseman was at university in the late 1940s, when New Criticism was at its height, and has always spoken for the importance of the principle of 'close reading' in his filmmaking practice; his last feature, *At Berkeley* (2013), ended with a professor's exegesis of John Donne's poem 'To His Mistress Going to Bed' (1669). In *National Gallery*, Wiseman has set his sights on another institution experiencing the funding pinch, though this time he scales back *At Berkeley*'s emphasis on trustee politicking to concentrate instead on close read-ings of the objects all the politicking is about: the paintings.

The museum and the cinema, two exhibition models eternally insecure about their relevance, seem increasingly to be clinging together for reassurance.

The film begins at the tail end of the blockbuster show 'Leonardo da Vinci: Painter at the Court of Milan', and carries through to the beginning of 'Turner Inspired: In the Light of Claude' and the 'multi-arts project' 'Metamorphosis: Titian'. The National Gallery exists to democratize access to art, at least some of which is elitist by nature, and the tension inherent to this mission is a pervasive undercurrent that is even vocalized by

museum director Nicholas Penny as he discusses a particularly aloof work by Nicolas Poussin. We first see Penny holding the line against outreach, which he seems to view – not without justification – as a byword for 'dumbing down'.

Penny is one of the characters who comes to the fore during the course of the film, along with Head of Display, Dawson W. Carr (now curating the European collection at the Portland Art Museum), and Director of Restoration, Larry Keith. These higher-ups receive no more introduction than the visitors we see looking at the canvases. The film's other stars are the museum's lecturers and guides, whose discourse directs both the sight of museum patrons and the camera-eye. The first that we encounter asks her audience to imagine a medieval altarpiece animated by the flicker of 13th-century candlelight – 'You're not in the National Gallery, you're inside that church' – and, time and again, the subject of context returns in discussions over placement of works, or their removal from their original settings. This puts me in mind of the 2008 film by French filmmaker Olivier Assayas, *Summer Hours*. Assayas's

film hinges on the debate among a recently deceased woman's surviving grandchildren as to what to do with her estate – which includes relics relating to her uncle, a noted painter – and is never more poignant than when lingering on the last view of her heirlooms, removed from a home environment and housed in an antiseptic display case in the Musée d'Orsay, Paris.

Summer Hours sprang from a proposed omnibus film financed by the Musée d'Orsay, as did Hou Hsiao-Hsien's *Flight of the Red Balloon* (2007) and Hong Sangsoo's *Night and Day* (2008). Not to be outdone, the Louvre underwrote 2009's *Face* by Taiwanese director Tsai Ming-Liang, who has recently looked towards galleries and museums as exhibition spaces. The museum and the cinema, two exhibition models eternally insecure about their relevance, seem increasingly to be clinging together for reassurance. The result is not only a museification of film culture, but an unprecedented openness of museums to being transcribed in film. Along with *National Gallery* and the forthcoming *Vatican Museums in 3D* (2014), we have recently seen Oeke Hoogendijk's four-hour *The New Rijksmuseum* (2013) and Johannes Holzhausen's *The Great Museum* (2014), filmed during the reopening of the Kunstkammer rooms in Vienna's Kunsthistorisches Museum. This last venue is also the setting for *Museum Hours*, a 2012 film by the American director Jem Cohen, who stages one of the movie's key scenes in the famous 'Brueghel Room'. (In it, an unfailingly pleasant guide deflects conflict with a couple of thick, conservative North American tourists who take exception at her secular-humanist reading of the 1567 painting *Conversion of Paul*. These foils are as obvious as the tenor of her speech is subtle.)

Pieter Brueghel the Elder seems to exhibit a particular appeal to filmmakers. In Lech Majewski's 2011 *The Mill and the Cross*, another painting in the Kunsthistorisches Museum, *The Procession to Calvary* (1564), is subject to a reading of an entirely different level of depth. The film shows Rutger Hauer's Brueghel bearing witness to the vignettes that he will eventually combine in his canvas. The peasant painter is also the muse for French director Marcel Hanoun in *Le Regard* (The

Gaze, 1977). The film begins with a couple in bed in a hotel room in Brussels; upon her leaving him alone to go out, it establishes a pattern of shifting between the man having sex with another (possibly imagined) woman and his female companion in that city's Musée des Beaux-Arts, examining *Landscape with the Fall of Icarus* (c.1560). Her attention to the canvas is accompanied by musings which echo W.H. Auden's 1938 poem 'Musée des Beaux-Arts', briefly alluded to by guides in both *Museum Hours* and *National Gallery*. ('In Breughel's *Icarus*, for instance: how everything turns away / Quite leisurely from the disaster.')

Recent scholarship suggests that the painting is possibly not by Brueghel at all, but the work of one of his followers. And provenance and authentication are the subjects of a 'gallery film' of quite another sort – *Art and Craft* (2014), a very funny documentary by Mark Becker, Sam Cullman and Jennifer Grausman. The film's 'star' is Mark Landis, a solitary resident of Laurel, Mississippi, who for a number of years has been using cheap, over-the-counter art supplies to make highly skilled forgeries of Old Master paintings – forgeries that he then gives, free of charge, to unsuspecting museum and university collections across the US.

That one degree or another of falsification is intrinsic to the gallery experience is a theme that carries through Wiseman's film, which concludes with attempts to 'translate' Titian into other forms: a *pas-de-deux* in front of his *Diana and Actaeon* (1556–59) to William Byrd's *Miserere mei, Deus* (Have Mercy on Me, Oh God, 1591), with verse by Jo Shapcott, who confesses 'every poem is a crude translation of something else'. This translation occurs every time a film camera is pointed at a canvas – and we should expect to see a great deal more of it if the cinema and the gallery continue to coalesce.

Nick Pinkerton lives in New York, USA. He writes regularly for Artforum, Film Comment, Sight & Sound *and* Little White Lies.

Mark Becker, Sam Cullman and Jennifer Grausman *Art and Craft*, 2014

Olga Chernysheva

6-10 LEXINGTON STREET
26 NOVEMBER 2014 – 17 JANUARY 2015

PACE LONDON

Let's assume there is a crisis in art writing. The past decade saw a number of essays, books, panel discussions and events debating the state of criticism, the death of the critic and the demise of art publishing. So, let's imagine that crisis: reviews always simply describe what is on view rather than say anything about it; catalogue essays never produce new knowledge, only serve to promote an artist's market value; and the language of press releases, so often derided as hollow, has taken over. All those roundtables that bring critics back from the dead and onto the podium reflect a growing anxiety over the communicative possibilities of writing.

Gilda Williams worries about all of the above. Call it by any name – her slightly derogatory 'art-patois', mystical 'speaking in tongues', or plain old 'artspeak' – it's all barely comprehensible to Williams. She sets out to correct this problem in a new book, *How to Write About Contemporary Art* (published by Thames & Hudson) which is structured to untangle the linguistic mess we have supposedly got ourselves into. In countless bullet points, she describes the field, its key players and its particular penchants (citing, amongst other things, a number of *frieze* articles), and then moves on to discuss style, the work of pitching and the different forms of writing in the contemporary-art context. Williams's methodology is flawless. She brings in some 50 examples of texts, ranging from exhibition reviews to snippets of catalogue essays and artist statements, and attentively analyzes them. She highlights the use of active verbs, points out specific nouns, deconstructs complex grammatical structures and, all in all, seems to read these samples more closely than anyone has done before. In confident style – 'Unless discussing a certain shark floating in a tank, or that porcelain bathroom fixture signed "R. Mutt", never assume your reader remembers or has seen the art' – Williams stresses that the essential approach to writing about art should be to answer three questions, easily summed up: (1) What is it? (2) What might this mean? and (3) So what? This formula is meant to answer what Williams sees as the inherent paradox of writing about art – 'stabilizing art through language risks killing what makes art worth writing about in the first place' – but her three-ingredient recipe is not a solution, it's a formula so simple that it could work just as well for nutritionists as it could for contemporary art writers. (Quinoa: a popular supergrain that can be eaten in salads, soup and stews; this may lead to a food shortage in Bolivia, but it provides a good source of protein for westerners.)

The book has its flaws: some ill-chosen examples of supposedly good writing practice, including a paragraph from Claire Bishop's 2012 book, *Artificial Hells*, in which the academic manages to use the dated term 'surf the web' not once, but twice. There is a use of emphasis (bold, italics, colour) so liberal that every other sentence is presented as if it is the end-all of literary flare. Williams also has the bad habit of comparing totally disparate things – a memorable passage contrasts Dave Hickey discussing the 1970s: 'limos, homos, bimbos, resort communities', to the 'pile-ups of *Kunsthalles* and *Kunstvereins* some art-writers try to pass off as a legitimate paragraph'. Still, her systematic analysis of the current state of art writing is a first and, when looking beyond her textual analysis, her examples can serve as a jumping-off point from which to review the field, its terms of engagement and what is at stake.

In the world Williams describes, the old-school critic is gone, replaced by a 'jack of all trades', but she does not dwell on the origin of this disappearance – the reality of writing about art, which is low pay, freelance hustle and a constant struggle to keep one's ethics in check – or its consequences. While Williams acknowledges that writers are implicated in some way in the larger art economy, the conclusion she draws is that 'today's critics are not as powerful as they once were [...] Occupying almost the bottom economic tier of the art-industry pyramid, critics are least affected by cycles of boom and bust. When art bubbles burst, art-writers often have more to write about and nothing special to worry about. As Boris Groys asserts, since nobody reads or invests in art-criticism anyway, its authors can feel liberated to be as frank as they please, writing with few or no strings attached.' Does a position of power enslave a writer? Not necessarily. In fact, it could give the critic further traction and support his/her role as someone that should – and potentially could – keep the market in check. As for Groys's assessment that no one reads criticism anymore, the conclusion that should be drawn from it is that what we urgently need right now is not more writing, but more critical writing.

No book could teach a writer to be interesting, opinionated, engaged or passionate. And that isn't the objective of this one. Its goal is to take a discipline that Williams conceives of as highly unregulated – and professionalize it. In outlining exactly how an auction catalogue differs from a museum's wall label and a magazine review, down to the vocabulary and tone each should accommodate, Williams gives insight to the inner workings of very different industries:

Books

Orit Gat

Gilda Williams's new book on how to write about contemporary art academia, auction houses and mainstream and professional press. With an eye on the rise of numerous academic programmes in art writing, a book on the subject could be seen as a democratizing entity, but the difference between a book and a school is interaction. Even if one recoils at the idea of needing an MFA in art criticism in order to write for a magazine – another instance of an art world in which the terms of participation are a secondary degree, often accompanied by academic debt that few can financially justify – at least those programmes allow students a sense of community. Whether found in a graduate programme

or not, it is the participation in discourse and interest in one's contemporaries that makes someone a critic. Williams's technique is married to the work of art – let the work lead you – which risks resulting in formulaic art writing that neglects the intellectual context from which the artwork emerges.

Art writing is not an industry in crisis – quite the opposite. Art publishing has developed into a realm complementary to the work, not one that merely describes it. The physical and conceptual expansion of what art can be has also produced a publishing landscape with a positive anything-goes ethos, which

we should promote, rather than suffocate. Writing about art has become a space in which good writers can discuss anything, lofty or mundane, from politics to neckties, philosophical trends to internet memes. While Williams claims that art writing needs to be grounded in descriptions of the art – the 'what's there' – I'd argue that this extended field of publishing is what makes for vibrant reading material, whether or not it ever mentions that this or that video installation has two screens and a total running time of 15 minutes. Art writing should be sharp and opinionated, but also sometimes flimsy and erratic. Art writing doesn't need to be

professionalized further – it needs to be granted room to experiment and expand. These more wayward forms of writing create an art world that is more perceptive, where what we read is equal in its intellectual ambition to the work we look at.

Orit Gat is a writer and contributing editor of Rhizome. *She lives in New York, USA.*

Illustration
by Pablo Helguera,
2014

'We needed to find a new secret code that would be impossible
to decipher, so we switched to artspeak.'

Tom of Finland
Early Work: 1944 – 1972
January 17 –
March 7, 2015

DAVID KORDANSKY GALLERY

info@davidkordanskygallery.com
www.davidkordanskygallery.com
T: 323.935.3030   F: 323.935.3031

Tom of Finland, Untitled, 1947,
gouache on paper, 11.31 x 8.19 inches (28.7 x 20.8 cm)

Toby Ziegler

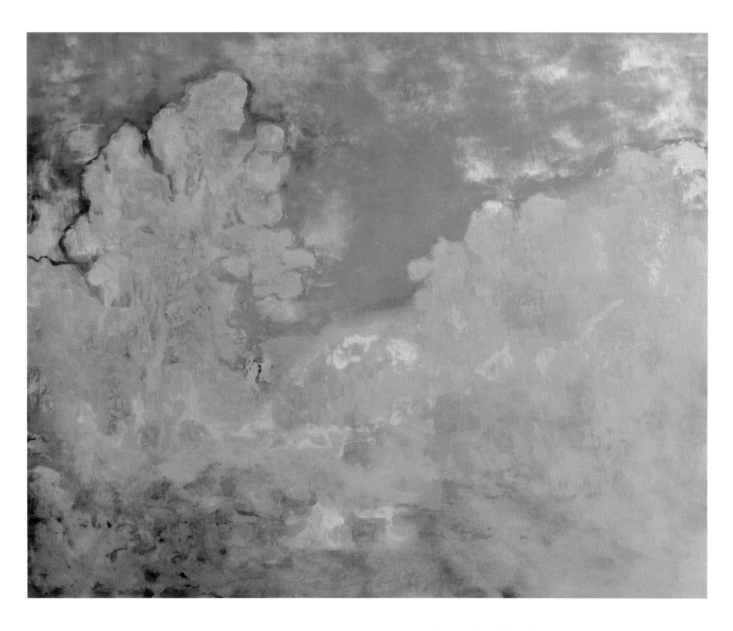

November 27 – January 24, 2015

57, rue du Temple, 75004 Paris
maxhetzler.com

LYNETTE YIADOM-BOAKYE *THE LOVE WITHIN*
November 21, 2014 – January 10, 2015

JACK SHAINMAN GALLERY
513 West 20th Street New York, NY 10011 | Tel: 212 645 1701 | Fax: 212 645 8316 | www.jackshainman.com | @jackshainman.com

In 1994.

May
When the first genetically modified tomato becomes available on the market in the United States, in Austria the artists group Gelitin fights against mass-produced food.

October
The Joshua Tree National Park in the Californian desert is proclaimed a nature reserve. Years later Andrea Zittel moves there to live and work.

September
First show at MDC of a great Italian master: Ettore Spalletti. In 2014 we continue this tradition by representing Gianfranco Baruchello.

MILANO { MDC } LONDON

MASSIMO DE CARLO
FOUNDED IN 1987

www.massimodecarlo.com   info@massimodecarlo.com   @mdcgallery   massimodecarlogallery

7 November – 20 December 2014

Polly Apfelbaum

COLOUR SESSIONS

Frith Street Gallery
GOLDEN SQUARE

17–18 Golden Square, London W1F 9JJ T +44 (0)20 7494 1550
F +44 (0)20 7287 3733 www.frithstreetgallery.com info@frithstreetgallery.com

Detail: Colour Sessions, 2013

Julian Stair

Quotidian

November 2014

Corvi-Mora

1A KEMPSFORD ROAD   LONDON   SE11 4NU
TELEPHONE 020 7840 9111 FAX 020 7840 9112   WWW.CORVI-MORA.COM

DANIEL LIPP
SLOWMO DRAMA
28 NOV–17 JAN

7 ROYALTY MEWS, SOHO   LONDON W1D 3AS   SOUTHARDREID.COM

Cibelle
Cavalli
Bastos

Mendes
Wood
DM

Rua da Consolação 3358
Jardins São Paulo
SP 01416–000 Brazil
+ 55 11 3081 1735
www.mendeswooddm.com
facebook.com/mendeswood
@mendeswooddm

R. Marco Aurélio, 311
Vila Romana São Paulo
SP 05048–000 Brazil

KENDALL KOPPE

LAURA ALDRIDGE

GRIER EDMUNDSON

ELLA KRUGLYANSKAYA

NIALL MACDONALD

CRAIG MULHOLLAND

CHARLOTTE PRODGER

CORIN SWORN

Suite 1/2, 6 Dixon Street, Glasgow G1 4AX
t +44 (0)141 248 8177 | m + 44 (0)7412 589163
info@kendallkoppe.com | www.kendallkoppe.com

KK

October 26
to December 21, 2014

Josh Faught
Christmas Creep

107 Norfolk Street
New York, New York 10002

Lisa Cooley

212-680-0564
lisa-cooley.com

JOÃO ONOFRE

TACET

Contemporary

19 November
10 January

6 Albemarle Street
London W1S 4BY

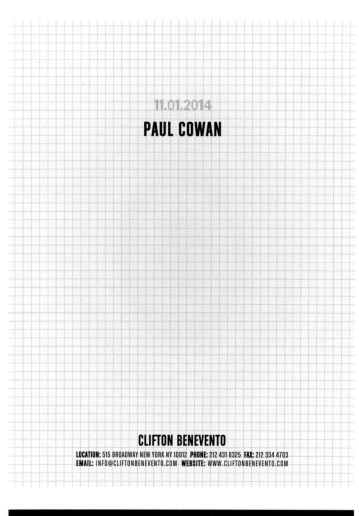

11.01.2014

PAUL COWAN

CLIFTON BENEVENTO

LOCATION: 515 BROADWAY NEW YORK NY 10012 PHONE: 212 431 6325 FAX: 212 334 4703
EMAIL: INFO@CLIFTONBENEVENTO.COM WEBSITE: WWW.CLIFTONBENEVENTO.COM

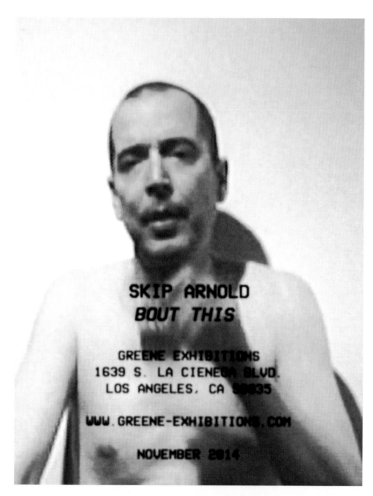

SKIP ARNOLD
BOUT THIS

GREENE EXHIBITIONS
1639 S. LA CIENEGA BLVD.
LOS ANGELES, CA 90035

WWW.GREENE-EXHIBITIONS.COM

NOVEMBER 2014

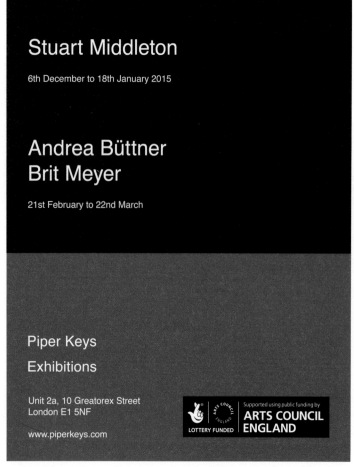

Stuart Middleton

6th December to 18th January 2015

Andrea Büttner
Brit Meyer

21st February to 22nd March

Piper Keys

Exhibitions

Unit 2a, 10 Greatorex Street
London E1 5NF

www.piperkeys.com

LOTTERY FUNDED · ARTS COUNCIL ENGLAND

Supported using public funding by
ARTS COUNCIL ENGLAND

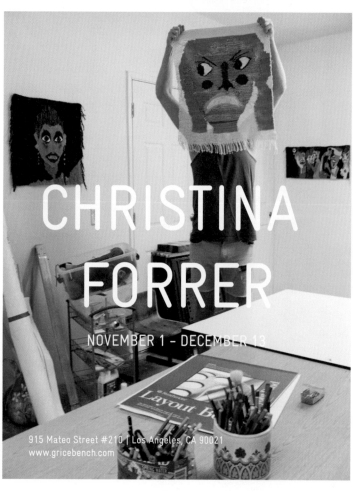

CHRISTINA FORRER

NOVEMBER 1 – DECEMBER 13

915 Mateo Street #210 | Los Angeles, CA 90021
www.gricebench.com

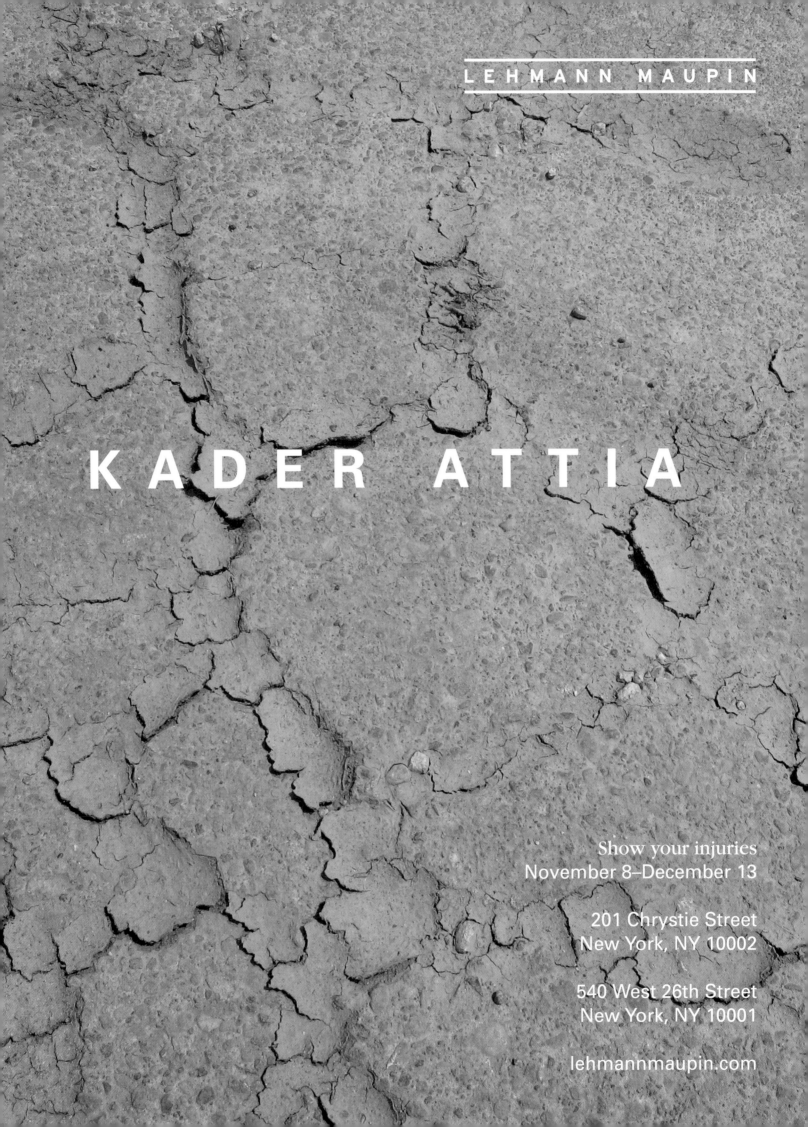

LEHMANN MAUPIN

KADER ATTIA

Show your injuries
November 8–December 13

201 Chrystie Street
New York, NY 10002

540 West 26th Street
New York, NY 10001

lehmannmaupin.com

ALFREDO JAAR   THE SOUND OF SILENCE

13.11.2014 - 23.1.2015

The Sound of Silence, 2006

GALERIA PATRICIA READY

Espoz 3125, Vitacura Santiago de Chile +56 2 2953 6210

www.galeriapready.cl

WITH SUPPORT FROM THE CULTURAL FUNDING LAW OF CHILE

Constantin Brancusi
THE PHOTOGRAPHS

October 25, 2014–January 1, 2015
Special programming during Art Basel Miami

The Margulies Collection at the Warehouse
591 NW 27th Street
Miami, Florida
www.margulieswarehouse.com

BRUCE SILVERSTEIN

RA

Royal Academy of Arts
Allen Jones RA

13 November 2014 –
25 January 2015

royalacademy.org.uk
#AllenJones
Friends of the RA go free

Allen Jones RA, *Body Armour*, 2013. Photograph, 127 x 127 cm
London, Private Collection. Image courtesy of the artist. © Allen Jones

Chris Ofili, *Rodin...The Thinker,* 1997–98 (detail). Acrylic, oil, polyester resin, glitter, map pins, and elephant dung on linen, 96 × 72 in (243.8 × 182.8 cm).
Courtesy David Zwirner, New York/London, and Victoria Miro, London. Photo: Stephen White

Chris Ofili
NIGHT AND DAY

**NEW
235 BOWERY
NEW YORK NY
10002 USA
MUSEUM**
newmuseum.org

ON VIEW | October 29, 2014–February 1, 2015

UNDER THE PATRONAGE OF
**His Highness General Sheikh
Mohamed bin Zayed Al Nahyan**
Crown Prince of Abu Dhabi
Deputy Supreme Commander of the UAE Armed Forces

ABU DHABI TOURISM & CULTURE AUTHORITY PRESENTS

SEEING THROUGH LIGHT

Selections from the Guggenheim Abu Dhabi Collection

5 November 2014 - 19 January 2015
Manarat Al Saadiyat, Saadiyat Cultural District
Abu Dhabi, UAE

Yayoi Kusama, *Infinity Mirrored Room, Filled with the Brilliance of Life*, 2011. Mirror-panelled installation with LED lights and water, edition 2/3, 500 x 617.5 x 645.5 cm. ©Guggenheim Abu Dhabi ©Tate, London 2011

SAADIYATCULTURALDISTRICT.AE

جوجنهايم أبوظبي
GUGGENHEIM ABU DHABI

هيئة أبوظبي للسياحة والثقافة

Katharina Fritsch, *Elefant / Elephant*, 1987
© Katharina Fritsch, VG BILD-Kunst, Bonn. Photo: Thomas Ruff

FRITSCH/KOONS/RAY

SCULPTURE
AFTER
SCULPTURE

11 October–18 January 2015

www.modernamuseet.se

MODERNA MUSEET

MIGROSMUSEUM
für Gegenwartskunst

Dorothy
Iannone

Censorship And
The Irrepressible Drive
Toward Love And Divinity

Wu
Tsang

migrosmuseum.ch
migros-culture-percentage.ch

30.08.–09.11.

22.11.–08.02.2015

Migros Museum für
Gegenwartskunst
Limmatstrasse 270
CH–8005 Zurich

Etel Adnan
Forrest Bess
Marcel Broodthaers
Gustave Courbet
Hanne Darboven
Henri Matisse
Reinard Mucha
Paul Thek
Lawrence Weiner
Katharina Wulff

the sea
salut d'honneur Jan Hoet

ostend

Dirk Braeckman, D.Z.-V.U.-2013, photo ©Dirk Braeckman

23.10.2014 - 19.04.2015 / **dezee-oostende.be**

© Kaat Flamey

puddle, pothole, portal

Olga Balema, Joachim Bandau, Camille Blatrix, Teresa Burga, Antoine Catala, Abigail DeVille, Jos de Gruyter & Harald Thys, Judith Hopf, Jamian Juliano-Villani, Allison Katz, Mark Leckey, Maria Loboda, Win McCarthy, Danny McDonald, Marlie Mul, Mick Peter, Chadwick Rantanen, Lucie Stahl, Saul Steinberg, Keiichi Tanaami, Lina Viste Grønli, and Jordan Wolfson

October 2, 2014 – January 5, 2015

Co-curated by
Ruba Katrib, Curator,
SculptureCenter,
and artist Camille Henrot

SculptureCenter
44-19 Purves Street
Long Island City, NY 11101
718.361.1750

Gallery Hours
Thursday–Monday
11am–6pm
sculpture-center.org

WILL BENEDICT
CORRUPTION FEEDS

31 OCTOBER – 14 DECEMBER
BERGEN KUNSTHALL

madre

napoli

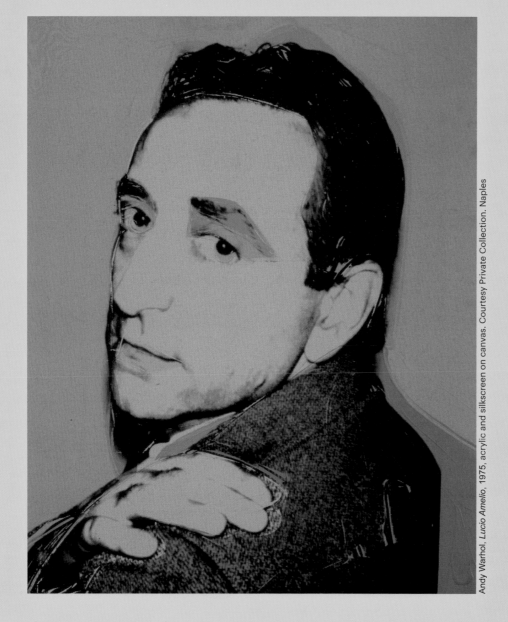

Andy Warhol, *Lucio Amelio*, 1975, acrylic and silkscreen on canvas. Courtesy Private Collection. Naples

21.11.2014 OPENING

Lucio Amelio
From the Modern Art Agency to the Genesis of Terrae Motus *(1965-1982) Documents, Works, a Story...*

22.11.2014 – 09.03.2015

ON VIEW

Walid Raad
Preface / Prefazione

In collaboration with
Carré d'Art-Musée d'art contemporain, Nîmes

11.10.14 — 19.01.15

Per_forming a collection #3

11.10.14 — in progress

PROGETTO XXI

**La scrittura visuale
La parola totale**

12.09.14 — 15.01.15
Fondazione Morra, Museo Nitsch
Vico Lungo Pontecorvo 29/d, Napoli

**Franco Vaccari
Rumori Telepatici**

09.10.14 — 30.11.14
Fondazione Morra Greco
Largo Proprio di Avellino 17, Napoli

In collaboration with

---

fondazione donnaregina
per le arti contemporanee

madre · museo d'arte
contemporanea donnaregina

via Settembrini, 79
80139 Napoli, Italia
www.madrenapoli.it

Organizzazione e gestione

Tim Head
Fictions
—
28 November 2014 — 24 January 2015

PARAFIN

18 Woodstock Street
London W1C 2AL
+44 (0)20 7495 1969
info@parafin.co.uk

DERRICK ADAMS

ELIJAH BURGHER

HOWARDENA PINDELL

HUNTER REYNOLDS

JACOLBY SATTERWHITE

CAROLEE SCHNEEMANN

DAVID WOJNAROWICZ

Here Today...

Sir Peter Blake

George Condo

Douglas Gordon

Carsten Höller

Bharti Kher

Mari Mahr

Julian Opie

Diana Thater

Gavin Turk

United Visual Artists

Andy Warhol

And many more...

AN INTERNATIONAL
CONTEMPORARY ART
EXHIBITION, FEATURING
OVER 50 ARTISTS, CURATED
BY ARTWISE, CHAMPIONING
THE 50TH ANNIVERSARY
OF THE **IUCN** RED LIST OF
THREATENED SPECIES

The Old Sorting Office, London
25 Nov 2014 - 17 Dec 2014

www.heretoday.org

International
Dialogue for
Environmental
Action

Gavin Turk, Pandy Warhol, 2014 © the artist & House of Fairytales

WERNER MANNAERS   THE SCENT OF MIMOSA

ROBERTO POLO GALLERY

20.11.2014 | 01.02.2015
CATALOGUE WITH TEXT BY MARTIN HERBERT AVAILABLE
RUE LEBEAU 8–12 1000 BRUSSELS +32(0)25025650
GALLERY@ROBERTOPOLO.COM WWW.ROBERTOPOLOGALLERY.COM
Very Cliché (Listening to Mendelssohn), 2014, acrylic, oil & spray on canvas, 152 x 121.5 cm

Stan Douglas
7 November 2014 – 15 February 2015

Possibilities of the Object: Experiments in Modern and Contemporary Brazilian Art
13 March – 25 May 2015

Market Street, Edinburgh
Always free

The Fruitmarket Gallery

www.fruitmarket.co.uk

JERWOOD**VISUAL**ARTS

Suspicion

NATHAN CASH DAVIDSON / STEPHEN CHAMBERS RA /
DAN COOMBS / SIMON LINKE / GAVIN LOCKHEART /
KATE LYDDON / DARREN MARSHALL / DAMIEN MEADE /
BENJAMIN SENIOR / GERALDINE SWAYNE / NEAL TAIT /
COVADONGA VALDES / FREYJA WRIGHT

A JERWOOD ENCOUNTERS EXHIBITION CURATED BY DAN COOMBS
5 NOVEMBER—7 DECEMBER 2014

Supported by

Jerwood Space
171 Union Street
London SE1 0LN

Admission Free
#JVASuspicion
@JerwoodJVA

jerwoodvisualarts.org

JERWOOD CHARITABLE FOUNDATION | JERWOOD SPACE

Damien Meade, Tunnel Music, 2013, Private collection Zurich. Courtesy the artist and Scheublein + Bak Gallery, Zurich

JUDITH LAUAND

Brazilian Modernist, 1950s–2000s

Through December 20, 2014

DRISCOLL | BABCOCK   525 West 25th Street, New York 212-767-1852 info@driscollbabcock.com

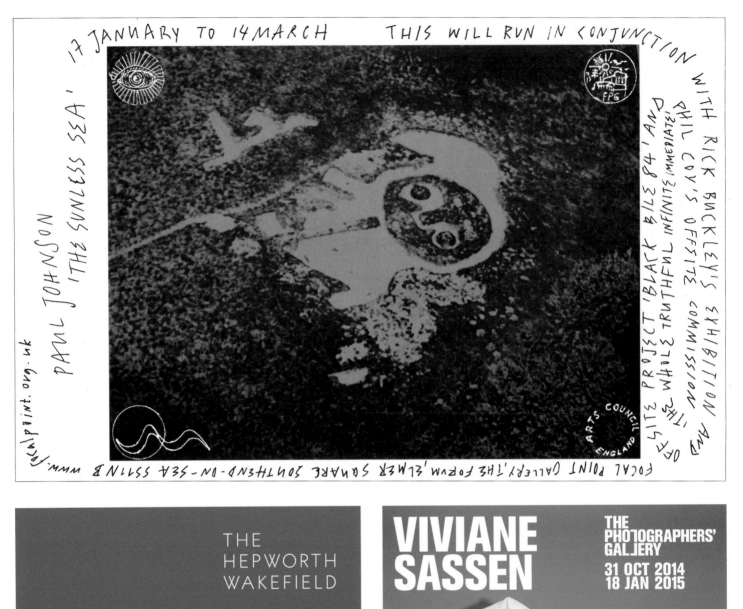

17 JANUARY TO 14 MARCH   THIS WILL RUN IN CONJUNCTION WITH RICK BUCKLEY'S EXHIBITION AND PHIL COY'S OFFSITE COMMISSION 'THE WHOLE TRUTHFUL INFINITE IMMEDIATE' AND OFFSITE PROJECT 'BLACK BILE 84' AND

PAUL JOHNSON 'THE SUNLESS SEA'

www.focalpoint.org.uk

FOCAL POINT GALLERY, THE FORUM, ELMER SQUARE, SOUTHEND-ON-SEA SS11NB

THE
HEPWORTH
WAKEFIELD

CONFLICT AND COLLISIONS:
NEW CONTEMPORARY SCULPTURE
1 OCT 2014 – 25 JAN 2015

THREE NEW SOLO
EXHIBITIONS BY:

ALEXANDRA BIRCKEN:
ESKALATION

FOLKERT DE JONG:
THE HOLY LAND

TOBY ZIEGLER/
CHARLES JAGGER

Free Admission
www.hepworthwakefield.org

Funded by Wakefield Council and Arts Council England.
Registered charity number 1138117.

VIVIANE SASSEN

THE
PHOTOGRAPHERS'
GALLERY
31 OCT 2014
18 JAN 2015

VIVIANE SASSEN
ANALEMMA,
FASHION PHOTOGRAPHY
1992–2012

Also showing:
EDWARD STEICHEN
IN HIGH FASHION,
THE CONDE NAST YEARS
1923–1937

16–18 Ramillies Street
London W1F 7LW
⊖ Oxford Circus
tpg.org.uk

LOTTERY FUNDED   Supported using public funding by
ARTS COUNCIL
ENGLAND

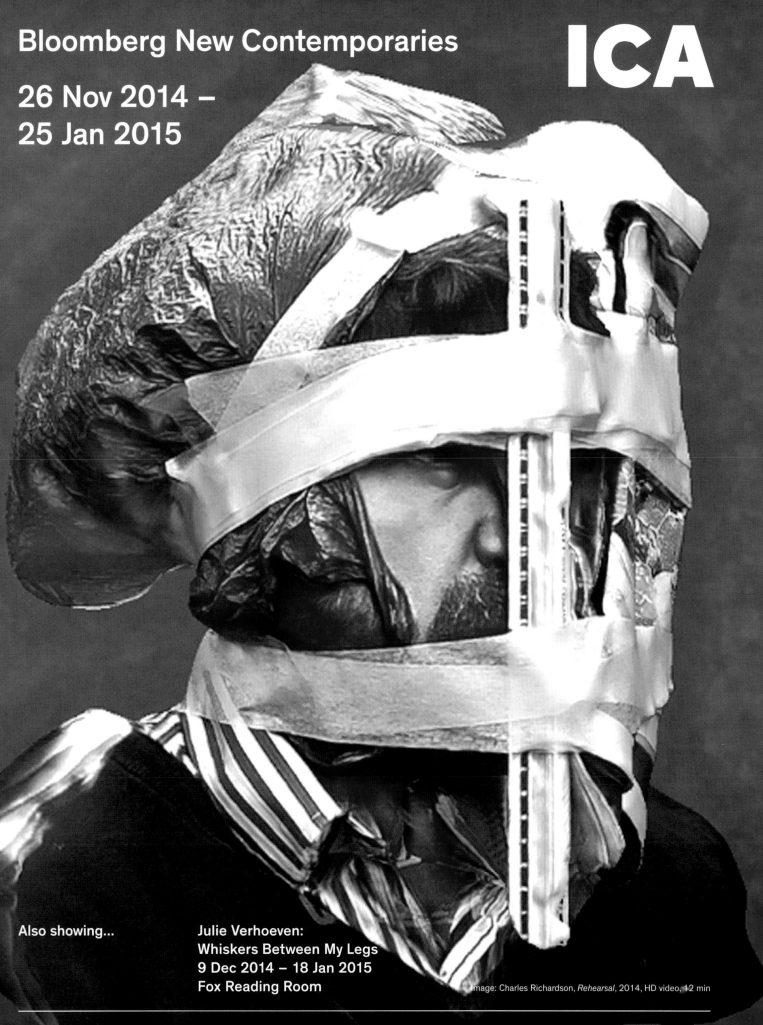

Bloomberg New Contemporaries

26 Nov 2014 –
25 Jan 2015

ICA

Also showing...

Julie Verhoeven:
Whiskers Between My Legs
9 Dec 2014 – 18 Jan 2015
Fox Reading Room

Image: Charles Richardson, *Rehearsal*, 2014, HD video, 12 min

Institute of Contemporary Arts,
The Mall, London, SW1Y 5AH
020 7930 3647
www.ica.org.uk

Bloomberg Supported by
ARTS COUNCIL
ENGLAND

ICA is a registered charity number: 236848

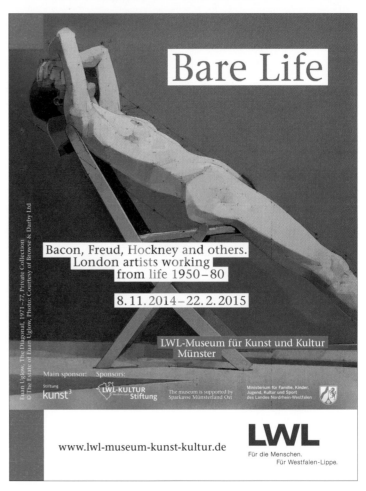

MUSEO JUMEX

DANH VO: وادي الحجارة
13.NOV.[2014]—25.FEB.[2015]

ABRAHAM CRUZVILLEGAS:
THE AUTOCONSTRUCCIÓN SUITES*
13.NOV.[2014]—08.FEB.[2015]

*Abraham Cruzvillegas: The Autoconstrucción Suites is organized by the Walker Art Center, Minneapolis.
Major support for the exhibition is provided by the Andy Warhol Foundation for the Visual Arts.
Additional support is generously provided by Nelly and Moisés Cosío Espinosa, the Rose Francis Foundation,
Gabriela and Ramiro Garza, Eugenio López, Leni and David Moore, Jr., Donna and Jim Pohlad,
Mike and Elizabeth Sweeney, and Marge and Irv Weiser.

FUNDACIONJUMEX.ORG

※ MUSEO JUMEX
MIGUEL DE CERVANTES SAAVEDRA 303
COLONIA AMPLIACIÓN GRANADA
11600 MEXICO CITY

MARKUS SCHINWALD

02·10·14 ✕ 08·02·15

WWW.MLEUVEN.BE

M VAN
**MUSEUM
LEUVEN**

frieze d/e

Magazin für zeitgenössische Kunst und Kultur
Magazine for contemporary art and culture

ONE TWO THREE FOUR FÜNF

5 AUSGABEN / ISSUES IN 2014

WWW.FRIEZE-MAGAZIN.DE / ABONNIEREN

AB / FROM € 40

SUSANNE VON FALKENHAUSEN
on Digital Circulation

PETER PILLER – a portrait

Monographs on **ELLEN GRONEMEYER,
JAN PETER HAMMER & MICHAEL SCHMIDT**

as well as 20 reviews
from Germany, Austria and Switzerland

ISSUE 17 OF FRIEZE D/E IS PUBLISHED 14 NOVEMBER

PARASOPHIA

Kyoto
International
Festival
of
Contemporary
Culture

2015·KYOTO PARASOPHIA

Parasophia: Kyoto International Festival of Contemporary Culture 2015
Saturday, March 7– Sunday, May 10, 2015
Venues: Kyoto Municipal Museum of Art,
The Museum of Kyoto, and other locations in Kyoto **www.parasophia.jp**

ART ACROSS THE CITY
SWANSEA, UK

Public Art Open Submission

Locws International is pleased to announce its second Open Submission competition for UK and international artists interested in working in the public realm.

Two selected artists will receive a £1,000 fee and a budget up to £2,500 to cover design, production, materials and installation.

Selection Panel: **Bob & Roberta Smith RA**, Artist; **Jane Simpson**, Artist, Director, Galerie Simpson; **David Hastie**, Director, Locws International and **Gordon Dalton**, Project Manager, Locws International.

Deadline: **1st December 2014**. For details of how to apply visit: *www.artacrossthecity.com/opensubmission*

www.artacrossthecity.com
e: locws@locwsinternational.com | t: +44 (0)1792 468979
t: @Locws_Art | f: Locws International

a LOCWS International production with support from:

EX—FACTORY

8—29 November 2014

Leigh Clarke

Chloe Cooper

Leslie Deere

Shaun Doyle and
Mally Mallinson

**Olympus Engineering,
College Road, Shelton,
Stoke-on-Trent, ST1 4DQ**

Supported using public funding by
**ARTS COUNCIL
ENGLAND**

ART.CITY

www.ex-factory.co.uk

museabrugge.be

BRU
GGE
MUSEA
BRUGGE

Ellen Harvey
the unloved

GROENINGEMUSEUM BRUGES (BE)

02.10.2014
01.02.2015

20 MAY

Save the date

WWW.TRIENNALEBRUGGE.BE

**TRIENNALE
BRUGGE 2015**

✦✦✦✦✦

**CRACKING THE
CITY GENE**

Contemporary art
and architecture

in the historical
city of Bruges

18 OCT

Vrienden
Musea Brugge

ERKEND
MUSEUM

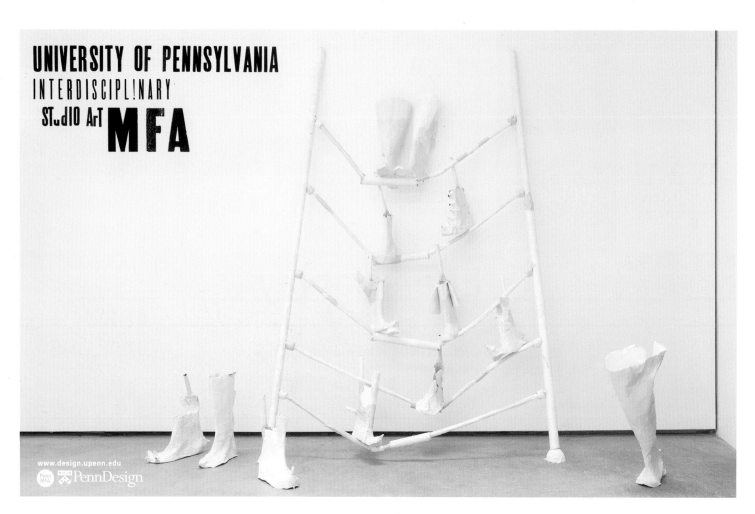

UNIVERSITY OF PENNSYLVANIA
INTERDISCIPL!NARY
STUdIO ARt MFA

www.design.upenn.edu

Penn MFA · PennDesign

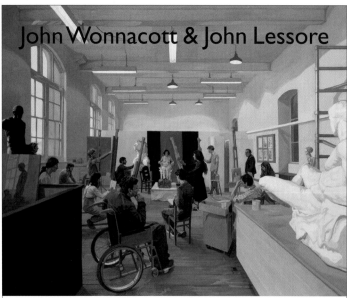

John Wonnacott & John Lessore

The Life Room and the City

4 October – 4 January 2015
Norwich Castle Museum and Art Gallery

About Life

4 November – 10 January 2015
The Gallery at Norwich
University of the Arts
www.nua.ac.uk/wandl

 NORWICH UNIVERSITY OF THE ARTS Norwich Castle Museum & Art Gallery Norfolk Museums Service ARTS COUNCIL ENGLAND heritage lottery fund LOTTERY FUNDED Bringing great art to the East · East Anglia Art Fund

---

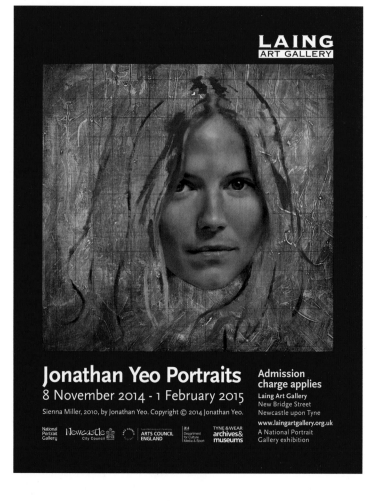

LAING
ART GALLERY

Jonathan Yeo Portraits
8 November 2014 - 1 February 2015

Sienna Miller, 2010, by Jonathan Yeo. Copyright © 2014 Jonathan Yeo.

National Portrait Gallery · Newcastle City Council · ARTS COUNCIL ENGLAND · Department for Culture Media & Sport · TYNE & WEAR archives & museums

Admission charge applies

Laing Art Gallery
New Bridge Street
Newcastle upon Tyne
www.laingartgallery.org.uk

A National Portrait
Gallery exhibition

WARNING
THIS EXPOSITION
CAN CHANGE YOUR LIFE

21
Quartier
Belvedere

21erHaus.at

"THE MEDIA ARE THE MEASURE OF THE WORLD"

★★★★
PETER WEIBEL

PETER WEIBEL
MEDIA REBEL

DIRECTOR **AGNES HUSSLEIN-ARCO** ARTIST **PETER WEIBEL** EXHIBITION-MAKER **ALFRED WEIDINGER** SPECIAL EFFECTS **WILLI NEUNER**

PHOTO **MORITZ SCHELL** CAMERA **FERDINAND STEININGER** MEDIA PARTNERS **DER STANDARD, FALTER** CO-OPERATION-PARTNER **UNIQA** EXHIBITION-VENUE **21ER HAUS**

DER STANDARD   FALTER   ꞏꞯ UNIQA

17 OCTOBER 2014 – 18 JANUARY 2015

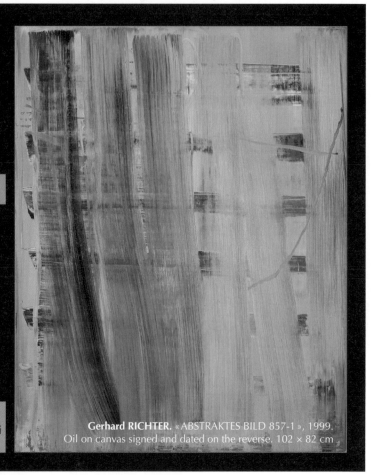
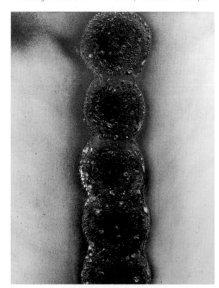

"No-one can read *frieze* and remain unchanged."

HANS ULRICH OBRIST

Never miss an issue of *frieze*! Subscribe from just £37
www.frieze.com/subscribe

BRD

Contemporary Art
from Germany

28 November 2014

Catalogue online now at
www.villa-grisebach.de

GRISEBACH

"A manifesto for anyone who cares about art"

NADA
MIAMI BEACH

Collins Ave & 67th St

Dec 4–7, 2014

NADA   newartdealers.org

Art | Basel
Miami Beach | Dec | 4–7 | 2014

Galleries | 303 Gallery | A | A Gentil Carioca | Abreu | Acquavella | Alexander and Bonin | Ameringer McEnery Yohe | Approach | Arnaud | Art : Concept | Artiaco | B | Baudach | benítez | Benzacar | Berggruen | Bernier/Eliades | Blum & Poe | Boesky | Bonakdar | Boone | Bortolami | BQ | Brito | Gavin Brown | Buchholz | C | Campoli Presti | Carberry | Casa Triângulo | Casas Riegner | Cheim & Read | Chemould | Chouakri | Cohan | Contemporary Fine Arts | Continua | Cooper | Corbett vs. Dempsey | CRG | Crousel | D | DAN | Dane | Davidson | De Carlo | de Osma | Dee | E | Eigen + Art | elbaz | F | Faria | Foksal | Fortes Vilaça | Freeman | Friedman | G | Gagosian | Galerie 1900 – 2000 | Gavlak | Gladstone | Gmurzynska | González | Marian Goodman | Goodman Gallery | Grässlin | Alexander Gray | Richard Gray | Greenberg | Greene Naftali | Greve | Guerra | Gupta | H | Hammer | Hauser & Wirth | Herald St | Hetzler | Hirschl & Adler | Hoffman | Houk | Hufkens | I | Ingleby | J | Jacques | Rodolphe Janssen | Juda | K | Kaplan | Kasmin | kaufmann repetto | Kelly | Kern | Kewenig | Kicken | Kilchmann | Kohn | König | Kordansky | Kreps | Krinzinger | Kukje / Kim | kurimanzutto | L | Landau | Lee | Lehmann Maupin | Lelong | Lévy | Lisson | Long March | Luhring Augustine | M | Maccarone | Magazzino | Mai 36 | Mara La Ruche | Marconi | Marks | Marlborough | Martin | Mathes | Mayer | McCaffrey | Meier | Meile | mennour | Metro Pictures | Meyer Riegger | Mezzanin | Millan | Miro | Mitchell-Innes & Nash | Mnuchin | Modern Art | Modern Institute | N | nächst St. Stephan | Nahem | Nahmad | Naumann | Navarro | neugerriemschneider | Noero | Nolan | Nordenhake | O | OMR | P | P.P.O.W | Pace | Pace/MacGill | Parrasch | Perrotin | Petzel | Presenhuber | Proyectos Monclova | R | Rech | Reena Spaulings | Regen Projects | Roberts & Tilton | Roesler | Ropac | Rosen | Rosenfeld | Rumma | S | Sadie Coles | Salon 94 | SCAI | Schipper | Schulte | Shainman | ShanghART | Sicardi | Sies + Höke | Sikkema Jenkins | Skarstedt | Snitzer | Sperone Westwater | Sprüth Magers | Staerk | Standard (Oslo) | Stein | Stevenson | Strina | Sur | T | Taylor | team | Thomas | Thumm | Tilton | Tornabuoni | V | Van de Weghe | Van Doren Waxter | Vermelho | Vielmetter | W | Waddington Custot | Wallner | Washburn | Wentrup | Werner | White Cube | Wolff | Z | Zeno X | ZERO | Zwirner | Nova | 47 Canal | 80m2 | Altman Siegel | Beijing Commune | Bureau | Cervera | Cherry and Martin | Cintra + Box 4 | Instituto de visión | Labor | Layr | Leighton | Leme | Liprandi | Maisterravalbuena | Meessen De Clercq | Mendes Wood | Michael Jon | Francesca Minini | mor charpentier | MOT International | mother's tankstation | Parra & Romero | Peres Projects | Real Fine Arts | Anita Schwartz | Silverman | SKE | Société | Supportico Lopez | T293 | Take Ninagawa | Travesía Cuatro | Wallspace | Positions | Carroll/Fletcher | Central | Clifton Benevento | Crèvecoeur | Fraser | Freedman Fitzpatrick | Gunn | Jongma | Kalfayan | RaebervonStenglin | Ramiken Crucible | Razuk | Revolver | SlyZmud | SpazioA | Subal | Edition | Cristea | Crown Point | GDM | Gemini G.E.L. | Knust | Nitsch | Pace Prints | Paragon | Polígrafa | Stolper | STPI | Two Palms | Survey | Bergamin | Bjerggaard | Broadway 1602 | Charim | de Torres | Edlin | espaivisor | Fuentes | Greenan | Menconi + Schoelkopf | Tonkonow | Vallois | Y++ Wada

✳ UBS

Curated by
Omar López-Chahoud
Christophe Boutin
Melanie Scarciglia

Architecture
by K/R

Art.
Curated.
International.

UNTITLED.

Miami Beach
Ocean and 12th
Dec
3/4/5/6/7
2014

art-untitled.com

Twitter
@untitledmiami

Facebook
/untitledartfair

Instagram
@untitledartfair

#untitled2014

MIAMIBEACH

PACIFIC CENTURY

E HOʻOMAU NO MOANANUIĀKEA

An international exhibition of contemporary art featuring artists from Hawaiʻi, Oceania, and Asia-Pacific

FEB 18 —MAY 8 2022

Honolulu, Oʻahu, Hawaiʻi

HAWAIʻI TRIENNIAL 2022

HAWAIʻI CONTEMPORARY

hawaiicontemporary.org

PACIFIC CENTURY

E HO'OMAU

NO MOANANUIĀKEA

An international exhibition of contemporary art featuring artists from Hawai'i, Oceania, and Asia-Pacific

FEB 18 —MAY 8 2022

Honolulu, O'ahu, Hawai'i

HAWAI'I TRIENNIAL 2022

HAWAI'I
CONTEMPORARY

hawaiicontemporary.org

a departure from consensus reality

Ministério da Cultura, SP-Arte,
Itaú, Oi and Iguatemi São Paulo present

sp-arte
/2015

April 08 to 12
Pavilhão da Bienal

São Paulo International Art Fair
April 08 [Preview]
April 09 to 12 [Open to the public]

 #sparte2015
www.sp-arte.com

Master Sponsorship

Itaú

IGUATEMI
SÃO PAULO

Cultural Support

Execution
sp-arte
Ministério da
Cultura

 **BRASIL**
PAÍS RICO É PAÍS SEM POBREZA

Art | Basel
Hong Kong | March | 15–17 | 2015

Australia & New Zealand

Dominik Mersch Gallery

Sydney, Australia
75 McLachlan Ave, Rushcutters Bay, 2011
tel. +61 2 9368 1999
www.dominikmerschgallery.com

JON CATTAPAN
'I'll be your mirror'
through 16 November
HELEN PYNOR
20 November – 20 December

Lab:
JENNY IHN
20 November – 20 December

Galerie Elisabeth & Klaus Thoman

Innsbruck
Maria-Theresien-Straße 34, 6020
tel. +43 512 575 785
www.galeriethoman.com

JOHN M ARMLEDER
through 10 January
Galerie Elisabeth & Klaus Thoman VIENNA,
Seilerstätte 7, 1010:
'LITTLE NEMO'
Curated by Max Hollein.
through 8 November
HERMANN NITSCH
'70. Malaktion'
21 November – February

**GAGPROJECTS /
Greenaway Art Gallery**

Adelaide, Australia
39 Rundle Street, Kent Town, 5067
tel. +61 8 8362 6354
www.greenaway.com.au

ARIEL HASSAN
'Capitulation of Discourse'
through 16 November

JENNY WATSON
19 November – 19 December

Roslyn Oxley9 Gallery

Sydney, Australia
8 Soudan Lane, off Hampden Street, 2021
tel. +61 2 9331 1919
www.roslynoxley9.com.au

**CAROLINE ROTHWELL
DEL KATHRYN BARTON**
13 November – 13 December

Austria

**ZEIT KUNST
NIEDERÖSTERREICH**

St. Polten
Kulturbezirk 5, 3100
tel. +43 2742 908 090
www.zeitkunstnoe.at

K.U.SCH.
'A Palette of Themes'
through 22 February

**Australian Centre for
Contemporary Art**

Melbourne, Australia
111 Sturt Street Southbank, 3006
tel. +61 3 9697 9999
www.accaonline.org.au

'FRAMED MOVEMENTS'
through 23 November

'MENAGERIE'
International, trans-historical survey tapping
into the link between humans and other animals.
Curated by Juliana Engberg.
13 December – 1 March

**Sherman Contemporary
Art Foundation**

Sydney, Australia
16-20 Goodhope Street, Paddington, 2021
tel. +61 2 9331 1112
www.sherman-scaf.org.au

**COLLECTION+: PINAREE SANPITAK
FUGITIVE STRUCTURES 2014**
'AR-MA: Trifolium'
In association with BVN Donovan Hill.
through 13 December

**Kunsthaus Graz,
Universalmuseum Joanneum**

Graz
Lendkai 1, 8020
tel. +43 316 80 17 9200
www.museum-joanneum.at/kunsthaus

**'DAMAGE CONTROL. ART AND
DESTRUCTION SINCE 1950'**
Organised by the Hirshhorn Museum and
Smithsonian Institution (Washington DC)
in association with Mudam Luxembourg.
14 November – 15 February

Galerie Thaddaeus Ropac

Salzburg
Mirabellplatz 2, 5020
tel. +43 662 881 3930
www.ropac.at

JACK PIERSON
through 15 November
GILBERT & GEORGE
through 17 January

Abu Dhabi Art Fair
4 – 8 November
Paris Photo
12 – 16 November
Art Basel Miami Beach
4 – 7 December

Gallery Gabrielle Pizzi

Melbourne, Australia
51 Victoria Street, 3065
tel. +61 3 9416 4170
www.gabriellepizzi.com.au

JULIE GOUGH
'HUNTING PARTY
incorporating Barbeque Area'
CHRISTIAN THOMPSON
'POLARI'
through 15 November

**LISA UHL
LORRAINE CONNELLY-NORTHEY**
19 November – 20 December

Te Tuhi

Auckland, New Zealand
13 Reeves Road, 2010
tel. +64 9 282 3967
www.tetuhi.org.nz

'OTHER WATERS'
A selection of New Zealand & international
contemporary artists.
15 November – 15 February

**Neue Galerie Graz,
Universalmuseum Joanneum**

Graz
Joanneumsviertel, 8010
tel. +43 316 80 17 9100
www.museum-joanneum.at/neue-galerie-graz

'DIE KUNST DES HERRN NESTLER'
through 22 February

**'EMERGENCE INTO MODERNISM?
PAUL SCHAD-ROSSA AND THE ARTS
IN GRAZ'**
7 November – 22 February

Galerie Nikolaus Ruzicska

Salzburg
Faistauergasse 12, 5020
tel. +43 662 630 360
www.ruzicska.com

KATJA STRUNZ
through 15 November

AXEL HUETTE
'Venezia'
21 November – 17 January

Anna Schwartz Gallery

Melbourne, Australia
185 Flinders Lane, 3000
tel. +61 3 9654 6131
www.annaschwartzgallery.com

KATHY TEMIN
'Pet Cemetery'
through 8 November
DANIEL VON STURMER
13 November – 20 December
Sydney, 245 Wilson Street, Darlington, 2008:
'COLD INTIMACY'
Nina Beier, Simon Denny, Alicia Frankovich
and Marlie Mul
15 November – 20 December

Galerie im Taxispalais

Innsbruck
Maria-Theresien-Straße 45, 6020
tel. +43 512 508 3171
www.galerieimtaxispalais.at

DANIEL RICHTER
'Chromos goo bugly'
through 23 November

**'LIVING IN THE MATERIAL WORLD –
MATERIALITY IN CONTEMPORARY ART'**
Lara Almarcegui, Michael Beutler, Karla Black,
Berta Fischer et al.
6 December – 15 February

Salzburger Kunstverein

Salzburg
Hellbrunner Straße 3, 5020
tel. +43 662 842 2940
www.salzburger-kunstverein.at

BEDWYR WILLIAMS
'Echt'
BEA MCMAHON
'Cover'
through 30 November

**'ANNUAL EXHIBITION 2014'
THOMAS HÖRL**
13 December – 1 February

Benelux

Hilger BROTKunsthalle
Vienna
Absberggasse 27, Stair 1, 1100
tel. +43 1 512 53 15200
www.hilger.at

Ö1 TALENTESTIPENDIUM FÜR BILDENDE KUNST 2014'
7 – 15 November

OSWALD OBERHUBER
18 December – 28 February

mumok – Museum of Modern Art Ludwig Foundation Vienna
Vienna
Museumsplatz 1, 1070
tel. +43 1 525 000
www.mumok.at

COSIMA VON BONIN
'HIPPIES USE SIDE DOOR. THE YEAR 2014 HAS LOST THE PLOT.'
through 18 January

'THE PRESENT OF MODERNISM'
through 8 February

Mu.ZEE
Oostende, Belgium
11 Romestraat, 8400
tel. +32 59 564 589
www.muzee.be

'THE SEA – SALUT D'HONNEUR JAN HOET'
Etel Adnan, Forrest Bess, Marcel Broodthaers, Gustave Courbet, Hanne Darboven, Henri Matisse, Reinard Mucha, Paul Thek, Lawrence Weiner, Katharina Wulff et al.
through 19 April

Gallery Ernst Hilger Wien 01
Vienna
Dorotheergasse 5, 1010
tel. +43 1 512 5315
www.hilger.at

'CURATED BY_VIENNA: THE CENTURY OF THE BED'
Curated by Alenka Gregoric.
through 8 November
JOAN MIRO
'Drawings, Prints, and Sculptures'
12 November – 13 December
FRIEDRICH PLAHL
17 December – 31 January

Secession
Vienna
Friedrichstraße 12, 1010
tel. +43 1 587 5307
www.secession.at

**CHTO DELAT?
RENATA LUCAS
PETER BARTOŠ**
21 November – 25 January

Tim Van Laere Gallery
Antwerp, Belgium
Verlatstraat 23-25, 2000
tel. +32 3 257 1417
www.timvanlaeregallery.com

HENK VISCH
through 29 November

ANTON HENNING
4 December – 24 January

DEWEER gallery
Otegem, Belgium
Tiegemstraat 6A, 8553
tel. +32 56 644 893
www.deweergallery.com

MICHAËL AERTS
'It was like so, but wasn't'
GEORGE LITTLE
'Wagon/Damask'
5 November – 14 December

Gallery Hilger NEXT Wien 10
Vienna
Absberggasse 27, Stair 2, 1010
tel. +43 1 512 53 15200
www.hilger.at

OLIVER DORFER
'wasteland'
7 November – 6 December
IAN BURNS
'Moment – Fragment'
18 December – 28 February
Project Room @ NEXT, Vienna
Absberggasse 27/2.3, 1100:
DOUGLAS HOEKZEMA
'Tangible Time'
7 November – 6 December

Galerie Hubert Winter
Vienna
Breite Gasse 17, 1070
tel. +43 1 524 0976
www.galeriewinter.at

'SLEEPLESS NIGHTS'
Curated by Abigail Solomon-Godeau.
through 8 November

FRANCESCA WOODMAN
13 November – 20 December

AEROPLASTICS
Brussels, Belgium
32 rue Blanche, 1060
tel. +32 2 537 2202
www.aeroplastics.net

'THE REMARKABLE LIGHTNESS OF BEING'
30 artists.
13 November – 20 December

1646
Den Haag, Netherlands
Boekhorststraat 125, 2512 CN
www.1646.nl

SHANA MOULTON
'Mindplace Thoughtstream'
through 30 November

HANNE LIPPARD
Performance.
3 December

ZIN TAYLOR
12 December – 25 January

Christine König Galerie
Vienna
Schleifmühlgasse 1a, 1040
tel. +43 1 585 7474
www.christinekoeniggalerie.com

'CURATED BY_VIENNA: THE CENTURY OF THE BED'
Curated by Luca Lo Pinto.
through 8 November

PER DYBVIG
'behind the house or in the bar at least '
13 November – 23 December

Almine Rech Gallery
Brussels, Belgium
Abdijstraat, 20, rue de l'Abbaye, 1050
tel. +32 2 648 5684
www.alminerech.com

AYAN FARAH
'Notes on Running Water'
**JOEL SHAPIRO
PIERO GOLIA**
'The Comedy of Craft (Intermission)'
through 12 November

JOHN ARMLEDER
'La Bruche du Haricot'
20 November – 14 February

Stroom Den Haag
Den Haag, Netherlands
Hogewal 1-9, 2514 HA
tel. +31 70 365 8985
www.stroom.nl

SUSAN SCHUPPLI
'Evidence on Trial'
through 16 November

'A GLASS DARKLY'
through 23 November

ANGELA FERREIRA
7 December – 22 February

Galerie Krinzinger
Vienna
Seilerstätte 16, 1010
tel. +43 1 513 3006/11
www.galerie-krinzinger.at
FRANK THIEL
through 11 November
ANJA RONACHER
through 15 November
THOMAS ZIPP / ISTVAN CSAKANY
18 November – 13 December
Krinzinger Projekte, Vienna
Schottenfeldgasse 45, 1070:
'CURATED BY_VIENNA: THE CENTURY OF THE BED'
Curated by Olga Sviblova.
through 23 November

Galerie Daniel Templon
Brussels, Belgium
Veydtstraat, 13A, Rue Veydt, 1060
tel. +32 2 537 1317
www.danieltemplon.com

JIM DINE
'New Paintings'
Opening: 6 November, 5.30-8.30pm
6 November – 20 December

West Den Haag
Den Haag, Netherlands
Groenewegje 136, 2515 LR
tel. +31 70 392 5359
www.westdenhaag.nl

'VOLKSPALEIS'
Konrad Smolenski, Cut Hands, Brutaz, Nic Collins, Noa Shadur, Mark Bain et al.
through 16 November
DENICOLAI & PROVOOST
'MORE'
through 6 December
MASSIMO GRIMALDI
'Morir Soñando'
12 December – 24 January

Marres – House for Contemporary Culture

Maastricht, Netherlands
Capucijnenstraat 98, 6211 RT
tel. +31 43 327 0207
www.marres.org

'THE UNWRITTEN'
Adela Babanova, Zachary Formwalt,
Annie Kevans, Gert Jan Kocken, Carlos Motta,
Óscar Muñoz, Song Ta, Koki Tanaka
through 23 November
'MARRES CURRENTS #2'
Recently graduated artists from academies
in BE, DE and NL.
11 December – 15 February

Jessica Bradley

Toronto
74 Miller Street, M6N 2Z9
tel. +1 416 537 3125
www.jessicabradleyinc.com

TRICIA MIDDLETON
'Making friends with yourself'
Sculpture & installation.
through 8 November

REBECCA BELMORE
13 November – 10 January

Contemporary Art Gallery

Vancouver
555 Nelson Street, V6B 6R5
tel. +1 604 681 2700
www.contemporaryartgallery.ca

JÜRGEN PARTENHEIMER
'The Archive – The Raven Diaries'
through 9 November

GUNILLA KLINGBERG
'Brand New View (Vancouver)'
through 11 January

SHIMABUKU
21 November – 11 January

MOCAK Museum of Contemporary Art in Krakow

Krakow, Poland
ul. Lipowa 4, 30-702
tel. +48 12 634 000
www.mocak.pl

JULIAN OPIE
'Sculptures, Paintings, Films'
through 25 January

Beta Gallery:
KAROL RADZISZEWSKI
'America Is Not Ready For This'
through 25 January

Diaz Contemporary

Toronto
100 Niagara Street, M5V 1C5
tel. +1 416 361 2972
www.diazcontemporary.ca

JOSEPH TISIGA
'A Sacred Game: Escape is Perpetual'
through 15 November

CHRIS KLINE
20 November – 10 January

UGM Maribor Art Gallery

Maribor, Slovenia
Strossmayerjeva ul. 6, 2000
tel. +386 2 229 5860
www.ugm.si

'HEROES WE LOVE'
Socialist-realism in Yugoslavia and
contemporary reactions.
19 December – 11 May

UGM Studio Maribor, Slovenia
Trg Leona Štuklja 2, 2000:
NINA SLEJKO BLOM & CONNY BLOM
'On the Shoulders of Giants'
13 November – 19 December

Canada

Daniel Faria Gallery

Toronto
188 St Helens Avenue, M6H 4A1
tel. +1 416 538 1880
www.danielfariagallery.com

MARK LEWIS
'Invention au Louvre'
At the Louvre, Paris.
through 5 January

KRISTINE MORAN
'Affairs and Ceremonies'
13 November – 10 January

Central & Eastern Europe

galerie antoine ertaskiran

Montréal
1892 rue Payette, H3J 1P3
tel. +1 514 989 7886
www.galerieantoineertaskiran.com

JON RAFMAN
'HOPE SPRINGS ETERNAL II'
through 22 November

UNTITLED. Miami
Andrea Sala
3 – 7 December

Susan Hobbs Gallery

Toronto
137 Tecumseth Street, M6J 2H2
tel. +1 416 504 3699
www.susanhobbs.com

SCOTT LYALL
through 22 November

ALTHEA THAUBERGER
'Preuzmimo Benčić'
27 November – 10 January

Galerie Rudolfinum

Prague, Czech Republic
Alsovo Nábrezí 12, 110 10
tel. +420 227 059 205
www.galerierudolfinum.cz

ANA MENDIETA
'Traces'
through 4 January

China

Birch Contemporary

Toronto
129 Tecumseth St, M6J 2H2
tel. +1 416 365 3003
www.birchcontemporary.com

RICHARD STORMS
'can't get there from here'
through 22 November

RENEE VAN HALM
'Depth of Field'
JANICE GURNERY
'Translations & Alliances'
29 November – 24 January

MKG127

Toronto
1445 Dundas Street West, M6J 1Y7
tel. +1 647 435 7682
www.mkg127.com

'WHAT BOX?'
Laura Kikauka with Carl Hamfelt
through 15 November
LISS PLATT
TEGAN MOORE
22 November – 20 December
MKG127 Front Space:
SYLVIA MATAS
through 15 November
UNTITLED. Miami
3 – 7 December

Contemporary Art Centre

Vilnius, Lithuania
Vokieciu Street 2, 01130
tel. +370 5 260 8960
www.cac.lt

'PROTOTYPES'
through 6 December

DAINIUS LIŠKEVIČIUS
'Labyrinthus'
14 November – 4 January

'THE OTHER SIGHT'
Curated by Julija Cistiakova.
21 November – 11 January

Boers-Li Gallery

Beijing
1-706 Hou Jie, 798 Art District
No.2 Yuan, Jiuxianqiao Lu, 100015-116
tel. +86 10 6432 2620
www.boersligallery.com

Artissima
7 – 9 November
Art021 Shanghai
12 – 16 November

Chambers Fine Art

Beijing
Red No.1-D, Caochangdi
Chaoyang District, 100015
tel. +86 10 5127 3298
www.chambersfineart.com
'GROUP SHOW'
Curated by Cui Cancan.
1 November – 7 December
YE NAN
13 December – 25 January
Chambers Fine Art New York,
522 W 19th Street, 10011:
AI WEIWEI
through 1 November
WU JIAN'AN
6 November – 20 December

Amy Li Gallery

Beijing
No. 54 Caochangdi (old Airport Road)
Chaoyang District, 100015
tel. +86 10 6434 0616
www.amyligallery.com
LI JIKAI
'Waste Picker'
YE YONGQING
'Hidden in the Grass'
through 9 November
HENNING OLAV ESPEDAL
15 November – 31 December
Art Taipei
through 3 November
Context Miami
2 – 7 December

Galerie Urs Meile Beijing

Beijing
104 Chaochangdi Cun, Cui Gezhuang Xiang
Chaoyang District, 100015
tel. +86 10 6433 3393
www.galerieursmeile.com

CHRISTIAN SCHOELER
MENG HUANG
8 November – 11 January

Art Taipei
through 3 November
Art021 Shanghai
12 – 16 November
Art Basel Miami Beach
4 – 7 December

Pékin Fine Arts

Beijing
No. 241 Cao Changdi Village, Cui Ge Zhuang
Chaoyang District, 100015
tel. +86 10 5127 3220
www.pekinfinearts.com

'POST-PHOTOGRAPHY'
through 11 November

Pékin Fine Arts Hong Kong:
'WAR ROOM'
through 18 November

Red Brick Art Museum

Beijing
Hegezhuang, Cuigezhuang Village
Chaoyang District, 100103
tel. +86 10 8457 6669
www.redbrickartmuseum.org

HUANG YONGPING
'The Conclusion of Tales from the Taiping Era –
the Arrival of the Circus'
HUANG SUNQUAN
'u-topophilia: Art in Field and Societal Space'
through 16 January

Ullens Centre for Contemporary Art

Beijing
798 Art District, No. 4 Jiuxianqiao Lu
Chaoyang District, 100015
tel. +86 10 5780 0200
www.ucca.org.cn

THE LOS ANGELES PROJECT
through 9 November

WHITE SPACE BEIJING

Beijing
No.255 Caochangdi, Airport Service Road
Chaoyang District, 100015
tel. +86 10 8456 2054
www.whitespace-beijing.com

HE XIANGYU
'Dotted Line'
XIE FAN
'Back to the Footlights Tomorrow'
through 7 December

Art021 Shanghai
12 – 16 November

Simon Lee Gallery Hong Kong

Hong Kong
304 Pedder Building
12 Pedder Street, Central
tel. +852 2801 6252
www.simonleegallery.com

MERLIN CARPENTER
'Decades'
through 15 November

SHERRIE LEVINE
Opening preview: 22 November
23 November – 3 January

Edouard Malingue Gallery

Hong Kong
8 Queen's Road, Central
tel. +852 2810 0317
www.edouardmalingue.com

CUI XINMING
through 15 November
Taipei Artist Village:
'NEVER ODD OR EVEN'
through 9 November
Art Taipei
through 3 November
Art021 Shanghai
12 – 16 November
Singapore Art Fair
27 – 30 November

Lehmann Maupin Hong Kong

Hong Kong
407 Pedder Building
12 Pedder Street, Central
tel. +852 2530 0025
www.lehmannmaupin.com

ROBIN RHODE
'having been there'
through 8 November

UDOMSAK KRISANAMIS
'Planet Caravan'
7 November – 20 December

Galerie Perrotin

Hong Kong
50 Connaught Road, Central
tel. +852 3758 2180
www.perrotin.com

JOHAN CRETEN
'Fireworks'
through 15 November
SOPHIE CALLE
MAKOTO AIDA
26 November – 10 January
Art021 Shanghai
12 – 16 November
Art Basel Miami Beach
4 – 7 December

White Cube Hong Kong

Hong Kong
50 Connaught Road, Central
tel. +852 2259 2000
www.whitecube.com

LARRY BELL
'Light and Red'
through 15 November

FRIEDRICH KUNATH
'Earth to Fuckface'
21 November – 17 January

AIKE DELLARCO

Shanghai
50 Moganshan Road, F2, Building 1
tel. +86 21 5252 7164
www.dearco.it

0 Space Shanghai, Room 102, Bldg 0,
50 Moganshan Rd, 200060:
TANG DIXIN
13 November – 13 December

Artissima
7 – 9 November
Art021 Shanghai
12 – 16 November

Power Station of Art

Shanghai
200 Huayuangang Road
Huangpu District, 200011
tel. +86 21 3110 8550
www.powerstationofart.com

**'THE 1ST PSA'S EMERGING
CURATORS PROGRAM'**
through 8 March

**'SOCIAL FACTORY: THE 10TH
SHANGHAI BIENNALE'**
23 November – 31 March

ShanghART Gallery and H-Space

Shanghai
50 Moganshan Road
Building 16 & 18, 200060
tel. +86 21 6359 3923
www.shanghartgallery.com

Please contact the gallery for information.

Leo Xu Projects

Shanghai
Lane 49, Building 3, Fuxing Xi Road
Xuhui District, 200031
tel. +86 21 3461 1245
www.leoxuprojects.com

CUI JIE
'Recent Works'
14 November – 11 January

OCAT Shenzhen

Shenzhen
Enping Road, Overseas Chinese Town, 518053
tel. +86 755 2691 6199
www.ocat.org.cn

**'WORLD FACTORY: AS A THEATRE OF
SOCIAL STUDIES AND PRACTICES'**
Curated by Zhaochuan.
17 – 23 November

France

Galerie Chantal Crousel

Paris
10, rue Charlot, 75003
tel. +33 1 4277 3887
www.crousel.com

SETH PRICE
'Animation Studio'
through 6 December
MELIK OHANIAN
'Stuttering'
12 December – 31 January

La Douane, 11F, rue Léon Jouhaux, Paris 75010:
'GALERIE NEU AT LA DOANE'
through 3 December

Germany

Jousse Entreprise

Paris
6, rue Saint Claude, 75003
tel. +33 1 53 82 10 18
www.jousse-entreprise.com
THOMAS GRÜNFELD
8 November – 13 December
18, rue de Seine, 75006:
**ANTOINE PHILIPPON
& JACQUELINE LECOQ**
through 1 November
ANDRÉ BORDERIE
7 November – 6 December
The Salon: Art + Design
14 – 17 November
Design Miami
3 – 7 December

Galerie Perrotin

Paris
76, rue de Turenne, 75003
tel. +33 1 42 16 79 79
www.perrotin.com

PARK SEO-BO
6 November – 20 December
New York, 909 Madison Avenue, 10021:
JOHN HENDERSON
through 15 November
CLAUDE RUTAULT
20 November – 3 January
Art021 Shanghai
12 – 16 November
Art Basel Miami Beach
4 – 7 December

Galerie Almine Rech

Paris
64, rue de Turenne, 75003
tel. +33 1 45 83 71 90
www.alminerech.com

RICHARD PRINCE
'New Figures'
through 20 December

Galerie Thaddaeus Ropac

Paris
7, rue Debelleyme, 75003
tel. +33 1 42 72 99 00
www.ropac.net

LIZA LOU
through 19 November
STURTEVANT
22 November – 20 December
Galerie Thaddaeus Ropac, Paris-Pantin
69, av. du Général Leclerc, 93500:
OLIVER BEER
through 15 November
'THE POWER OF PAINTING'
Georg Baselitz, Anselm Kiefer, Yan Pei-Ming
23 November – 30 January

Galerie Patrick Seguin – 20th Century Furniture and Architecture

Paris
5, rue des Taillandiers, 75011
tel. +33 1 47 00 32 35
www.patrickseguin.com

'CARTE BLANCHE KURIMANZUTTO, MEXICO'
Gabriel Orozco, Rirkrit Tiravanija, Gabriel Kuri, Damian Ortega, Jimmie Durham, Gabriel Sierra, Jonathan Hernandez.
through 26 November

Sultana

Paris
12, rue Ramponeau, 75020
tel. +33 1 44 54 08 90
www.galeriesultana.com

NAUFUS RAMIREZ FIGUEROA
through 20 December

Artissima
Pia Camil, Emmanuel Lagarrigue, Gavin Perry
7 – 9 November

Suzanne Tarasieve Paris

Paris
7, rue Pastourelle, 75003
tel. +33 1 42 71 76 54
www.suzanne-tarasieve.com

MARKUS LÜPERTZ
'Promenade'
through 20 December
LOFT19 Paris, Passage de l'Atlas
5 Villa Marcel Lods, 75019 :
STANISLAS GUIGUI
'Cabaret New Burlesque'
through 29 November
Paris Photo
Boris Mikhaïlov, Juergen Teller
13 – 16 November

Galerie Daniel Templon

Paris
30, rue Beaubourg, 75003
tel. +33 1 42 72 14 10
www.danieltemplon.com

DAVID LACHAPELLE
'LAND SCAPE'
through 24 December

Galerie Georges-Philippe & Nathalie Vallois

Paris
36, rue de Seine, 75006
tel. +33 1 46 34 61 07
www.galerie-vallois.com

**ALAIN BUBLEX
JEAN-YVES JOUANNAIS**
through 8 November
RICHARD JACKSON
14 November – 20 December
Abu Dhabi Art
5 – 8 November
Art Basel Miami Beach
4 – 7 December

Ludwig Forum Aachen

Aachen
Jülicher Strasse 97-109, 52070
tel. +49 241 180 7104
www.ludwigforum.de

'MODERN ICONS. PAINTING FROM THE COLLECTION'
through 8 February
**'EASTWARDS. FREEDOM, BORDERS, PROJECTIONS'
ALMAGUL MENLIBAYEVA**
'Transoxiana Dreams'
16 November – 22 February
MICHAEL DEAN
16 November – ongoing

Künstlerhaus Bethanien GmbH

Berlin
Kottbusser Straße 10, 10999
tel. +49 30 616 9030
www.bethanien.de
**MASASHI ECHIGO
PRISCILA FERNANDES
EMMA WALTRAUD HOWES
PRAJAKTA POTNIS
RON TRAN**
through 2 November
'OPEN STUDIOS'
19 November, 7-10pm
**CHIA-WEI HSU
'FALKENROT PREIS 2014:
MICHAELA MEISE'**
20 November – 14 December

Galerie Buchholz

Berlin
Fasanenstraße 30, 10719
tel. +49 30 886 24056
www.galeriebuchholz.de

RICHARD HAWKINS
27 November – 24 January

Deutsche Bank KunstHalle

Berlin
Unter den Linden 13-15, 10117
tel. +49 30 202 0930
www.deutsche-bank-kunsthalle.com

MESCHAC GABA
Museum of Contemporary African Art in cooperation with Tate Modern.
through 16 November

'HÖHERE WESEN BEFEHLEN...'
Baselitz, de Kooning, Polke, Rainer, Rauch, Richter. Works on paper from the Collection Frieder Burda.
5 December – 8 March

Sprüth Magers Berlin

Berlin
Oranienburger Straße 18, 10178
tel. +49 30 2888 4030
www.spruethmagers.com

'ARTE POVERA AND 'MULTIPLI', TORINO 1970-1975'
through 17 January
**LOUISE LAWLER
ROBERT ELFGEN**
15 November – 17 January 2015
Sprüth Magers London
7a Grafton Street, W1S 4EJ:
JOSEPH KOSUTH
26 November – February 2015

Neuer Berliner Kunstverein

Berlin
Chausseestraße 128-129, 10115
tel. +49 30 280 7020
www.nbk.org

LUCA VITONE
through 9 November
NAIRY BAGHRAMIAN
13 December – 25 January

n.b.k. Showroom:
KATHARINA GROSSE
through 7 November
LAURE PROUVOST
16 December – 23 January

me Collectors Room Berlin / Olbricht Foundation

Berlin
Auguststraße 68, 10117
tel. +49 30 8600 8510
www.me-berlin.com

'FRAGILE SENSE OF HOPE – ART COLLECTION TELEKOM'
through 23 November

'EXOTICA AND 4 OTHER CASES OF THE SELF'
through 22 February

Haus am Waldsee – Internationale Kunst in Berlin

Berlin
Argentinische Allee 30, 14163
tel. +49 30 801 8935
www.hausamwaldsee.de

MICHAEL SAILSTORFER
'B-Side'
through 9 November

HAUS-RUCKER-CO
'Architectural Utopia Reloaded'
22 November – 22 February

Bonner Kunstverein

Bonn
Hochstadenring 22, 53119
tel. +49 228 693 936
www.bonner-kunstverein.com

GABRIEL LESTER & HAEGUE YANG
'Follies, manifold'
through 23 November

JANA EULER
6 December – 22 February

LISTINGS

Kunstverein Braunschweig

Braunschweig
Lessingplatz 12, 38100
tel. +49 531 49556
www.kunstverein-bs.de

Villa Salve Hospes:
CLEMENS VON WEDEMEYER
through 16 November
WILFREDO PRIETO
6 December – 15 January
Remise:
KEVIN SCHMIDT
through 16 November
FLORIAN AUER
6 December – 15 February

Künstlerhaus Bremen

Bremen
Am Deich 68/69, 28199
tel. +49 421 508 598
www.kuenstlerhausbremen.de

ARMANDO ANDRADE TUDELA
'Nomadismus beginnt zu Hause'
through 30 November

'PRESENTATION OF THE ANNUAL EDITIONS'
12 December

GAK Gesellschaft für Aktuelle Kunst

Bremen
Teerhof 21, 28199
tel. +49 421 500 897
www.gak-bremen.de

KOENRAAD DEDOBBELEER
'A Quarrel in a Faraway Country Between People of Whom We Know Nothing'
1 November – 25 January

Galerie Buchholz

Cologne
Neven-DuMont-Straße 17, 50667
tel. +49 221 257 4946
www.galeriebuchholz.de

LIZ DESCHENES / FLORIAN PUMHÖSL
12 November – 10 January

Elisenstraße 4-6, 50667:
'MA-RE MOUNT'
Carl Andre, Liz Deschenes, Richard Prince, R.H. Quaytman
12 November – 10 January

GALERIE CHRISTIAN LETHERT

Cologne
Antwerpener Strasse 4, 50672
tel. +49 221 356 0590
www.christianlethert.com

LUTZ FRITSCH
'gerade gebogen'
through 20 December

Nada Miami
Rana Begum, Fergus Feehily, Imi Knoebel, Daniel Lergon
4 – 7 December

Museum Ludwig

Cologne
Heinrich-Böll-Platz, 50667
tel. +49 221 2212 6165
www.museum-ludwig.de

'INTRACTABLE AND UNTAMED: DOCUMENTARY PHOTOGRAPHY AROUND 1979'
'THE MUSEUM OF PHOTOGRAPHY: A REVISION'
through 16 November
'LUDWIG GOES POP'
through 11 January
ANDREA BÜTTNER
'2'
through 15 March

Galerie Thomas Zander

Cologne
Schönhauser Straße 8, 50968
tel. +49 221 934 8856
www.galeriezander.com

'DOUBLE ELEPHANT'
Manuel Álvarez Bravo, Walker Evans, Lee Friedlander, Garry Winogrand
through 10 November

LEE FRIEDLANDER & PIERRE BONNARD
through 15 November

ROBERT ADAMS / RUDOLF SCHWARZ
22 November – 14 February

Kunsthalle Düsseldorf

Dusseldorf
Grabbeplatz 4, 40213
tel. +49 211 899 6243
www.kunsthalle-duesseldorf.de

THOMAS RUFF
'LICHTEN'
through 11 January

KIT – Kunst im Tunnel
Mannesmannufer 1b, 40213:
'TAU'
A project by the class of Prof. Katharina Grosse.
29 November – 15 February

Julia Stoschek Collection

Dusseldorf
Schanzenstraße 54, 40549
tel. +49 211 585 8840
www.julia-stoschek-collection.net

'NUMBER NINE: ELIZABETH PRICE'
through 1 February

MMK Museum für Moderne Kunst

Frankfurt
Domstraße 10, 60311
tel. +49 69 2123 0447
www.mmk-frankfurt.de
MMK1, Domstraße 10, 60311:
SUBODH GUPTA
through 18 January
STURTEVANT
through 1 February
MMK2, Taunustor 1, 60310:
'BOOM SHE BOOM. WORKS FROM THE MMK COLLECTION'
through 14 June
MMK3, Domstraße 3, 60311:
DAYANITA SINGH
through 4 January

Portikus

Frankfurt
Alte Brücke 2 / Maininsel, 60594
tel. +49 69 9624 4540
www.portikus.de

LUCY RAVEN
'Curtains'
through 23 November

ELIF ERKAN
'Konzentration der Kräfte'
6 December – 1 February

SCHIRN KUNSTHALLE FRANKFURT

Frankfurt
Römerberg, 60311
tel. +49 69 299 882 112
www.schirn.de

HELENE SCHJERFBECK
ANDREAS SCHULZE
'Pea Roads'
through 11 January
'GERMAN POP'
Thomas Bayrle, Christa Dichgans, Karl Horst Hödicke, Konrad Klapheck, Ferdinand Kriwet, Uwe Lausen, Sigmar Polke, Gerhard Richter et al.
6 November – 8 February

Kunstverein in Hamburg

Hamburg
Klosterwall 23, 20095
tel. +49 40 322 157
www.kunstverein.de

LISA OPPENHEIM
'Forever is Composed of Nows'
KARL LARSSON
'North Western Prose'
through 18 January

Badischer Kunstverein

Karlsruhe
Waldstraße 3, 76133
tel. +49 721 28226
www.badischer-kunstverein.de

GRACE SCHWINDT
'Only a Free Individual Can Create a Free Society'
BEATE ENGL
'APPARAT'
through 23 November

'EDITIONS 2014/2015'
9 December – 6 January

Kunstverein München

Munich
Galeriestraße 4, 80539
tel. +49 89 221152
www.kunstverein-muenchen.de

'REGENERATE ART'
Chris Evans, Aleksandra Domanovic, Lukas Duwenhögger, Alan Kane & Simon Periton, Scott King, Joanna Rajkowska
through 30 November

'JAHRESGABEN 2014'
5 – 14 December

Kunsthalle Nürnberg

Nuremberg
Lorenzer Straße 32, 90402
tel. +49 911 231 2853
www.kunsthalle.nuernberg.de

TATIANA TROUVÉ
'I TEMPI DOPPI'
13 November – 8 February

Kunstmuseum Wolfsburg

Wolfsburg
Hollerplatz 1, 38440
tel. +49 5361 26690
www.kunstmuseum-wolfsburg.de

IMI KNOEBEL
'Works 1966 – 2014'
through 15 February

India

Experimenter

Kolkata
2/1 Hindusthan Road, 700 029
tel. +91 33 4001 2289
www.experimenter.in

GAURI GILL & SEHER SHAH
'Ways of Seeing'
through 29 November

31st Bienal de São Paulo
Prabhakar Pachpute
through 7 December
Montréal Biennial
Hajra Waheed
through 4 January

Jhaveri Contemporary

Mumbai
2, Krishna Niwas
58A Walkeshwar Road, 400 006
tel. +91 22 2369 3639
www.jhavericontemporary.com

SHAMBHAVI KAUL
through November

Japan

SCAI THE BATHHOUSE

Tokyo
6-1-23 Yanaka, Taito-ku, 110-0001
tel. +81 3 3821 1144
www.scaithebathhouse.com

NATSUYUKI NAKANISHI
'Chiasme'
through 8 November

JULIAN OPIE
'Street Portraits'
14 November – 20 December

Scandinavia

Project 88

Mumbai
BMP Building, Ground Floor
N. A. Sawant Marg, Colaba, 400 005
tel. +91 22 2281 0066/99
www.project88.in

PALLAVI PAUL
'mistaking <> for direction signs'
13 November – 31 December

Taka Ishii Gallery

Tokyo
1-3-2-5F Kiyosumi, Koto-ku, 135-0024
tel. +81 3 5646 6050
www.takaishiigallery.com
NOBUYA HOKI
through 8 November
**SILKE OTTO-KNAPP AND
FLORIAN PUMHÖSL**
22 November – 20 December
Taka Ishii Gallery Photography / Film, Tokyo:
LEO RUBINFIEN
through 6 December
LINA SCHEYNIUS
13 December – 31 January
Paris Photo
13 – 16 November

ShugoArts

Tokyo
5th Floor, 1-3-2
Kiyosumi Koto-ku, 135-0024
tel. +81 3 5621 6434
www.shugoarts.com

YUKIO FUJIMOTO
through 1 November

**'3 ARTISTS SHOW: TEPPEI KANEUJI,
KESANG LAMDARK, LEE KIT'**
15 November – 20 December

Martin Asbaek Gallery

Copenhagen, Denmark
Bredgade 23, 1260
tel. +45 33 15 40 45
www.martinasbaek.com

JESPER CARLSEN
through 29 November

CORNELIUS QUABECK & PAUL MCDEVITT
5 December – 3 January

Paris Photo
Trine Søndergaard, Elina Brotherus,
Astrid Kruse Jensen, Nicolai Howalt,
Martin Liebscher, Ebbe Stub Wittrup
13 – 16 November

Exhibit 320

New Delhi
F-320, Lado Sarai, 110030
tel. +91 11 4613 0637
www.exhibit320.com

MITO GEGIČ
'Encryption'
Winner of the Laguna Awards.
through 14 November

**'ARTCHIVING: THE ARTIST'S
PERSPECTIVE'**
Remen Chopra, Probir Gupta, Pooja Iranna,
Muktinath Mondal, Vibha Galhotra
Curated by Ranjita Chaney Menezes.
20 November – 5 January

Aoyama Meguro

Tokyo
2-30-6 Kamimeguro, Meguro, 153-0051
tel. +81 3 3711 4099
www.aoyamameguro.com

TASTUMI ORIMOTO
'Carrying a baby pig on my back'
15 November – 6 December

HIROFUMI ISOYA
'Lag'
13 December – 10 January

Wako Works of Art

Tokyo
Piramide Bldg. 3F
6-6-9 Roppongi, Minato-ku, 106-0032
tel. +81 3 6647 1820
www.wako-art.jp

GREGOR SCHNEIDER
'it's all Rheydt'
through 22 November

Art Taipei
Miriam Cahn, Gerhard Richter,
Gregor Schneider, Wolfgang Tillmans,
Luc Tuymans, Nana Yokoi
through 3 November

Galleri Bo Bjerggaard

Copenhagen, Denmark
Flaesketorvet 85a, 1711
tel. +45 33 93 42 21
www.bjerggaard.com

ERWIN WURM
'Some of this and some of that'
7 November – 20 December

PER KIRKEBY
'Architecture'
21 November – 20 December

Latitude 28

New Delhi
F 208 GF, Lado Sarai, 110030
tel. +91 11 4679 1111
www.latitude28.com

'PERMANENT COLLECTION'
Kartik Sood, Deepjyoti Kalita, Dilip Chobisa,
Gigi Scaria, Baiju Parthan, Prajakta Palav,
Anupam Sud, Muhammad Zeeshan, Shweta
Bhattad and Mohammad Ali Talpur.
Ongoing.

MUJIN-TO Production

Tokyo
2-12-6 Miyoshi, Koto-ku, 135-0022
tel. +81 3 6458 8225
www.mujin-to.com

CHIM↑POM
'YAJIRUSHISOVIETORU –
Chim and Pom's paradox'
1 – 29 November

Nada Miami
Lyota Yagi, Chim ↑ Pom, Sachiko Kazama,
Yukihiro Taguchi, Tsubasa Kato
4 – 7 December

hiromiyoshii roppongi

Tokyo
5-9-20 Roppongi, Minato, 106-0032
tel. +81 3 5772 5233
www.hiromiyoshii.com

HIRO SUGIYAMA
through 6 December

Kunsthal Charlottenborg

Copenhagen, Denmark
Nyhavn 2, 1051
tel. +45 33 74 46 00
www.kunsthalcharlottenborg.dk

JENNIFER TEE
'Occult Geometry'
through 2 November

ROSE ENGLISH
'The Eros of Understanding'
KEREN CYTTER
through 1 January

Take Ninagawa

Tokyo
2-12-4 Higashi Azabu, Minatoku, 1060044
tel. +81 3 5571 5844
www.takeninagawa.com

TARO IZUMI
'The Combine PI, The Liberty PO'
8 November – 30 January

Art Basel Miami Beach, Booth N32
Ryoko Aoki, Shinro Ohtake, Tsuruko Yamazaki
4 – 7 December

Den Frie Centre of Contemporary Art

Copenhagen, Denmark
Oslo Plads 1, 2100
tel. +45 33 12 28 03
www.denfrie.dk

**'KE14 – THE ARTISTS' AUTUMN
EXHIBITION'**
through 9 November
SUSAN HILLER
14 November – 1 March
**'THE CARL NIELSEN & ANNE MARIE
CARL-NIELSEN ART PRIZE 2014'**
22 November – 4 January

Overgaden

Copenhagen, Denmark
Overgaden Neden Vandet 17, 1414
tel. +45 32 57 72 73
www.overgaden.org

YVETTE BRACKMAN
'AGIT FLIGHT'
**'REVISIT: MUSIKERNE MALER,
MALERNE MUSICERER OG DIGTERNE
HOLDER KÆFT'**
15 November – 11 January

Louisiana Museum of Modern Art

Humlebaek, Denmark
Gl Strandvej 13, 3050
tel. +45 49 19 07 19
www.louisiana.dk

OLAFUR ELIASSON
'Riverbed'
through 4 January

PAULA MODERSOHN-BECKER
5 December – 6 April

ARKEN Museum of Modern Art

Ishoj, Denmark
Skovvej 100, DK 2635
tel. +45 43 54 02 22
www.arken.dk

PALLE NIELSEN
'THE MODEL'
through 7 December

MICHAEL ANCHER AND P.S. KRØYER
'Friends and rivals'
through 12 April

Bergen Kunsthall

Bergen, Norway
Rasmus Meyers allé 5, 5015
tel. +47 55 55 93 10
www.kunsthall.no

KNUT HENRIK HENRIKSEN
'Notes to Stones'
through 9 November

WILL BENEDICT
'Corruption Feeds'
JULIA WACHTEL
through 14 December

Kunstnernes Hus

Oslo, Norway
Wergelandsveien 17, 0167
tel. +47 22 85 34 10
www.kunstnereshus.no

ELISE STORSVEEN & JON GUNDERSEN
'Tellus Tell Us'
14 November – 4 January

CHRIS MARKER
'A Grin Without a Cat'
Organised by Whitechapel Gallery.
through 11 January

Kunsthall Trondheim

Trondheim, Norway
Dronningens Gate 28, 7011
tel. +47 4064 0758
www.kunsthalltrondheim.no

LINA SELANDER
'A Series of Images About You'
At Kalmar Konstmuseum, Sweden.
through 23 November

DAN PERJOVSCHI
'Freedom of Expression'
through 14 December

Trondheim kunstmuseum

Trondheim, Norway
Bispegata 7B, 7013
tel. +47 7353 8180
www.trondheimkunstmuseum.no

JOÃO PENALVA
through 18 January
JENS JOHANNESSEN
'Retrospective'
8 November – 22 February
TKM Gråmølna Trondheim
Trenerys gt 9, 7042:
CHRISTINE ÖDLUND
'Music for Eukaryotes'
through 25 January

Borås konstmuseum

Borås, Sweden
Kulturhuset, PA Halls Terrass, SE-501 80
tel. +46 33 35 35 05
www.boras.se/konstmuseum

SVEN-ERIK JOHANSSON
through 9 November
'SISTER'
Sharon Hayes, Sisters of Jam, Roxy Farhat,
Jenny Wilson et al.
through 11 January
'FROM GRÜNEWALD TO FERNSTRÖM'
From the museum collection.
through 1 February

Lunds konsthall

Lund, Sweden
Mårtenstorget 3, 223 51
tel. +46 46 35 52 95
www.lundskonsthall.se

**'RANDOM INTERNATIONAL.
STUDIES IN MOTION'**
through 16 November

NINA CANELL
'Free-Space Path Loss'
ERIC M NILSSON
'Apropå ord'
29 November – 25 January

Lilith Performance Studio

Malmö, Sweden
Bragegatan 15, 214 30
tel. +46 40 78997
www.lilithperfomancestudio.com

TORI WRÅNES
A new site-specific large-scale live performance.
4 – 6 December

Malmö Konsthall

Malmö, Sweden
S:t Johannesgatan 7, 205 80
tel. +46 40 34 60 00
www.konsthall.malmo.se

**'THE ALIEN WITHIN – A LIVING
LABORATORY OF WESTERN SOCIETY'**
In partnership with Goethe-Institut. The
realisation of Christoph Schlingensief's
Animatograph is in collaboration with Thyssen-
Bornemisza Art Contemporary, Vienna.
Opening: 13 November, 6-9pm
14 November – 1 March

Moderna Museet Malmö

Malmö, Sweden
Ola Billgrens plats 2-4, 211 29
tel. +46 40 685 7937
www.modernamuseet.se

**'THE MODERNA EXHIBITION 2014 –
SOCIETY ACTS'**
Emily Roysdon, Janek Simon, Visible Solutions
LLC, Tris Vonna-Michell, Mette Winckelmann,
Agnieszka Kurant et al.
through 25 January

'A WOUNDED DREAM'
6 December – 11 January

Tensta konsthall

Spånga, Sweden
Taxingegränd 10, 163 04
tel. +46 8 36 07 63
www.tenstakonsthall.se

ANE HJORT GUTTU
'This Place Is Every Place'
DAVE HULLFISH BAILEY
'School Section'
Both as part of 'The New Model'.
'TENSTA MUSEUM CONTINUES'
With Jakob Kolding, writer Mekonen Tekeste and
stories about Eritrea, and The Silent University:
Language Café.
through 11 January

Bonniers Konsthall

Stockholm, Sweden
Torsgatan 19, 113 90
tel. +46 8 736 42 48
www.bonnierskonsthall.se

**'EXPERIENCES OF BRAZILIAN ART AND
FILM FROM THE 1960s AND 70s'**
through 23 November
LAURA LIMA
'The Naked Magician'
through 30 November
**'GRANT RECIPIENTS 2014: MARIA
BONNIER DAHLIN FOUNDATION'**
30 November – 21 December

Index – The Swedish Contemporary Art Foundation

Stockholm, Sweden
Kungsbro Strand 19, 112 26
tel. +46 50 219838
www.indexfoundation.se

**MALIN ARNELL, FIA BACKSTRÖM,
IMRI SANDSTRÖM**
through 15 November

ELIZABETH PRICE
'SUNLIGHT'
29 November – 31 January

Galleri Magnus Karlsson

Stockholm, Sweden
Fredsgatan 12, 111 52
tel. +46 8 660 4353
www.gallerimagnuskarlsson.com

BRUNO KNUTMAN
'Serious Times'
through 9 November

HELENE BILLGREN
'heart h'
13 November – 21 December

MAGASIN III – Museum & Foundation for Contemporary Art

Stockholm, Sweden
Frihamnen, 115 56
tel. +46 8 545 68040
www.magasin3.com

'WIZZ EYELASHES'
Katharina Grosse, Sol LeWitt, Walter De Maria
'I'M STILL HERE'
Curated by Richard Julin and Tessa Praun.
'THE DRAWING ROOM'
Curated by David Neuman.
through 14 December

Moderna Museet Stockholm

Stockholm, Sweden
Skeppsholmen, 103 27
tel. +46 8 5202 3500
www.modernamuseet.se

NINA CANELL
'Mid-Sentence'
through 4 January
MERIÇ ALGÜN RINGBORG
'Becoming European'
through 11 January
**'SCULPTURE AFTER SCULPTURE:
FRITSCH, KOONS, RAY'**
through 18 January
'A WAY OF LIFE'
through 15 February

Marabouparken

Sundbyberg, Sweden
Löfströmsvägen 8, 172 66
tel. +46 8 294 590
www.marabouparken.se

'NO SOUND IS INNOCENT'
Erik Bünger, The Great Learning Orchestra,
Angelica Mesiti
through 30 November

Bildmuseet

Umeå, Sweden
Östra Strandgatan 30 B, SE-903 33
tel. +46 90 786 7400
www.bildmuseet.umu.se/en

'SEARCHING FOR SMOOTH SPACE'
through 2 November
GEIR TORE HOLM
through 18 January
ANDERS SUNNA
through 1 February
CAMPANAS
2 November – 1 February
RAFAEL LOZANO-HEMMER
2 November – 3 May

Schools & Colleges

Galeria Luisa Strina
São Paulo, Brazil
Rua Padre João Manuel, 755, 01411–001
tel. +55 11 3088 2471
www.galerialuisastrina.com.br

ANNA MARIA MAIOLINO
MAGDALENA JITRIK
through 14 November

'GROUP SHOW'
Curated by Fernanda Arruda.
25 November – 14 February

School of the Museum of Fine Arts, Boston
Boston
230 The Fenway, MA 02115
tel. +1 617 267 6100
www.smfa.edu

'SMFA ART SALE'
Featuring works by alumni, faculty and students sold to benefit scholarships.
Reception: 20 November.
20 – 23 November

South America

Galeria Fortes Vilaça
São Paulo, Brazil
Rua Fradique Coutinho, 1500, 05416-001
tel. +55 11 3032 7066
www.fortesvilaca.com.br
GUILLERMO KUITCA
through 6 December
'MONOCROMO'
13 December – 30 January
Galpão São Paulo - Brasil
Rua James Holland, 71, 01138-000:
EFRAIN ALMEIDA
1 November – 20 December
Independent Projects
7 – 9 November
Art Basel Miami Beach
4 – 7 December

South Korea

Herron School of Art and Design IUPUI
Indianapolis
735 West New York Street, IN 46202
tel. +1 317 278 9477
www.herron.iupui.edu

Herron Library:
'AL-MUTANABBI STREET ARTISTS' BOOK COLLECTION'
through 19 November

Baró Galeria
São Paulo, Brazil
Rua Barra Funda, 216, 01152-000
tel. +55 11 3666 6489
www.barogaleria.com

SONG DONG
through 20 December

White Cube São Paulo
São Paulo, Brazil
Rua Agostinho Rodrigues Filho 550
tel. +55 11 4329 4494
www.whitecube.com

JULIE MEHRETU
'The Mathematics of Droves'
through 1 November

DAMIEN HIRST
'Black Scalpel Cityscapes'
11 November – 31 January

Gallery Baton
Seoul
65 Apgujeong-ro 29-gil
Gangnam-gu, 135-901
tel. +82 2 597 5701
www.gallerybaton.com

AXEL GEIS
'Persona'
through 6 December

BIN, WOO HYUK
'Arkadia'
17 December – 17 January

Pennsylvania Academy of the Fine Arts
Philadelphia
128 North Broad Street, PA 19102
tel. +1 215 972 7600
www.pafa.edu

'DAVID LYNCH: THE UNIFIED FIELD'
through 11 January

'PETER BLUME: NATURE & METAMORPHOSIS'
14 November – 5 April

Dan Galeria
São Paulo, Brazil
Rua Estados Unidos, 1638, 01427-002
tel. +55 11 3083 4600
www.dangaleria.com.br

FERREIRA GULLAR
'The Revelation of the Reverse'
12 November – 13 December

Mendes Wood DM
São Paulo, Brazil
Rua da Consolação, 3358, 01416-000
tel. +55 11 3081 1735
www.mendeswood.com

ANNA BELLA GEIGER
GUILLERMO KUITCA
through 22 November

Hakgojae Gallery
Seoul
50 Samcheong-ro, Jongno-gu, 110-200
tel. +82 2 739 4937
www.hakgojae.com

CHUNG HYUN
through 9 November
SONG HYUN-SOOK
19 November – 31 December

Hakgojae Shanghai
No 101, Building 9, Moganshan Road #50,
M50 Art Zone, Putuo District:
NAM JUNE PAIK
'Meeting Nam June Paik in Shanghai'
through 2 November

Parsons The New School for Design
New York
72 5th Avenue, NY 10011
tel. +1 800 292 3040
www.newschool.edu/parsons

Please see website for information on academic programmes, public events and exhibitions.

Galeria Nara Roesler
São Paulo, Brazil
Avenida Europa 655, 01449-001
tel. +55 11 3063 2344
www.nararoesler.com.br

ISAAC JULIEN
'Playtime'
through 15 November
VIRGINIA DE MEDEIROS
'Studio Butterfly e outras fábulas'
through 29 November

Rio de Janeiro, Rua Redentor 241, 22241-030:
TOMIE OHTAKE
through 22 November

Galería Patricia Ready
Santiago, Chile
Espoz 3125, Vitacura, 7630192
tel. +56 2 2953 6210
www.galeriapready.cl

ALFREDO JAAR
'THE SOUND OF SILENCE'
12 November – 23 January

Gallery Hyundai
Seoul
14 Samcheong-ro, Jongno-gu, 110-190
tel. +82 2 2287 3500
www.galleryhyundai.com

SEUNG-TAEK LEE
'Think Reform'
Sculpture, video and installation.
through 9 November
LEE BAE
Painting.
18 November – 14 December
DONGI LEE
Painting.
20 November – 28 December

Kukje Gallery
Seoul
54 Samcheong-ro, Jongno-gu, 110-200
tel. +82 2 735 8449
www.kukjegallery.com

DONALD JUDD
through 30 November

**LEE KWANG HO
DAVID NASH**
16 December – 25 January

One and J. Gallery
Seoul
130-1 Gahoe Dong, Jongro Gu, 110-260
tel. +82 2 745 1644
www.oneandj.com

TAEYOON KIM
'Erratic Routines'
through 16 November

KWANGHO LEE
28 November – 26 December

Gallery Skape
Seoul
58-4 Samcheongro Jongnogu, 110-200
tel. +82 2 747 4675
www.skape.co.kr

SUNGSOO KIM
5 November – 19 December

Spain & Portugal

CAM – Calouste Gulbenkian Foundation
Lisbon, Portugal
Rua Dr. Nicolau Bettencourt, 1050-079
tel. +351 21 782 3474
www.cam.gulbenkian.pt

ANTÓNIO DACOSTA
'1914 | 2014'
SALETTE TAVARES
'Spacial Poetry'
'ANIMALIA AND NATURE IN THE CAM'S COLLECTION'
through 25 January

Culturgest
Lisbon, Portugal
Edifício CGD
Rua Arco do Cego, 50, 1000-300
tel. +351 21 790 5155
www.culturgest.pt

'HONEY, I REARRANGED THE COLLECTION... BY ARTIST'
Posters from the Lempert Collection
(Chapter 1 / Part 1).
through 15 March

Culturgest Porto, Avenida dos Aliados, 104:
CARLOS NOGUEIRA
'Out of the nature of things all this will end'
through 27 December

Galeria Filomena Soares
Lisbon, Portugal
Rua da Manutenção, 80, 1900-321
tel. +351 21 862 4122/3
www.gfilomenasoares.com

KILUANJI KIA HENDA
'A city called mirage'
through 29 November

HELENA ALMEIDA
'Drawing'
4 December – 1 March

Galería Juana de Aizpuru
Madrid, Spain
Barquillo, 44, 28004
tel. +34 91 310 5561
www.juanadeaizpuru.es

TIM PARCHIKOV
'Dead Sea'
through 30 November

galería elba benítez
Madrid, Spain
San Lorenzo, 11, 28004
tel. +34 91 308 0468
www.elbabenitez.com

FRANCISCO RUIZ DE INFANTE
'La Línea de los Ojos (The Death Line)'
through 9 November

ERNESTO NETO
21 November – 31 January

Art Basel Miami Beach
4 – 7 December

Switzerland

Aargauer Kunsthaus
Aarau
Aargauerplatz, 5001
tel. +41 62 835 2330
www.aargauerkunsthaus.ch
SOPHIE TAEUBER-ARP
'Today is Tomorrow'
'DOCKING STATION'
Contemporary artists work with artworks from
the Aargauer Kunsthaus and the Nationale
Suisse Collection.
'CARAVAN 3/2014: MAX LEISS'
Series of Exhibitions of Young Art
through 16 November
'AUSWAHL 14'
Aargau artists.
5 December – 4 January

von Bartha
Basel
Kannenfeldplatz 6, 4056
tel. +41 61 322 1000
www.vonbartha.com

SARAH OPPENHEIMER
'P-02'
through 8 November
KARIM NOURELDIN
'Play'
22 November – 31 January
von Bartha S-chanf
Somvih 46, 7525:
FLORIAN SLOTAWA
28 December – 24 January

Kunsthalle Basel
Basel
Steinenberg 7, 4051
tel. +41 61 206 9900
www.kunsthallebasel.ch

'FESTIVAL OF THE ELEVENTH SUMMER'
through 16 November
'50 JAHRE ATELIERGENOSSENSCHAFT BASEL'
30 November – 18 January
'REGIONALE 15'
30 November – 25 January
Kunsthalle Basel - Back wall:
NEVIN ALADAG
'Marsch'
through 30 April

Kunsthalle Bern
Bern
Helvetiaplatz 1, 3005
tel. +41 31 350 0040
www.kunsthalle-bern.ch

SHIRANA SHAHBAZI
'MONSTERA'
through 7 December

Kunstmuseum Bern
Bern
Hodlerstraße 8-12, 3000
tel. +41 31 328 0944
www.kunstmuseumbern.ch
YVES NETZHAMMER
through 31 December
BETHAN HUWS
'Reading Duchamp, Research Notes
2007-2014'
through 1 February
AUGUSTO GIACOMETTI
'Colour and I'
through 8 February
'IN THE HERE AND NOW! COLLECTION KUNST HEUTE'
through 26 April

Kunsthaus CentrePasquArt
Biel Bienne
Seevorstadt 71-73 Faubourg Du Lac, CH-2502
tel. +41 32 322 5586
www.pasquart.ch

'MOUVEMENT III – THE CITY PERFORMED'
The 12th edition of the Swiss Sculpture Exhibition
focuses on the body in movement and shows
works from the 60s until today.
through 2 November

Fri Art – Kunsthalle Fribourg
Fribourg
Petites-Rames 22, 1701
tel. +41 26 323 2351
www.fri-art.ch

BORIS DENNLER
'Design from the Lab'
through 16 November

HAYAN KAM NAKACHE
28 November – 8 February

BLONDEAU & CIE

Geneva
5, rue de la Muse, 1205
tel. +41 22 544 9595
www.blondeau.ch

VIKTOR KOPP
through 20 December

FONDATION BEYELER

Riehen
Baselstrasse 101, 4125
tel. +41 61 645 9700
www.fondationbeyeler.ch

GUSTAVE COURBET
through 18 January

PETER DOIG
23 November – 22 March

ALEXANDER CALDER GALLERY III
through 6 September 2015

Hauser & Wirth

Zurich
Limmatstrasse 270, 8005
tel. +41 44 446 8050
www.hauserwirth.com
BHARTI KHER, ANRI SALA
22 November – 10 January
Hauser & Wirth London:
**BERLINDE DE BRUYCKERE,
PIPILOTTI RIST**
27 November – 10 January
Hauser & Wirth Somerset:
FRANZ WEST
through 9 November
**PIPILOTTI RIST, JOHN CHAMBERLAIN,
RICHARD TUTTLE**
29 November – 22 February

Galerie Mark Müller

Zurich
Hafnerstrasse 44, 8005
tel. +41 44 211 8155
www.markmueller.ch

JUDY MILLAR
'Paintings'
through 15 November

'MARKSMALLOW'
Paintings.
22 November – 10 January

MAMCO – Museum of Modern and Contemporary Art

Geneva
10, rue des Vieux-Grenadiers, 1205
tel. +41 22 320 6122
www.mamco.ch

**'THE NEVER ENDING STORIES CYCLE:
AUTUMN-WINTER 2014-2015 SEQUENCE'**
Ulla von Brandenburg, Marcia Hafif,
Sonia Kacem, Amy O'Neill, Stéphane Zaech,
Tribute to Claude Rychner & Collections.
through 18 January

Kunst Halle Sankt Gallen

St. Gallen
Davidstrasse 40, 9000
tel. +41 71 222 1014
www.k9000.ch

**'THE DARKNET – FROM MEMES TO
ONIONLAND. AN EXPLORATION'**
Anonymous, Cory Arcangel, !Mediengruppe
Bitnik, Aram Bartholl, Heath Bunting,
Simon Denny, Eva and Franco Mattes,
Seth Price et al.
through 11 January

Museum Haus Konstruktiv

Zurich
Selnaustrasse 25, CH-8001
tel. +41 44 217 7080
www.hauskonstruktiv.ch

**'LOGICAL EMOTION – CONTEMPORARY
ART FROM JAPAN'**
Aoki, Hirata, Ikeda, Kusama, Miyajima, Kaneuji,
Sugito, Watanabe, Yokoyama et al.
HAROON MIRZA
'Zurich Art Prize 2014'
through 11 January

Galerie Eva Presenhuber

Zurich
Diagonal Building, Zahnradstraße 21, 8005
tel. +41 43 444 7050
www.presenhuber.com

ALEX HUBBARD
'Urethane Paintings'
22 November – 24 January
Galerie Eva Presenhuber, Löwenbräu Areal
Zurich, Limmatstrasse 270, 8005:
CANDIDA HÖFER
'Closer'
**JUSTIN MATHERLY, OSCAR MURILLO,
DAVID OSTROWSKI, TOBIAS PILS**
22 November – 24 January

Kunsthaus Glarus

Glarus
Im Volksgarten, 8750
tel. +41 55 640 2535
www.kunsthausglarus.ch

**'KUNSTSCHAFFEN GLARUS UND
LINTHGEBIET R – Z 2014'**
Regional artists showing their works.
'FOKUS: KARIEL'
KARIEL
Winner of the Fokus Prize 2013.
7 December – 18 January

Kunstmuseum St Gallen

St. Gallen
Museumstrasse 32, 9000
tel. +41 71 242 0671
www.kunstmuseumsg.ch
'ELEMENTARE MALEREI'
through 25 January
ALICJA KWADE
'Warten auf Gegenwart'
21 November – 15 February
Lokremise:
MATHIEU MERCIER
'everything but the kitchen sink'
through 9 November
MICHEL VERJUX
'Anschaulichkeit'
through 26 April

Lullin + Ferrari

Zurich
Limmatstraße 214, 8005
tel. +41 43 205 2607
www.lullinferrari.com

MICHAEL BAUCH
'Paintings'
through 6 December

'BEAUTY OF INDIFFERENCE'
Alexander Heim, Lena Hilton, Mamiko Otsubo,
wiedemann/mettler and guests.
13 December – 7 February

Kunsthalle Zürich

Zurich
Limmatstrasse 270, 8005
tel. +41 44 272 1515
www.kunsthallezurich.ch

JANA EULER
'Where the energy comes from'
SLAVS AND TATARS
'Mirrors for Princes'
through 9 November

AVERY SINGER
'Pictures Punish Words'
TFT MÜLLENBACH
22 November – 25 January

Kunstmuseum Luzern

Lucerne
Europaplatz 1, 6002
tel. +41 41 226 7800
www.kunstmuseumluzern.ch
'INS OFFENE!'
GABRIELE BASILICO
'Urbanscapes'
through 23 November
CANDIDA HÖFER
'Düsseldorf'
1 November – 8 February
SABIAN BAUMANN
'Horizontales Paradies'
**'JAHRESAUSSTELLUNG
ZENTRALSCHWEIZER KUNSTSCHAFFEN'**
6 December – 8 February

Kunstmuseum Thun

Thun
Hofstettenstraße 14, 3602
tel. +41 33 225 8420
www.kunstmuseumthun.ch

GEORGE STEINMANN
'Call and Response. A Dialogue with
George Steinmann'
**PROJECT ROOM ENTER:
'HERITAGE 1. ARTISTS AS ETHNOGRAPHS'**
through 23 November

**'CANTONALE BERNE JURA 2014'
'HERITAGE 2'**
13 December – 25 January

Mai 36 Galerie

Zurich
Rämistraße 37, 8001
tel. +41 44 261 6880
www.mai36.com

MICHEL PÉREZ POLLO
through 20 December

Art Basel Miami Beach
4 – 7 December

Galerie Urs Meile Lucerne

Lucerne
Rosenberghöhe 4, 6004
tel. +41 41 420 3318
www.galerieursmeile.com

AI WEIWEI
13 November – 17 January

Art Taipei, Booth D-35
through 3 November
Art021 Shanghai
12 – 16 November
Art Basel Miami Beach, Booth M-02
4 – 7 December

Kunstmuseum Liechtenstein

Vaduz
Städtle 32, FL-9490
tel. +423 235 0300
www.kunstmuseum.li

GARY KUEHN
'Between Sex and Geometry'
**'FROM THE COLLECTION: UNDER THE
MAGNIFYING GLASS. MINIMAL,
POST-MINIMAL AND POP IN DIALOGUE'**
through 25 January

Migros Museum für Gegenwartskunst

Zurich
Limmatstrasse 270, 8005
tel. +41 44 277 2050
www.migrosmuseum.ch

**DOROTHY IANNONE
'COLLECTION ON DISPLAY'**
John Armleder, Richard Jackson et al.
through 9 November

**WU TSANG
CHRISTOPH SCHLINGENSIEF**
'Collection on Display'
22 November – 8 February

WHAT'S SO FUNNY?

HOW HUMOUR FEEDS PAINTING
BY PAUL TEASDALE

Title font: Sign Painter House House Brush, courtesy House Industries

Writing in *The New York Times* in 2010, Roberta Smith observed a new-found optimism in painting. According to her, it had finally shaken off the hangover of the Modernist separation of abstraction and representation. Titled 'It's Not Dry Yet', her brief article succinctly catalogued the history of painting's anxiety in the face of the Clement Greenberg and Donald Judd-dominated theorizing of the 1960s and '70s. Charting the cautious, self-conscious return of figuration in the work of Sigmar Polke, David Salle and Julian Schnabel, and noting the long history in which abstraction and representation have found equilibrium – 'Byzantine mosaics; pre-Columbian and American Indian textiles and ceramics; Japanese screens; Mughal painting; and post-Impressionism' – Smith concluded that talk of a separation between abstraction and representation in painting is bunkum. 'With each generation of painters, the authority of Greenberg and Judd pales while the history of the pictorial expands,' she declared. It seems she was right. Over the past few years, painters have been mixing representation and abstraction in ways that have been increasingly bold. Gone are the nervous irony and apologetic jokes that often seemed to accompany representation and, in their place, is a figuration that is confident and playful, self-aware, expressive – and funny.

What's changed? Partly, it seems to me, it is the seriousness with which comics are being treated these days. To cite two examples: this year's spring issue of *Critical Inquiry*, edited by Hillary Chute and Patrick Jagoda, was dedicated to 'Comics and Media', and *Artforum*'s summer issue was themed around 'Art and Animation'. In different ways, both publications focused on the rich tradition of comic books in the US and its steady infiltration into other art forms – mostly digital, mainly video. Yet surprisingly, in both issues, the medium a mere side-step away from comic-book drawing – i.e. painting – was skipped over.

There are a number of prosaic explanations as to why comics and painting shouldn't mix and many are due to the art-historical hangover cited by Smith. We've been taught to think of comic books as a low art form and painting as a high one. Comics are cheap, mass-produced and serialized; paintings are unique and costly. Comics are crude and crass, whereas paintings are supposedly refined and reticent. But with the digitization of the once print-only comic tradition, an online depository of comic-book images now freely circulates. Even more tellingly, the translation of a comic-book style through animated cartoons has worn down a once fiercely underground art form to a lingua franca. With the simultaneity afforded by online image circulation, the Modernist sequestering

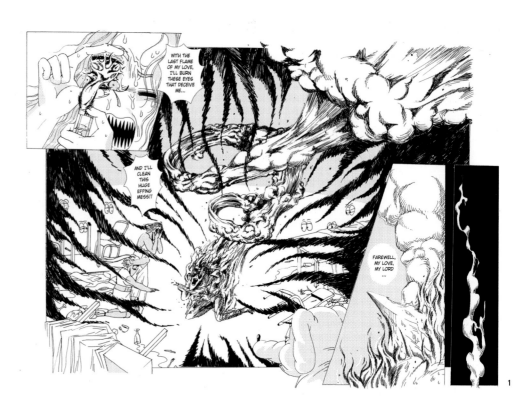

1

of discrete areas of artistic production now seems a quaint historical footnote. Today's landscape is chronologically flat and stylistically vast. A painting now is no more privileged than any other art form and shares the same rules of engagement – a fact made ever-more obvious by the increasingly hybrid stock of images that cohabit online.

The groundbreaking 1983 exhibition, 'The Comic Art Show', co-curated by John Carlin and Sheena Wagstaff at the Whitney Museum in New York, marked the first time that comics were taken seriously by an art institution. That validation was followed seven years later in the same city by MOMA's divisive 1990 show 'High and Low: Modern Art and Popular Culture'. A more recent (if disappointingly male-focused) exhibition 'Masters of American Comics' took place at the Hammer Museum and the Museum of Contemporary Art, Los Angeles, in 2005, co-curated by Carlin and Brian Walker. In 2010, 'Rude Britannia: British Comic Art' was held at Tate Britain and included work from William Hogarth and Aubrey Beardsley to David Shrigley and Sarah Lucas. Robert Crumb's *Book of Genesis Illustrated by R. Crumb* (2009) was shown in its entirety last year at the 55th Venice Biennale. The same year, Art Spiegelman had a retrospective at the Museum Ludwig Cologne, featuring his Pulitzer Prize-winning graphic novel *Maus* (1991). Crumb, Gary Panter, Spiegelman and Chris Ware are as well regarded in the art world as they are in the world of comics. In addition to the men, Chute reminds us in her 2010 book *Graphic Women: Life Narrative and Contemporary Comics* that many highly esteemed comic-book or graphic-narrative (the term she prefers to 'graphic novel') artists are female. She focuses on six: Lynda Barry, Alison Bechdel, Phoebe Gloeckner, Aline Kominsky-Crumb and Marjane Satrapi.

Previous page
Amelie von Wulffen, *Untitled*, 2012, watercolour and Indian ink on paper, 28 × 20 cm

1
Julien Ceccaldi
Less Than Dust (detail), 2014, comic book

2
Carroll Dunham
Late Trees #2, 2011–12, mixed media on linen, 2.2 × 1.7 m

Courtesy
previous page: the artist, Gió Marconi, Milan, and Galerie Meyer Kainer, Vienna; photograph: Roman März
• 1 the artist • 2 the artist, Blum and Poe, Los Angeles, Gladstone Gallery, New York, and Gerhardsen Gerner, Berlin

Of course, painting's flirtation with comics and cartoons started long before the Whitney show. Cartoon imagery has been visible in painting, in various guises, for as long as cartooning has existed. Some historians, such as Martin Barker in his 1989 book *Comics: Ideology, Power and the Critics*, have cited the Lascaux cave paintings as the Promethean moment for both art in general and the comic tradition of sequential art in particular. The word 'cartoon' came from the Italian *cartone* meaning large sheet of paper, a term that was commonly used from the Renaissance onwards to denote a preparatory drawing for a painting or tapestry, such as the series of 63 tapestry cartoons Francisco de Goya created for the Spanish crown in 1775. Cartooning as we currently know it was birthed in the early 18th century by the satirical political etchings of William Hogarth. Many major artists from the 20th century – including Willem de Kooning, Philip Guston and Roy Lichtenstein – have all, to greater or lesser extents, been influenced by comic figuration. That Pablo Picasso was famously an avid reader of newspaper comics is likewise evident in his drawings. John Wesley's clean, flat pictures invariably host Disney characters; Takashi Murakami's Superflat work is filled with manga and artists such as George Condo, John Currin, Carroll Dunham, Erró, Lisa Yuskavage and, more recently, Tala Madani, have all drawn upon cartooning's use of sexual imagery for political and formal purposes. More scrappy, intuitive comic appropriation can be found in the brilliant paintings of Armen Eloyan, Ansel Krut, Amy Sillman and Rose Wylie, to name just a few more contemporary practitioners.

If comics and cartoons already have a long tradition in art, what might explain their particular relevance to painting now? Two possible reasons: comics are unfettered by painting's angsty autobiography and unbothered by the tradition of

2

Some historians have cited the Lascaux cave paintings as the Promethean moment for both art in general and the comic tradition of sequential art in particular.

critical reception that painting has had to grapple with. And, importantly, comic stylization – grounded in reduction and caricature – has an easy approachability that painting has often been accused of ignoring. At a time of cross-platform, cross-channel communication the legibility and power of cartoonish figuration follows the same logic as the pictogrammatic emoticons we use to communicate feelings. A reduced but wider-reaching lexicon for depicting social realities and expressing emotion – caricature for melo-drama; figuration abstracted to its most universal – has a poignant, current appeal.

Julien Ceccaldi's *Comics Collection 2010–2013* (2013) documents the episodic adventures of a group of young girlfriends interested in three things: going out, shopping and themselves. In each installment, their positive sass and front is punctured to reveal a legion of confusions and insecurities: 'Why do I give such terrible advice? / 'God, why is my friend such a huge bitch?' In a different style but similarly 'in-real-life' register, 'The Scene Report', an ongoing series from the *Wendy* comic by Montreal-based artist Walter Scott, charts the everyday worries, anxieties, fears and tragedies that play out in the life of the main character, Wendy, a wannabe artist trying to figure her way through an industry littered with rejection and regrets, complicated by friends, parties and boys. Amelie von Wulffen presented an autobiographical take on experiences of art-world anxiety, trauma and angst in her graphite-on-paper comic book *At the Cool Table* (2014), which was published to coincide with her concurrent shows at the Kunstverein Munich and Portikus, Frankfurt, earlier this year. Goya appears as her companion and muse on the voyages through her dream scenarios: watching a young bro-artist reading from his autobiography, surrounded by swooning girls ('the first chapter is about my awakening as a writer'); turning up at the opening of her own show (that she forgot to install) wearing nothing but an open trench coat; fighting with Goya over the meaning of still-life painting in her studio; visiting her non-artist sister who is somehow participating in Documenta. Von Wulffen's series of watercolours shown at Alex Zachary, New York, in 2011, and collected in the book *This Is How It Happened* (2011), take a more cartoony tone, filled with a colourful ensemble cast of anthropomorphic fruit, vegetables and tools in scenes as innocent as ice-cream cones sledding down a mountain to more sinister ones of tomatoes being brutalized by mean-eyed potatoes in a sex dungeon (both *Untitled*, 2011). For all three artists, language is key: Ceccaldi's caricatures rely on immersion in the perky patois of a 20-something US girl; Scott uses a similarly simple sucks-to-be-young-in-the-art-world inflection; and Von Wulffen's charming English/ German register uses a narrative form that flies through a constellation of personal and private situations made social.

Loosely grouped under the same social canopy – fraught relationships, personal anxiety, power dynamics and professional ennui – a number of painters, including Vittorio Brodmann, Sanya Kantarovsky, Ella Kruglyanskaya and Lucy Stein, as well as Von Wulffen, are taking a sidelong approach to comic appropriation, melding painterly abstraction with cartoonish representation. As with Von Wulffen's work, Brodmann's paintings depict scenes from a life at once recognizable and strange; sometimes coherent and sometimes anything but. In the Swiss artist's earlier works, the 1940s cartoon character Droopy appears as a mascot for failure – in life as well as in painting – but,

Ella Kruglyanskaya
Moustache Beach, 2013, egg tempera on panel, 61 × 81 cm

Courtesy
the artist, Gavin Brown's Enterprise, New York, and Kendall Koppe, Glasgow

more recently, self-invented characters have crowded his pictures: monstrous anthropomorphic blobs with hooves, bug-eyed moustachioed lurkers and grinning reptilian beings move around and morph into each other. In Brodmann's recent show at Gregor Staiger in Zurich, it felt like a dumpster truck's worth of cartoonish imagery had been mangled through a Surrealist subconscious. Brodmann says he is just as influenced by sitcoms as he is by cartoons, by the visual humour of a sudden entrance and door slam. He also told me that he's interested in the moment when people laugh at a picture before realizing they don't really get the joke. It's this insecurity and dislocation that plays out as both intention and method. Seemingly arbitrary faces are scattered across his figures at random, creating a number of competing focal points. Working directly onto canvas rather than from drawings, Brodmann bleeds and sweeps garish colours together in unresolved combinations. In *Drooping poorly* (2014) an arm becomes a foot while *Along the polished floorboards* (2014) reverses the situation. In *Putting one's tongue into a cheek* (2014) ghostly open-mouthed figures in the background haze into a large nose, mirrored by the snout of an apologetic-looking crocodile in the opposite corner – the title suddenly revealing an extra layer of humour behind the grotesqueness of the imagery.

Kruglyanskaya doesn't read comics, which is something of a surprise. Her particular stylistic language seems a compendium of familiar illustrative and comic-book dialects: the small lips, button noses and sharp chins of mid-20th-century fashion drawings, to the Crumb or Erró-evoking buxom, curvilinear bodies of the women she depicts. Drawn from imagination rather than life models, and citing references such as Pieter Bruegel the Elder, Albrecht Dürer and Lucas Cranach the Elder, her works focus on the body and portraiture as much as on implied narratives.

For Kruglyanskaya, as for cartoonists and illustrators, figuration is arrived at through a method of reduction: characters – mostly women, often in pairs – are cropped so tightly that their fleshy bodies fill the frame. They become the ground for cartoonish faces painted onto their clothing: the sly-looking guy in *Moustache Beach* (2013) or the

screaming mouth in *Zip It* (2014). Comic-book themes as well as styles emerge: girl-on-girl power relationships play out in dramatic clinches – the sassy figure throwing shade in *Crossed Out (in green)* (2013) or the pairs of women that, almost exclusively, featured in the canvases shown at her solo show at Studio Voltaire in London earlier this year, titled 'How to Work Together'. Men, if depicted at all, are reduced to mere clothing illustrations, predatory shadowy figures or, more amusingly, in *The Heist* (2013), a horizontally-hoisted statue or an about-to-be-disposed-of corpse. Echoing graphic-design motifs, Kruglyanskaya's canvases function as pages, closing off context by treating the figures as cut-outs. These appear associatively as *trompe l'oeil* pages, as with the painted drawing within a painting in *Bather on Yellow* (2013), included in her solo show at Kendall Koppe in Glasgow last year. Her bright palette and loose, fast brushstrokes replicate the colour range and felt-tip scribblings common to posters.

Unlike the unstable Surrealism of a Brodmann or a Kruglyanskaya punchline, Kantarovsky's paintings seem to move at a different clip. For his 2012 show 'Dear Dilletante' at Tanya Leighton in Berlin, *petite bourgeoisie* scenes, rendered in a muted blue-grey palette, added to the silent-movie-era elegance of a set of ornate sculptures: a well-heeled man walking through a wall, only his feet visible (*A Situation*, 2012), an umbrella balanced in a baroquely curved hand (*A Missplaced Name*, 2012). A series of waspish men in elegant poses – putting on a coat (*The Other One Never Waits*, 2012), throwing open shutters (*A Joke That's Hard to Understand*, 2012), clicking long fingers to summon his cat (*Untitled*, 2012) – were punctuated by ghostly abstract canvases. If this show demonstrated Kantarovsky's skill in restrained period-piece immersion, then his exhibition 'Allergies' at Casey Kaplan in New York this summer saw freer associations. Painted in garish colours using oils, watercolours and pastels (influenced by a Natalia Goncharova show in Moscow that the artist had seen, as well as the *Agitplakat* posters which were mass-produced in the Soviet Union during the period of de-Stalinization), animistic imagery and a range of cartoonishly simplified faces appeared, complicating his usually elegant scenes. Kantarovsky recently told me that he likes images that look initially familiar but then aren't – that hold something back and then demand something more. Hybrid traditions and styles, reflecting his Russian then US upbringing, bump up against each other in *When Things*

For Kruglyanskaya, as for cartoonists and illustrators, figuration is arrived at through a method of reduction: characters — mostly women, often in pairs — are cropped so tightly that their fleshy bodies fill the frame.

1

Don't Work Out (2014): a wisp-slim girl in a man's shirt leans back against a bedroom wall while a clownish little imp peers up at her from under the blankets of the bed. If Kantarovsky's impulse is to stylize, his default mode has a certain 19th-century, literary, *New Yorker*-esque charm. And charm is key. As with the stand-up comic, charm carries the humour, and humour, however interpreted, is the glue for Kantarovsky's images: a nod and a wink to the vanity of painting but an expression of confidence and optimism in its existence.

Stein works in a similarly disarming comic mode that conceals a darker key. Blending a Surrealist approach to line, the London-based artist's paintings reformat art-historical symbolism, religious iconography and sexual innuendo into readable gags. Take the slip-wearing girl in her painting *Well*

Dressing (2013), ceremoniously dipping her forearms into a font-like basin that also forms the underpants of a torsoless male. Legs curl out from the left and right edges of the canvas, framed under the heraldic banner of two comically extended penises. In another painting, *O!* (2013), also included in her exhibition at Galerie Gregor Staiger in 2013, the female figure takes backstage, looking on mournfully (scornfully?) as a reclining egg-headed male plays with the drooping pot plant between his legs. In *Utopian Tubes* (2013) it's the regalia that dominates, two displaying swans oversee a woman comforting her faceless, bare-legged friend; two button-like faces hover in the centre of the picture grinning down facetiously.

As with the recognizability of Ceccaldi's head-in-hands girlfriends (reprised on the inside-cover page of his comic 'Silence Equals Death' in his new book *Less Than Dust*, 2014) or the hollow-eyed anger of Scott's Wendy, clichéd signals of melan-choly and despair are productive. Taking

the familiar Jesus-face-in-toast/coffee foam/cloud meme for her recent show at Piper Keys gallery in London, Stein used potatoes to print a host of shadowy oval marks over abstracted, noisy backgrounds. Her aim, she said, was for people to see a face in each one, though each person's private associations would, of course, be different. According to Henri Bergson, laughter is always the laughter of the group – a social gesture. Perhaps this idea points to where the joining of comics and paintings, abstraction and representation, becomes interesting: in that happy, confusing social moment of recognizing the joke, but not yet realizing what's so funny. ❦

Paul Teasdale is assistant editor of frieze *and managing editor of* frieze d/e. *He lives in Berlin, Germany.*

Gone are the nervous self-irony and apologetic jokes. In their place is a figuration that is confident and playful, self-aware, expressive — and funny.

2

3

1
Vittorio Brodmann
Not based on a backbone, 2014,
oil on canvas, 30 × 35 cm

2
Ansel Krut
Self Portrait with Bendy Balloons,
2007, oil on canvas, 120 × 90 cm

3
Lucy Stein
O!, 2013, oil and oil stick on
canvas, 90 × 90 cm

Courtesy
1 the artist and Galerie Gregor
Staiger, Zurich • 2 the artist and
Stuart Shave/Modern Art,
London • 3 the artist, Galerie Gregor
Staiger, Zurich, and Gimpel Fils,
London

After

the End

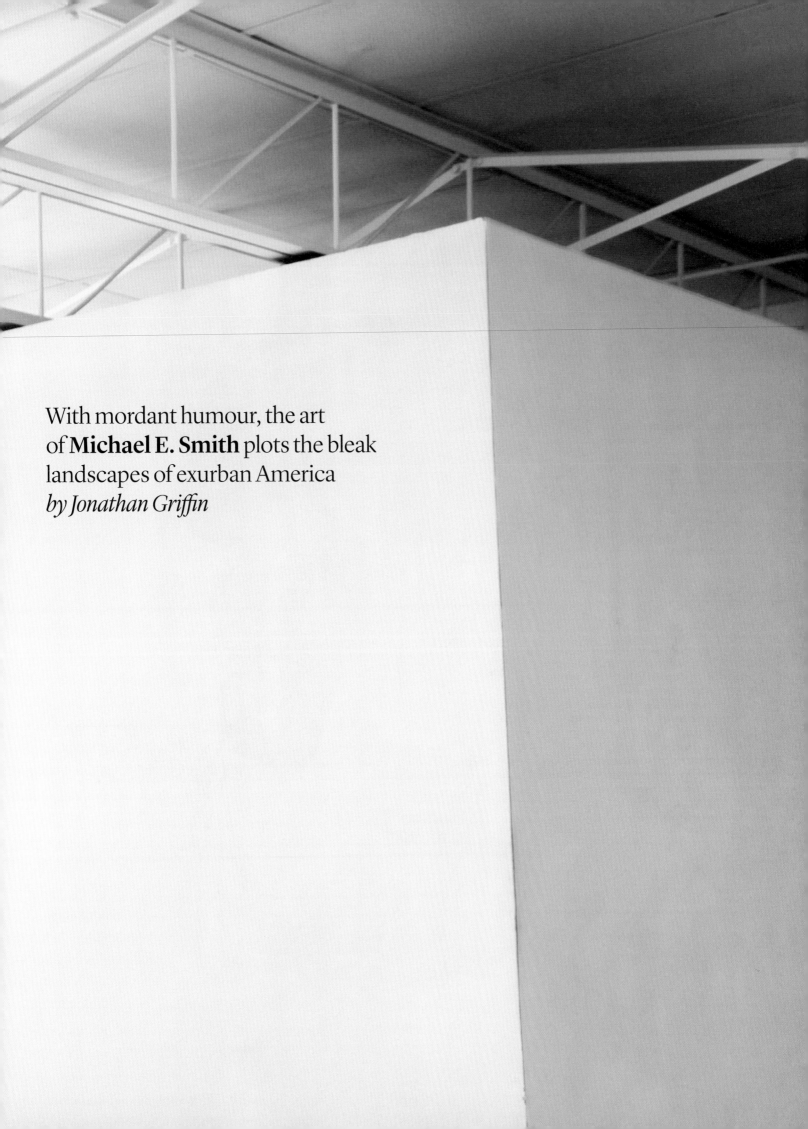

With mordant humour, the art
of **Michael E. Smith** plots the bleak
landscapes of exurban America
by Jonathan Griffin

At the start of Michael E. Smith's recent monograph, published in 2013 to accompany his exhibition at the Ludwig Forum in Aachen, there is a black page with two QR codes printed in white. Underneath each are the capitalized inscriptions: 'BEETLEJUICE' and 'FOR HEADS'. This is the artist's preface to the book.

Scanning the codes with a smartphone leads you to two video links. In *FOR HEADS* (2013), we are looking through the windscreen of a car on a grey winter's day as it moves down wide streets, on the edge of a town somewhere. We pass signs for Express Auto Repair, Lotto and Liquor, Kentucky Fried Chicken and Taco Bell. Snow flurries. The windows in many buildings are knocked out or boarded up. The cars have Michigan plates and a road sign points north to Flint, on the Interstate 75. Petrol here is US$2.98 a gallon. Our vehicle is following a white hearse with the word 'PEACE' written in its window and, on the radio, the R&B singer Maxwell sings his 1999 hit, 'Fortunate'.

BEETLEJUICE (2013) is altogether different. It is a close up of three battered old yellow Motorola phones – the kind that can also be used as two-way radios, and that are typically sold off-contract, pre-paid. Burner phones. Over their surfaces scrabble large black beetles, and the phones jostle as if riding on a seething mass of insect life.

These two videos may be the closest that the reticent Smith is likely to come to an expository essay on his work. Between them, they plot points around the US artist's aesthetic and thematic compass: the bleak landscapes of exurban America, specifically post-recessional Detroit; the tradition of black music; mordant humour; apocalyptic environmentalism; junk technology; cars; depression (in all its senses); horror.

By and large, Smith deals in objects and spaces rather than in representational images. While he has made a small number of videos and photographic works, even his paintings are typically two-sided, existing as objects to be sited – precisely and unexpectedly – within a given architectural environment. In his exhibition at the Ludwig Forum, the artist hung an untitled painting, made of T-shirt fabric encrusted with downy feathers, immediately beneath the counter of the museum shop, where it brushed against unsuspecting visitors' legs as they paid for their tickets. The small panel looks as if it were the scene of the recent murder of a delicate and vibrantly coloured bird.

Smith has become recognized for his ability to sharpen the atmospheric pitch of a space with the introduction of a few ultra-meagre sculptures, often seemingly made

1

2

from things he found by the roadside. In his exhibition at the 2014 Triennale di Milano, the building's large bright hall at first appeared to be empty. Smith's artworks, such as a length of old garden hose at the foot of a wall, or a bunched-up pair of sweatpants soaked in resin then sawed in two (both *Untitled*, 2014), were no more dominant than the gallery's fire-safety equipment and the lighting tracks on the ceiling. Other sculptures offset drabness with revulsion: *Untitled* (2014), from the same exhibition, consists of a length of steel pipe with a white-feathered cockatiel pelt jammed, headfirst, into one end. It is hard to relax in any room with an object like that leaning in the corner.

Smith troubles the stillness of his sculptures by charging them with the latent energy of something recently alive. He is drawn to a certain kind of weathered surface, a surface that looks corporeal even if it is vegetal or man-made. A dried gourd resembles psoriatic skin; dirty plastic looks like bone; a milky plastic resin recalls saliva, pus or semen. Ontologically, not all of these bodily substances are 'living' in the same sense. Skin is alive (it grows, heals itself, is sensitive) but what about tooth or bone? At what point do excreta no longer belong to their host? Saliva and blood and hair and feathers all occupy an animistic grey area, and are indicative of the ways that we, as bodies, are subjects and objects, nature and culture, amalgams of the food we eat, the chemicals we ingest and millions of bacteria. In Smith's hyper-sensitized world, the lines between animal, vegetable and mineral are kicked over.

Smith's films plot points around his aesthetic and thematic compass; they may be the closest the reticent artist is likely to come to an expository essay on his work.

Opening pages
Untitled, 2014, birdfeeder, rice, glue,
62 × 8 × 8 cm, installation view
at Susanne Hilberry Gallery, Detroit

1
Untitled, 2012,
altered weed trimmer, oatmeal,
plastic, 39 × 15 × 10 cm

2
FOR HEADS, 2013, video still

Courtesy
opening pages: the artist and Susanne
Hilberry Gallery, Detroit • 1 the artist,
Michael Benevento, Los Angeles, Clifton
Benevento, New York, Susanne
Hilberry Gallery, Detroit, KOW, Berlin;
photograph: Andres Ramirez •
2 the artist

Along with industrial materials, clothing and animal parts, food crops up a lot in Smith's art. It is usually inedible, like the dry oatmeal glued onto the plastic handles of two weed trimmers, in an untitled pair of wall-mounted sculptures from 2012. A favoured technique of the artist is to fill, or half-fill, a plastic milk or soda bottle with coloured resin or urethane foam, sometimes with feathers or fabric entombed within like flies in amber. Smith cuts off the bottle and grinds away part of the resulting stump. At the Ludwig Forum, he shrouded the gallery in a brownish fug by placing film printed with a pattern of writhing tinned spaghetti over a row of high windows. This is food for after the end: wheat and tomatoes processed to within an inch of their lives and preserved for eternity. It looks like minced meat or matted fur.

The politics of food, though diverse, touch on many of the wider preoccupations in Smith's work. The US promises of choice, safety and freedom are heinously reneged in the case of the country's corporatized food culture. Patently unhealthy mass-produced foods are marketed specifically to the young and the poor, with a callous disregard for

Despite the macabre quality of some of his materials,
such as human skull or fossilized whale ear bone, Smith does not believe in
spiritual possession.

environmental and social consequences. Smith's art often seems to stand as grim testament to the indifference of the world in which he grew up.

Smith left Detroit in 2012, but the atmospherics and mythology of the city in which he was born continue to hum, indelibly, in the background of his work. Though the media has begun to report cautiously on the bankrupt city's early renaissance, its ravaged infrastructure still tells its own story of abandonment.[1] The normal organizational dynamics of a metropolis no longer apply to this, a city that has emptied itself out from within. Wilderness is interleaved with zones of human habitation; deer, pheasants and falcons thrive in overgrown empty lots. Not that Smith has ever subscribed to a moral polarity between the natural (good) and the man-made (evil). As a child, he would spend summers on his grandparents' catfish farm in Mississippi; he describes the nature he encountered there – huge bugs, blood-red mud and a poisonous snake that his grandmother hacked to pieces on the living room carpet – as 'ferocious'.[2]

As with the American South, the saga of Detroit is also a story about race. When the Big Three automotive companies took their business elsewhere in the 1950s, the predominantly white middle class followed them or moved to the suburbs. The working-class population – predominantly black – stayed. Today, 83 percent of Detroit is African American. Smith, who is white, understands black music, historically, to be synonymous with suffering. Gospel, he told me, is 'a musical kind of crying' and 'all art is some variation on the blues'. He is influenced by the improvisation techniques of jazz and hip-hop, which have much in common with the economy of means evident in black assemblage art, especially that of the 1960s and '70s. When he stretches the torso of an infant's romper suit around a huge shovel, in the sculpture *Untitled* (2014), one cannot help but recall the devastating simplicity of David Hammons's *Bird* (1973), a saxophone with a metal spade head pushed into its stem. In another work by Smith, a spiked metal lightening rod connects with a frying pan to conjure a rudimentary stick figure.

Hammons is an artist who believes in the possession of objects by human spirits. Cut hair, bottles that have touched drinkers' lips, imprints of skin on paper: for him, indexicality is a means of bewitchment.[3] Other black assemblage artists, such as John Outterbridge and Noah Purifoy, both influences on Hammons, held to similar principles. Purifoy salvaged charred artefacts from the debris of the Los Angeles Watts Riots and used them, relatively unaltered,

in his earliest sculptures from the mid-1960s. Like Smith's work, assemblage by African Americans from this period is both searing social documentary and metaphysical poetry.

In his 2014 exhibition at The Power Station, Dallas, Smith placed six flat-screen monitors against a window in the industrial space's high ceiling. Visitors standing on the ground two storeys below could look up and watch a video clip, shot downwards from a helicopter hovering above the sea, that showed an orange stretcher being winched up out of the blue. The found footage was of a rescue mission in the wake of Hurricane Sandy, a detail that was neither available to the viewer nor essential to the piece. Beyond

1

the affective power of this mesmerizing image, it was apparent that here was an item of documentary significance: 'This has happened,' it told us.

Sometimes, the outside world forces its way in uninvited. For his exhibition at the Ludwig Forum, Smith included a low-mounted television showing the Cartoon Network, live. (Animation is a fitting corollary to his work, if one considers how perturbing the reality of a walking and talking

sponge or gumball or orange, would be.) Cable television was installed in the gallery especially for the exhibition. During the opening, on 15 April, the cheery transmission was interrupted by flash news reports showing the carnage caused by the two bombs that exploded during the Boston Marathon.

Unlike Hammons, Smith is not superstitious, and when coincidences occur in his work he puts it down to the inherent natures of things – of objects, substances or situations – rising to the surface. The sculpture *Mike* (2013), a matted ball of rooster feathers glued to a mannequin's cranium, shares its name both with the artist and two of his dealers (Clifton and Benevento) but is actually named after Mike the Headless Chicken, a freakish circus sideshow from the 1940s. Smith simply lays the coincidence at our feet, and leaves us to make of it what we will. Despite the macabre quality of some of his materials, such as human skull or fossilized whale ear bone, he does not believe in spiritual possession.

Smith is a rationalist, but his rationalism also leads him to speculate that the objects to which he is drawn must have accumulated something – not *a* soul but maybe just soul – along their journeys through the world. They are absorbent, he says, like the carbon filter in a fish tank. W.G. Sebald once wrote: 'Things outlast us, they know more about us than we know about them: they carry the experience they have had with us inside them and are – in fact – the book of our history opened before us.'[4] ◆●

1 For instance, Ben Austen, 'The Post-Post-Apocalyptic Detroit', *The New York Times*, 11 July 2014
2 All Michael E. Smith quotations from conversations with the author, May – September 2014
3 David Hammons, on hair: 'You've got tons of people's spirits when you handle that stuff. The same with the wine bottles. A black person's lips have touched each one of those bottles, so you have to be very, very careful.' Quoted in Kellie Jones, 'David Hammons', *Real Life Magazine*, 16, 1986, p. 8
4 W.G. Sebald, 'As Day and Night, Chalk and Cheese: On the Pictures of Jan Peter Tripp', in *Unrecounted: 33 Poems by W.G. Sebald, 33 Lithographs by Jan Peter Tripp*, New Directions, New York, p. 83

Jonathan Griffin is a contributing editor of frieze *based in Los Angeles, USA.*

Michael E. Smith is an artist living in Hopkinton, USA. In 2014, his solo exhibitions included The Power Station, Dallas, USA; Susanne Hilberry Gallery, Ferndale, Michigan, USA; Zabludowicz Collection, London, UK; La Triennale di Milano, Italy; and Lulu, Mexico City (opening December). In 2015, Smith will have solo exhibitions at: Etablissment d'en face, Brussels, Belgium; Sculpture Center, New York, USA; De Appel, Amsterdam, the Netherlands; and Kunstverein Hannover, Germany.

1
Mike, 2013, two roosters, plastic,
38 × 28 × 40 cm

2
Untitled, 2013, pigeon pelt, plastic,
26 × 10 cm

Courtesy
1 the artist and Clifton Benevento,
New York; photograph: Andres Ramirez •
2 the artist, Michael Benevento,
Los Angeles, Clifton Benevento, New York,
Susanne Hilberry Gallery, Detroit, KOW,
Berlin, and ZERO, Milan

Oscar Santillan

'Civilizations of the jaguar', vacuum cleaners and the human body

—

by Timotheus Vermeulen

1
Lost Star, 2012–13
blank copy of Alexander von
Humboldt's *Cosmos* with
extracted ink, 18 × 13 × 3 cm

2
Zephyr (detail)
2013–14, slide projection

3
A Hymn, 2013, production still

Courtesy
1 the artist, The Ridder,
Maastricht, and Cøpperfield,
London • 2 the artist and
Cøpperfield, London • 3 the artist
and The Ridder, Maastricht

I vividly recall the first time I saw work by the Ecuadorian artist Oscar Santillan. I was being given a tour of The Ridder gallery in Maastricht by its director, Ardi Poels, when I was suddenly drawn to a slideshow. It cut, puzzlingly, from a painting by Carl Jung of his astrological birth chart, to a black and white photograph of the psychoanalyst holding a three-dimensional model of that same chart, to an exploded diagram of a vacuum cleaner, to snapshots of a shaman in the Ecuadorian jungle, to images of someone walking around the jungle with a vacuum cleaner. *Zephyr* (2013–14) tells the surreal story of how Santillan posthumously realized Jung's desire – which remained unfulfilled during the psychoanalyst's lifetime – to see 'the civilizations of the jaguar'. He did so by installing a hollow replica of Jung's three-dimensional birth chart (which he devised around 1930, but subsequently lost), modelled to function as a dirt-catching bag, inside a vacuum cleaner. Travelling to the Ecuadorian jungle, Santillan – with the help of a shaman – used this machine to suck the scent of the jaguar out of the air. In the installation of *Zephyr* at The Ridder, the 'bag' that supposedly holds the scent was placed opposite the wall on which the slides were projected. What attracted me to this work was not the singularity of the story itself so much as the surprising way it is told.

The *Zephyr* slideshow lasts for just one minute and ten seconds, and consists of 11 still images, separated by cuts to black, linked by brief descriptive subtitles. While the black interludes draw attention to the extent to which the images seem to follow wildly different scripts, the subtitles suggest the opposite: that they are all, in fact, part of the same story. Indeed, what for me makes the work so mesmerizing, even magical, is that the seemingly antithetical fragments of the story play out in just the way one would expect them to – a birth chart holds the key to a person's life, a vacuum cleaner vacuums, a shaman gives guidance, jaguars emit a distinct scent in the Ecuadorian jungle, etc. – and build into a single incredible but coherent narrative. Here, everything is out of the ordinary because nothing is out of the ordinary; all becomes mysterious because mystery is conspicuously absent.

Santillan extracts elements from one context and reinserts them into another. In itself, that is nothing special: recycling has the same effect by, say, reusing the casing of a computer to make plastic cups. The plastic dies as one thing and is reincarnated as another, but it's still plastic. It's different with Santillan's recontextualization of Jung, the vacuum cleaner or the shaman: the material remains what it is while simultaneously becoming something else – we see the ghosts, so to speak, of other purposes rising from it.

Throughout his work, Santillan expresses a concern with materiality. At times, his particular focus is the human body. The video *Finale* (2012), for instance, documents a clairvoyant looking deep into the eyes of a curator to predict how he will die, followed by a short underwater glimpse of the curator seemingly enacting his own death by drowning. In *The Telepathy Manifesto* (2009–11), Santillan portrays two men, one of whom is trying to catch the tears that fall from the face of the other in his own eyes. *A Hymn* (2013) synchronizes the beat of a drum with a dancer's sweat as it drops to the floor. The materiality of the body is also foregrounded in the performance *Juana Inés de la Cruz* (2010–11), in which five people show only their hair through holes in a wall, creating a line of disembodied locks that suddenly appear strangely alien.

In other works, Santillan turns his attention to objects. For instance, in the installation *Daybreak* (2010), he scraped paint from the wall in the shape of a church window and applied it to the floor in the form of a shadow. For *Lost Star* (2013), Santillan used a chemical process to draw ink out of the pages of *Cosmos*

1

(1845–62) – geographer, naturalist
and explorer Alexander von
Humboldt's magnum opus on
science and nature – which was
then used to create a miniature
sculpture resembling a globe. Each
of these works calls to mind too
many debates – political (globali-
zation, exploitation, the politics
of place), philosophical (monism,
transcendence, hermeneutics)
and art historical (Modernism,
non-Western art) – and raises
too many questions to be reduced
in summary to a single trope.
However, the thread of repurposing
(or of creating new, parallel
purposes), runs through them: tears
falling from the eyes of one person
into another, hair displaced from
body to wall, the transmutation of
miniature things into grand narratives and back. Importantly, this
process of creating new purposes
is never present as an answer but as
a question, luring the viewer in.

Currently artist-in-residence
at the Jan Van Eyck Academie in
Maastricht, Santillan is developing
his practice. Recently restructured,
the Academie seems the perfect
place to help him achieve this.
Given the quality and imaginative-
ness of what Santillan has already
created, this would appear to be
less a case of the artist finding his
voice than about honing it. In the
six months since I first saw *Zephyr*,
the work has lost none of its power.
If anything, it has increased, continually percolating in my head,
resonating in my interactions with
other artworks, informing my
writing. I can't wait to see – and
hear – what Santillan does next.

*Timotheus Vermeulen is Assistant
Professor in Cultural Theory at
Radboud University Nijmegen, the
Netherlands, where he also heads
the Centre for New Aesthetics. He is
co-founding editor of the academic
arts and culture webzine* Notes on
Metamodernism.

*Oscar Santillan is currently artist-
in-residence at the Jan Van Eyck
Academie in Maastricht, the
Netherlands. Following a residency
at the Delfina Foundation, London,
UK, which begins in January 2015,
he will have his first solo exhibition at
Cøpperfield, London, in March 2015.*

2

3

*In Santillan's work, everything is out of the
ordinary because nothing is out of
the ordinary; all becomes mysterious because
mystery is conspicuously absent.*

1

Rachel Reupke

Taking stock
of stock images
—
by Dan Kidner

British artist Rachel Reupke's silent video *Wine and Spirits* (2013) begins with a close-up of a woman in profile, her hair tied back; she's looking off-camera as if listening to someone and nods her head almost imperceptibly. There follows a series of short establishing shots that show pints of Guinness being held, first by the woman – at a slightly cocked angle so that the white 'head' of the stout acts a little like a spirit level, almost matching the horizontals of the picture frame – and then by her male companion, who holds his glass at a perfect 90-degree angle. After several minutes of glasses being raised and lowered, the woman leans forward and her lips move. At this point, the first intertitle flashes up: 'Look who's here.' The man leans back to see and half his body leaves the frame. He doesn't respond, but the woman continues: 'I'm going to the museum this weekend. Do you want to come?' Again, he doesn't respond.

The video continues with a series of discrete scenes, each featuring the same actors playing different couples, in which their clothes, body language and choice of tipple change. They sit, stand or lean, surrounded by full, empty or half-empty glasses in elaborately constructed sets,

which have been modelled either on advertisements or on fashion photographs. The 'content' – the latent emotion conveyed through body language and snatches of conversation displayed on the intertitles – is drawn, according to the artist, from personal experience. The sense of unease in *Wine and Spirits* doesn't just come from this meshing together of unrelated source material. Reupke frequently has her actors stare off into the middle distance as she holds a shot for longer than is natural or expected. This creates a kind of surplus into which other emotions can be projected: boredom, hatred, love, regret or disappointment. In the final sequence, the couple, now puzzlingly nursing two half-pints of lager each, sit at a bar. The woman stares into the middle distance as if thinking, while the man looks at her with what could be love or desire. A half smile plays over his lips. Then, very slowly, she turns to face him with an expression that could be contentment. He suddenly appears unyielding and almost spiteful. He says something, which the intertitle indicates was: 'Don't get your hopes up.'

For some years, Reupke has been interested in the expressive properties of stock images,

advertisements and outtakes. In *10 Seconds or Greater* (2009) the artist had four actors perform various scenarios in a non-specific, Ikea-furnished, domestic environment, in the style of stock imagery. The scenes played out are generic enough to be employed for multiple uses. A young black woman sits with a white man and woman on a sofa looking through photographs on a digital camera; the man is then seen cross-legged on the floor, smiling and typing on his laptop. The last five minutes of the 15-minute video are taken up with a variety of drinking scenarios: a male/female couple drink red wine; two men drink beer; two women drink beer; two men drink wine. There are crisps, then crisps and peanuts. The permutations seem endless and completely banal. But, as in all of Reupke's work, there is a sense in which the artist is attempting to elicit feelings from, or inject meaning and emotion into, forms that have been emptied of these properties. Attuned to the way in which work, social interactions, entertainment and shopping have become intertwined within the same digital technologies, Reupke is on the lookout for the shafts of light that illuminate the points at which this digital hegemony is penetrated by the messy (analogue) world of feelings.

2

There is a sense that Reupke is attempting to elicit feelings from, or inject meaning and emotion into, forms that have been emptied of these properties.

As such, Reupke's recent work alights on the site of relationships, especially those that unfold in pre-digital social spaces; it is no coincidence that she focuses so much attention on that most analogue of all social lubricants: alcohol. Intoxication as an agent of transformation in the digital realm is also something that is explored in Ed Atkins's recent work, *Ribbons* (2014), whose avatar searches in vain for some kind of corporeal fulfilment at the bottom of a CGI cut-glass whisky tumbler. What both artists have in common is a desire to project emotion, sentiment and personal memories onto forms that appear to resist such projections. The spaces of advertising, technologically mediated social relations and computer-generated approximations of 'real life' are being mined by many artists today, but rarely with such attention to the thing that is most often left out of these spaces: human frailty.

In Reupke's *Deportment* (2011), a couple perch awkwardly behind a small table, on which two empty champagne flutes are set at an odd angle. After some moments, the frame shudders, as if someone has knocked the camera. Everything seems to teeter on the edge of collapse, an effect the artist achieved in part by shooting

the video twice, once with the couple and once without. Using the visual effects and compositing software 'After Effects', she layered the image of the empty room under the image of the couple and then redrew their profiles using a 'mask', giving the woman a button nose and elongated forehead. She then used Photoshop to alter the woman's jaw line with some skin-tone brush strokes, and adorned the couple with splodges of black paint to sculpt their hair. The unsettling aesthetic and extreme bathos of *Deportment* is something the artist intends to explore further in a new work, based on images of people writing letters of complaint, which will form the basis of her forthcoming solo show at London's Cubitt Gallery, opening in January 2015.

The images in Reupke's work oscillate between movement and stillness. Her work is about this movement, this transition from something still (an ideal) to something moving (reality). Using prosumer editing software, she consistently and deliberately fails to give her images the sheen of an ideal reality that high-grade digital processing has now made possible. Her videos are peppered with moments of stillness and awkwardness. In these instants, when the facade threatens to fall

away to reveal the messy analogue reality beneath, there is a kind of digital 'naked lunch' moment, which – as Jack Kerouac famously suggested to William Burroughs as the title for his seminal 1959 novel – is that frozen moment when you realize exactly what is on the end of your fork.

Dan Kidner is a curator and writer who lives in London, UK.

Rachel Reupke lives in London, UK. In 2013, she had a solo show at Cell Project Space, London. In 2014, her work has been shown at Ullens Center for Contemporary Art Beijing, China; Museum of Modern Art, Vienna, Austria; Wattis Institute, San Francisco, USA; Tate Britain, London; Whistable Biennial, UK; and South London Gallery. She has also been nominated for the 2014 Jarman Award. In January 2015, she will have a solo exhibition at Cubitt Gallery, London.

1 & 2
Wine and Spirits, 2013,
HD video stills

Courtesy
the artist, LUX and Cell
Project Space, London

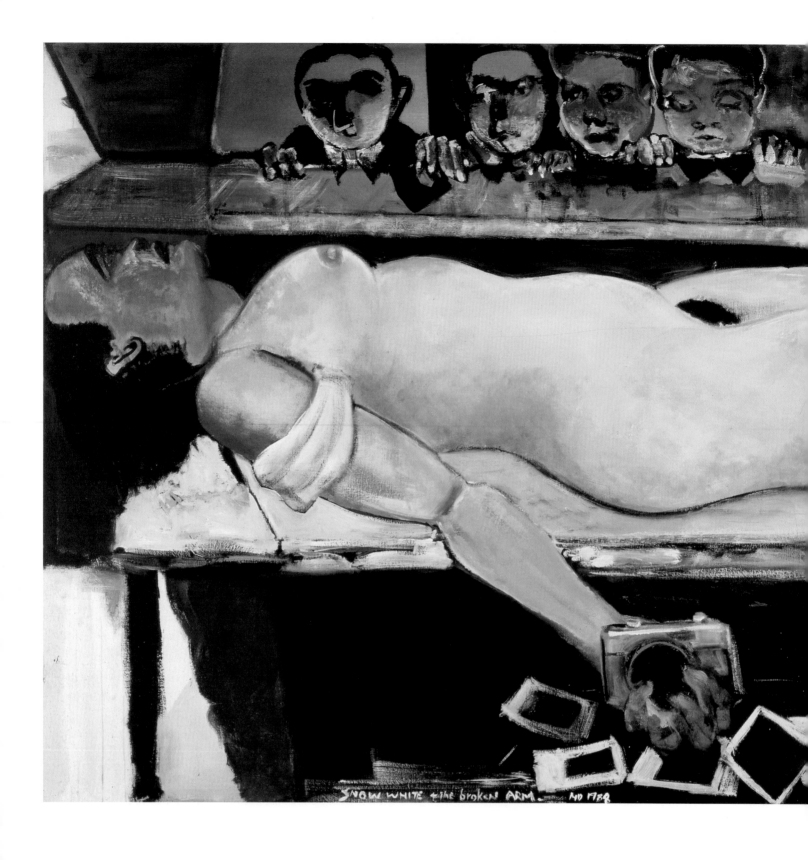

SNOW WHITE + the broken ARM. MD 1988

A WALL TO OBJECT TO

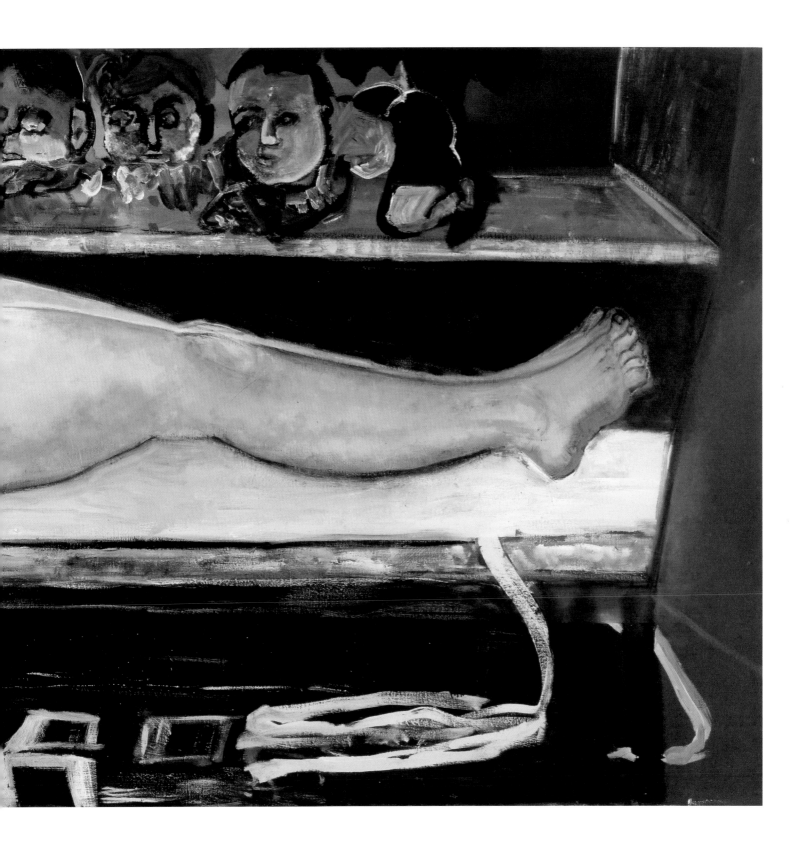

On the occasion of a major touring
retrospective, *Caoimhín Mac Giolla Léith*
examines the relationship
between image and painting in the
work of **Marlene Dumas**

'An image needs an edge to relate to, and a painting needs a wall to object to.'[1]
Marlene Dumas

Let us take a pair of portraits – one well known, one not – and see what they suggest about the work of Marlene Dumas. The first is an emblematic oil painting on canvas derived from a photograph, as ever with Dumas (aside from a few early works). *The Painter* (1994) depicts a naked child, standing alone, glowering defiantly, her paint-smeared hands hanging by her sides. This work graces the cover of the catalogue for Dumas's first European retrospective, 'Marlene Dumas: The Image as Burden', which opened in September at the Stedelijk Museum in Amsterdam, the artist's home since she arrived there from South Africa as a young woman in the mid-1970s.

The second image is a casual photograph reproduced as supplementary material in the exhibition's catalogue. Taken some years after the snapshot on which *The Painter* is based, it features the same little girl: Dumas's daughter Helena, aged nine. Dressed in white, she stands demurely in a corner of one of the Stedelijk's galleries, amid a group show of art from the Netherlands, dwarfed and hemmed in on both sides by huge paintings by her parents: Dumas and her Dutch partner Jan Andriesse. Her mother's two works, looming darkly to her right, are three-metre-tall portraits from the mid-1990s 'Magdalena' series, many of which are personifications of the archetypical 'fallen woman' redeemed. In the painting hanging nearest the little girl, *Magdalena (Manet's Queen/Queen of Spades)* (1995) – based on a magazine image of the model Naomi Campbell – the naked woman's ankles and feet are pale, as if blackness were a body-stocking that might be pulled on and off at will. A century and a half after the controversial reception of Édouard Manet's *Olympia* (1863), to which the work's subtitle alludes, it is hard to imagine a painting inciting a comparable mixture of moral outrage and aesthetic affront. That said, Dumas's picture is simultaneously alluring and disconcerting in its own (im)modest way. Given that the artist's rendering of the dark-skinned figure is barely distinguishable from the shadowy background, the viewer's natural inclination is to approach the painting to discern its detail. The giant Magdalena's crotch sits at eye level, and this close encounter is a bit like bumping into a naked Neytiri, from the 2009 film *Avatar*, down a dark alley. Meanwhile, to young Helena's left is a shimmering expanse of rainbow-like gradated colour in her father's signature mode of late-Modernist abstraction.

The Freudian 'family romance' staged in this obscure photo, when viewed in tandem with the iconic painting with which we began, offers the daughter as a character by turns empowered and overwhelmed by a heritage of picture-making, both figurative and abstract, which may be received as a blessing or a curse. The title of this retrospective, 'The Image as Burden' – borrowed from a small painting by Dumas from 1993 of a naked man carrying the inert figure of a woman in a flowing white

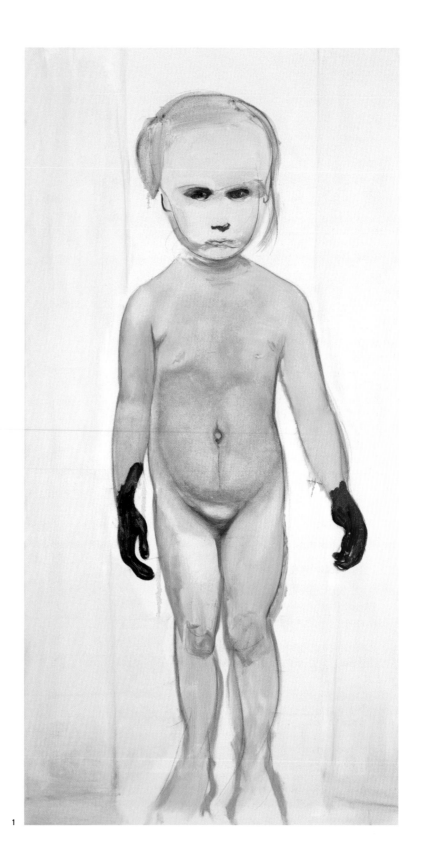

1

Marlene Dumas has insisted that, as a maker of paintings — as opposed to a taker of photographs, which of course she also is — her aim is to 'reveal' not to 'display'.

Opening pages
Snow White and the Broken Arm, 1988,
oil on canvas, 1.4 × 3 m

1
The Painter, 1994, oil on canvas,
200 × 99 cm

2
*Magdalena (Manet's Queen/
Queen of Spades)*, 1995,
oil on canvas, 3 × 1 m

All images courtesy (unless otherwise
stated) the artist, Frith Street,
London, Gallery Koyanagi, Tokyo, David
Zwirner, New York, Zeno X, Antwerp,
and Galerie Paul Andriesse, Amsterdam
• 1 MoMA, New York • 2 Stedelijk
Museum, Amsterdam • All photographs:
Peter Cox

robe (is she dead or has she fainted?) – favours
the second option. The source image for
this inverted *pietà*, it seems, is a film still of
Greta Garbo cradled in Robert Taylor's
arms in *Camille* (1936), the classic weepie of
golden-age Hollywood.

For decades, Dumas has supplied a running
commentary on the gap between her
work's intention and its reception via a stream
of aphoristic 'poems', often marked by
a mischievous literalism. In a similar vein, *The
Image as Burden*'s underhanded salute to a
movie icon who withdrew from public view at
the height of her fame is an intimation of how
traditional 'to-be-looked-at-ness' (i.e. woman
as image) can be literally difficult to bear. The
two most striking elements in the painting
are the ghoulish mask of impasto that is the
woman's face and the crudely rendered man's
hand as he awkwardly supports his charge,
while gazing at her with concerned affection.
His rude mitt is a stark patch of black paint
against the immaculate white of the woman's
robe, which, as the critic Wendy Steiner
once noted, effectively 'creates a dark pubis for
her, as her own sex is hidden': 'Unlike
Titian's *Venus of Urbino* or Manet's *Olympia*,
in which the woman's hand hides and at the
same time presents her pubis in a visual simula-
tion, here it is the man whose supporting
hand must perform this scandalous ostentation,
for she is no longer able to do so on her own.'[2]

This inability (and, indeed, inexplicitness)
is the exception rather than the rule, as any
number of paintings worked up from Dumas's
stockpile of print pornography and Polaroids
of working strippers can attest. A telling visual
rhyme with a later painting of precisely
the same dimensions as *The Image as Burden*,
titled *Fingers* (1999) – depicting a semi-clothed
woman on her knees, facing away from us, one
hand stretched around under her naked behind
to splay her sex and provide a better view –
may also serve as a reminder that modern
porn's repertoire of poses is no less codified
than that of the Old Masters. Dumas
has insisted that, as a maker of paintings –
as opposed to a taker of photographs, which

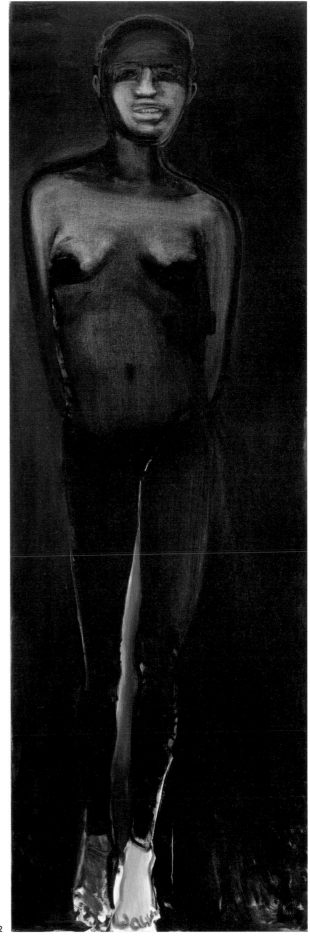

2

1

of course she also is – '[the] aim is to "reveal"
not to "display". It is the discourse of the
lover. I am intimately involved with my
subject matter […] I am not disengaged with
the subject of my gaze.'[3] From the viewer's
perspective, however, this may seem truer
of some of her paintings than of others, in
spite of the transformation of photographic
source materials involved in their production. Dumas's own defence of *Fingers*, as well
as related works drawn from 'pornobooks',
contrives to retrieve the requisite sense of
intimacy through a combination of displace-
ment and projection: 'Because I can't see
myself when I do the things I do, / I don't
know how I look when I look at you.'[4]

The variety of found imagery, augmented
by her own photographs, on which Dumas
bases her paintings is well documented and
longstanding, though there have been shifts
in emphasis over the years. From my one brief
trip to the artist's Amsterdam studio back in
1996, I remember a floor strewn with photo-
copied press images of models and celebrities,
including Campbell and Princess Diana,
the twin subjects of one of her oddest and most
arresting works of oblique social commentary,

the diptych *Great Britain* (1995–97). I also
recall a pub conversation I had with Dumas,
during which she delightedly reported that
her (female) assistant had turned up with some
porn mags containing 'images that even
I cannot use'. In fact, Dumas has always been
disarmingly generous in divulging her
sources, ever since the early *Love vs Death*
(1980). In this monumentally chaotic work
of collage and blueprint drawing, she first set
out her stall in an explosion of images and
text that includes the aforementioned film
still from *Camille*, as well as a photograph
of the aged, bedridden Peggy Guggenheim,
bluntly glossed: 'Is she dead yet?' In response
to a query by the critic Richard Shiff, as he
prepared a catalogue essay for her 2008 US
retrospective, Dumas revealed that her well-
known painting *The Kiss* (2003) was derived
from the closing image of the famous shower
scene in Hitchcock's *Psycho* (1960), adding
simply that nobody had asked her about the
source before.[5]

Which begs the question: how much does
the viewer gain when armed with such insider
knowledge? No amount of dutiful detective
work can account for the confounding

1
The Image as Burden,
1993, oil on
canvas, 40 × 50 cm

2
Fingers,
1999, oil on canvas,
40 × 50 cm

Courtesy
1 the artist and private
collection, Belgium

2

No amount of detective work can account for the confounding visceral impact of Marlene Dumas's consummate paintings and works on paper when encountered in person.

visceral impact of Dumas's most consummate paintings and works on paper when encountered in person. The veteran South African photographer David Goldblatt has spoken of his awestruck conversion to her work on finally seeing an exhibition of her paintings, after having spent some time puzzling over catalogue reproductions, unsure what the fuss was about. The boldly skittering drawn line that supplies Dumas's painted images' essential undergirding; the translucent washes, creamy swipes and clotted gobs of oil paint; the swiftly arcing, swerving and stabbing brushstrokes; the occasionally startling use of colour (an underappreciated aspect of Dumas's painting, obscured to some extent by the work's frequent thematization of blackness and whiteness); the virtuoso sloshing and puddling of watercolour on dexterously tipped and tilted sheets of paper, sometimes given extra sparkle by the admixture of metallic acrylic. To many viewers, these are the qualities that constitute the essence of Dumas the painter.

And yet, in spite of her commitment to the medium, any attempt to situate her work primarily in relation to the shifting fortunes

of painting (or indeed drawing) will always fall short. True, René Daniels was an early, local touchstone, and comparisons with Luc Tuymans were always inevitable, though a two-person show last year at Zeno X Gallery in Antwerp showcased intriguing divergences in form and content between the two artists, both on the gallery walls and in a recorded conversation. Shared concerns with other European contemporaries who work across several media, from Thomas Schütte to Rosemarie Trockel, seem equally pertinent. The tension between individual and type explored in Dumas's panoramic portrait grids, from *Models* (1994) to *Man Kind* (2005–06), owes much to a photographic lineage that runs from August Sander through Bernd and Hilla Becher to their celebrated students, and to Dumas's slightly younger Dutch contemporary Rineke Dijkstra. Casting the net across the Atlantic, a consideration of such Pictures Generation peers as Sarah Charlesworth, Barbara Kruger, Sherrie Levine and Cindy Sherman is surely crucial in assessing an artist who has always been alert to distinctions between taking and making pictures.

Measuring your own grave.

All of which suggests that, from the outset, lying at the root of Dumas's art is an exploration of the difference between an image and a painting. 'When looking at images,' she once claimed, 'I'm not lost, / but I'm uneasy.'[6] This disjuncture has been exacerbated by subsequent developments in the technological dissemination of imagery. That she should sometimes couch her thoughts on this matter in explicitly political terms is unsurprising, given her work's persistent engagement with questions of race, gender, violence, colonialism and ongoing conflicts in the Middle East. Somewhat more unexpected is her invocation of Ad Reinhardt as a father-figure – an irascible opponent of social injustice who was far better known as a proponent of endgame abstraction: 'Reinhardt felt that artists who try to make pictures that are also paintings usually fail to do either well. They do it "to avoid political responsibility and aesthetic criticism". Even though I try to solve this dilemma by trying to make works that look like pictures and act like paintings, I don't know if he would agree and his

approval means a lot to me.'[7] This brief *apologia* is from a commentary on the painting *Reinhardt's Daughter* (1994), which Dumas derived from a photograph of Helena sleeping, her skin painted a dark brown. A pendant work, *Cupid* (1994), based on the same photo, in which the girl's skin is white, confirms this as another play on essential versus incidental blackness – pigment as racial determinant as opposed to painting material.

If ever there were an artist with a natural inclination to attempt to do several things at once, it is Dumas. And it would be easy to dismiss this heartfelt ambition as misguided. She has certainly endured more than her fair share of critical sniping, especially in the US – one complaint being that her painting is insufficiently transformative of its source materials. Yet the very fact that she sometimes seems to add little to the found image compositionally – other than hemming it into its rectangular frame and turning it into a painting – is in itself striking. Her persistent emphasis on the picture plane's constraints is remarkable, as isolated bodies contort themselves in order to fit into its confines, or extend their limbs to push against its imaginary walls and ceiling. It is as if human bodies were just so much pictorial material – compliant forms ready to be stretched, folded or crammed into their rectangular cage. The title of Dumas's US retrospective came from the painting *Measuring Your Own Grave* (2003), in which the outstretched hands of a bent-over figure

claw at the edges of the canvas. No room was found in this European retrospective for Dumas's body of elongated horizontal paintings (the frame as coffin?), dating back to *Snow White and the Broken Arm* (1988), many of them modelled on Hans Holbein's *The Body of the Dead Christ in the Tomb* (1520–22). The point is that every one of Dumas's manifestly self-conscious paintings began life as an image of an entirely different order, and they should not be assessed without accounting for the dialogic nature of this double articulation.

Dumas came into her own as an artist at around the same time Thomas Lawson devised the astute analysis and perverse prognosis of his epochal essay 'Last Exit: Painting'. Announcing, in 1981, the exhaustion of late Modernism and (certain brands of) critical Postmodernism alike, Lawson advocated as the best way forward for the radical artist 'the appropriation of painting as a subversive method [that] allows one to place critical aesthetic activity at the centre of the marketplace where it can do most damage', adding that the 'discursive nature of painting is persuasively useful, due to its characteristic of being a never-ending web of representations'.[8] It is unlikely that Dumas's work was quite what Lawson had in mind back then, though it does fit the bill. Somehow, her paintings seems equally unlikely, more than 30 years later, to figure prominently in ongoing debates about the nature of the image and its various relations: to its mechanisms of production and circulation, to its disparate material 'carriers', to its potential sub-categorizations (e.g. *starke Bilder* or 'strong images'), to the general domain of art and its systems of evaluation. But if Dumas's work doesn't occupy a central place in this discourse, it will have been a missed opportunity. ❖

1 Cornelia Butler, *Marlene Dumas: Measuring Your Own Grave*, Museum of Contemporary Art, Los Angeles, 2008, p. 95
2 Wendy Steiner, 'The Burden of the Image', *Venus in Exile: The Rejection of Beauty in Twentieth-Century Art*, University of Chicago Press, Chicago, 2001, pp. 32–34
3 *Marlene Dumas: Miss Interpreted*, Stedelijk van Abbemuseum, Eindhoven, 1992, p. 43
4 Leontine Coelewij, Helen Sainsbury and Theodora Vischer, *Marlene Dumas: The Image as Burden*, Tate Publishing, London, 2014, p. 41
5 ibid., p. 122
6 ibid., p. 72
7 http://www.brooklynrail.org/special/AD_REINHARDT/artists-on-ad/why-i-called-a-painting-of-mine-reinhardts-daughter, last accessed 13 September 2014
8 Thomas Lawson, 'Last Exit: Painting', *Artforum* 20, no. 2 (October 1981), pp. 40–47

Caoimhín Mac Giolla Léith is a critic who teaches at University College Dublin, Ireland.

Marlene Dumas is a South African artist who lives in Amsterdam, the Netherlands. Her retrospective, 'Marlene Dumas: The Image as Burden', is on view until 4 January 2015 at the Stedelijk Museum in Amsterdam. From there, it will travel to Tate Modern, London, UK, from 5 February to 10 May 2015, and then to Fondation Beyeler, Riehen / Basel, Switzerland, later next year.

1
Measuring Your Own Grave,
2003, oil on
canvas, 1.4 × 1.4 m

*If ever there were an artist with a natural inclination to attempt
to do several things at once, it is Dumas.*

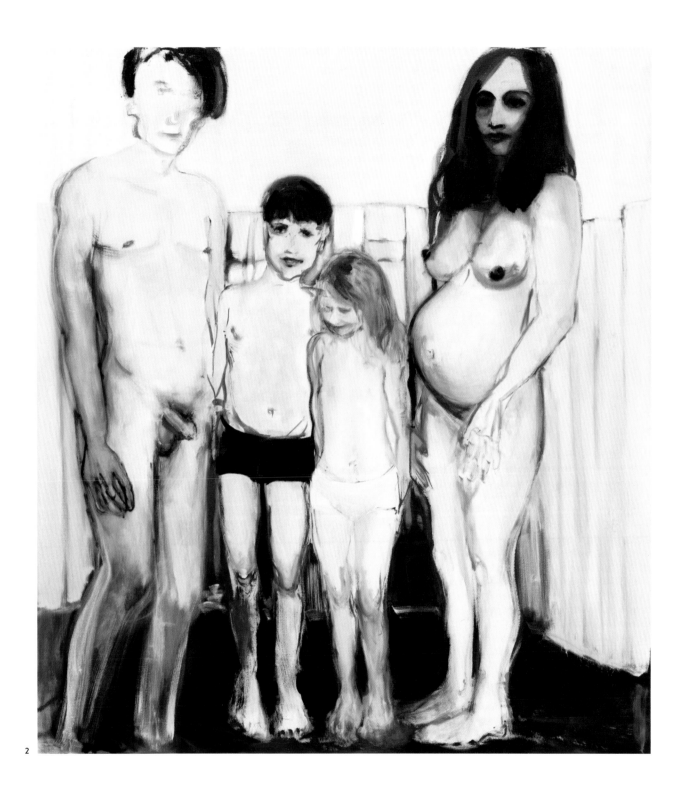

2

2
Nuclear Family,
2013, oil on canvas, 2 × 1.8 cm

Courtesy
2 the artist and Fondation
Beyeler, Basel

THE
CARTOON NETWORK

Illustration and art history
collide in **Sanya Kantarovsky**'s paintings
by Scott Roben

'Code-switching' is a term that describes the tendency of two or more multilingual speakers to alternate between languages, or language registers, during a single conversation or even a single sentence. More than just a question of toggling, code-switching itself can influence meaning, at least insofar as the exact point of the switch is often decided by subtle social and cultural cues. It crossed my mind while thinking about Sanya Kantarovsky's paintings, which slide so deftly, sometimes nearly imperceptibly, between visual idioms. They navigate not just styles but the particular histories that formed them and the distinct expressive structures that underlie them – all of this, more often than not, with a bit of a wink.

First and most obviously, there's an illustrational style in Kantarovsky's work that relies heavily on drawing: calligraphic marks outlining willowy figures in black shoes and bowlers, light bulbs and walking sticks. These characters seem to have arrived, if somewhat the worse for wear, from the world of gag cartoons, channelling the graphic wit of cartoonists such as Saul Steinberg or maybe even, with their dandyish charm and dreamlike appearances, the early-20th-century comics of Winsor McCay – to pose just two possibilities from what's surely an endless list of references. Then there are the highly mannered painted spaces they inhabit, which contain a great deal of visible brushwork and make references sprawling from Fauvism to postwar Russian poster design. Kantarovsky certainly isn't the only artist working today

who's putting cartoon illustration into contact with, or alongside, a painting practice. (Vittorio Brodmann, Trevor Shimizu, Amy Sillman and Amelie von Wulffen are some varied examples that reveal only the tip of the iceberg.) However, the peculiar ways in which he impels the two to make meaning together – within the bounds of the same frame, shape or even line – are what keep me looking.

Cartoons, especially the type of single-frame gag cartoons that Kantarovsky's canvases gesture toward, frequently depend on some kind of text for their meaning – a caption, a speech bubble, a magazine article. Kantarovsky's paintings, though, are resolutely mute. Take, for instance, *You Expected Something Different* (2013), in which a veil of transparent white paint covers up what appears to have been a very quick, all-over gestural composition, leaving only a small rectangle in the top-right corner. The exposed rectangle reads like an unframed canvas hanging on a wall, and its scale is suggested by two feet resting on a side table, added as a final layer in the foreground. There's something slightly precarious about the whole set-up: the half-concealed underpainting, the feet that seem prone to slip off the table at any moment, the table itself which appears to be missing one of its curved metal ornaments. There's a sense of a punchline, somewhere, but just when you feel as though you're on the verge of uncovering it, you're funnelled right back into the picture. You want to 'get' the joke,

but it's a dead end. In the same way that many paintings are devised with an inbuilt tension that discourages the eye from resting at any one point on their surfaces, here the brain scans continually for meaning and never finds it; in fact, the experience of the pictorial space and the search for the joke are wired together in the same circuit. This might be a way of saying Kantarovsky's paintings are not one-liners.

Often, and especially in the earlier work, it seems as though the 'joke' might be about representation itself, and the cartoonish style becomes a vehicle for a kind of parodic meta-discourse on painting. Super-charged signifiers – including paintings, windows, frames, masks and even projectors – appear frequently within Kantarovsky's canvases, as though laying the groundwork for a pun, but one that never actually lands. There's a certain sort of affect that self-referential structures are capable of producing on their own, by creating the illusion that the artwork itself is self-aware and thus able to 'think'. These paintings capitalize on that but with a healthy dose of irony and occasional cuteness. Sometimes paint itself passes over into the realm of signs and ciphers conjured by the cartoons, assuming the role of a character, or becoming a caricature of itself. This is the case in *You Expected Objects* (2013), where a vortex of tar-black brushstrokes materializes in front of another painting-within-a-painting, taking on the role of a viewer in front of the depicted work. Despite

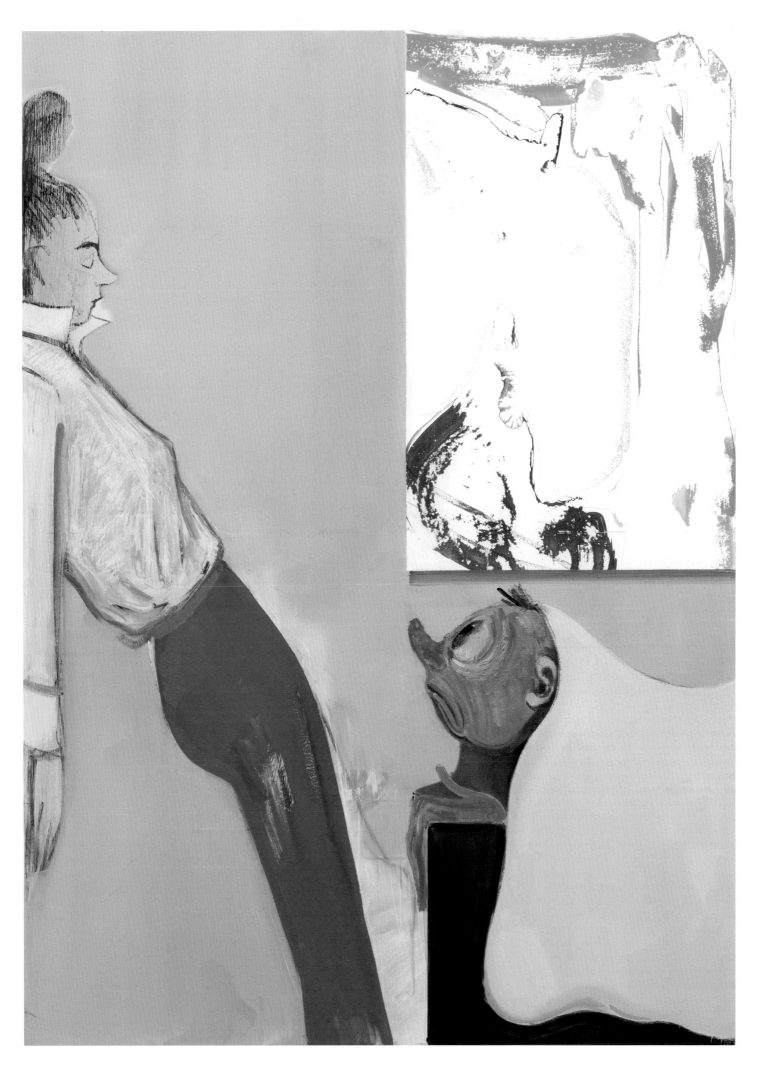

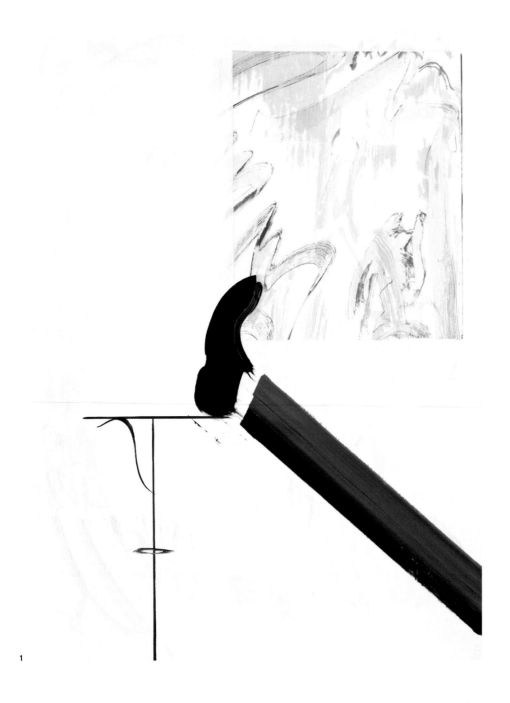

1

There's something slightly precarious about the whole set-up. You want to 'get' the joke, but it's a dead end.

the crotch, his face turned away, tossing us a smug side-eye. Meanwhile, the picture's construction noticeably evokes Matisse: wide, flat fields of brilliant colour comprised of feathery brushstrokes that either butt up against each other or peter out just before making contact with an adjacent shape. The figure and the interior share a certain visual logic up until the face, which shifts in key to something yellower, its profile coming to a point on a Pinocchio-like nose that has been pulled from yet another visual lexicon. Passages like these, where one language surfaces within the brackets of another, give the paintings a sort of schizophrenic voice that betrays a great deal of sensitivity.

Of course, although it's quite easy to be drawn into the worlds offered up by the paintings, not all of the meaning in Kantarovsky's work happens within the confines of the picture plane. For one thing, there's an ongoing insistence on installation. In the past, Kantarovsky has shunned traditional wall-based hangs and installed his works on panels suspended from the ceiling. In a quietly slapstick move, the panels' bases do not quite touch the floor, allowing the disembodied feet of fellow visitors to be seen from the other side. In an exhibition at the Badischer Kunstverein earlier this year, these 'floating' panels were dressed up to look like enormous men's shirts, with collars and buttons running vertically up and down their fronts, their collective, metonymic evocation of the male body in perfect harmony with the archetypal, genteel characters that tend to populate the artist's paintings. Sculpture, too, plays a role here and there. In Kantarovsky's 2012 exhibition at Marc Foxx Gallery in Los Angeles, for example, shapes and angles excerpted from a large, curling metal sculpture in the middle of the space resurfaced as motifs in the surrounding paintings. Repeatedly, Kantarovsky has sought ways of bringing his extremely two-dimensional painted figures into three-dimensional space, where they're poised for new kinds of

the reverence many artists and critics bear toward self-reflexivity, especially in painting, there's a lightness to these works that arises not only from their arch tone but also their palette, which is dominated by thin blues and greys, as well as their facture: wispy lines that demarcate forms with uncommon economy. If there's a struggle happening anywhere behind these paintings, it might arise less from the process of 'resolving' the picture than from the challenge of preserving its ambivalence.

While the language of cartoon illustration seems to speak loudest in Kantarovsky's earlier works, his most recent yield more fully to a language that's specific to painting. First off, there's a much more expansive range of mark-making showing up on their surfaces, with additive procedures (paint building in intensity through layers, or piling up in thick impastos) dovetailing with subtractive ones (bleaching, scraping, scumbling, abrading). Some pictures are unprimed, meaning the paint simply soaks into the linen, sometimes forming crisp contours, other times bleeding out of

control. They've become more laboured as well as more muscular in terms of their use of colour, the latter's role deepening both in establishing space and as a citational tool. In 'Allergies', an exhibition mounted earlier this year at Casey Kaplan in New York, the paintings adopted a vocabulary mined in large part from European painting around the turn of the last century: artists as disparate as Paul Gauguin, Ernst Ludwig Kirchner, Henri Matisse, Emil Nolde or early Max Beckmann cast shadows on these pictures, though again their invocation within Kantarovsky's tongue-in-cheek pictorial world borders on caricature.

The caricature stands in contrast to Kantarovsky's characters, who no longer seem to be just passing through, and instead have become more deeply entwined in the images' essential fibre – though they don't always look too content within it. In *Visitor* (2014), a man reclines nude on a couch in a pose that parodies Édouard Manet's *Olympia* (1863), one hand covering

Opening page
When Things Don't Work Out
2014, oil, watercolour, pastel, oilstick
on linen, 1.4 × 1 m
1
*You Expected Something
Different*, 2013, ink, watercolour, oil,
gesso on canvas, 1.4 × 1 m

2
'What Were You
Expecting, Mr. Milquetoast, a Plot?',
2014, installation view, Badischer
Kunstverein, Karlsruhe

3
Visitor, 2014
oil, watercolour, pastel, oilstick on
linen, 1.4 × 1 m

All images courtesy
Casey Kaplan, New York, Mark Foxx
Gallery, Los Angeles, and Tanya
Leighton, Berlin

collisions with historical genres. In *A Situation* (2012), for instance, a cartoonish man's lower trouser leg and shoe were cut out of steel and mounted low to create the illusion of a figure stepping through the wall, reproducing a motif already established in the paintings of people entering, exiting or passing through the frame. It's hard not to read it as a cover version of Robert Gober's beeswax leg sculptures from the late 1980s, the latter's eerie corporeality exchanged for the surreal experience of an embodied sign. (Performance, it's worth mentioning, has also started to appear in recent collaborations with artists Liz Magic Laser and Ella Kruglyanskaya.)

Kantarovsky's work may be teasing at times, and it carries a lot of heavy subject matter, but there's a sweetness to it that's pretty hard to miss. Some of the figures could have even been taken from children's book illustrations, like the pyjama-clad men in the pair of paintings *Homo Duplex I* and *II* (2013), who slump pensively in the corners of pale-pink and blue squares that block out the centres of two landscapes. One shows an expansive industrial scene, the other a soft forest, both of which register as the content of memories or dreams – just out of reach. Dreams tend to be places of mixed codes, and it might be nice to imagine this work as half-dreaming. Though, actually, Kantarovsky's project is far from sleeping. ❖●

Scott Roben is an artist and writer based in New York, USA.

Sanya Kantarovsky lives in New York, USA. In 2014, he had solo exhibitions at: 346 Mission, Los Angeles, USA; Casey Kaplan, New York; and kim? Contemporary Art Center, Riga, Latvia. In 2015, he will have solo shows at Marc Foxx Gallery, Los Angeles; Tanya Leighton, Berlin, Germany; and Studio Voltaire, London, UK.

In its Place

Decoding **Uri Aran**'s mysterious work-tables
by Declan Long

Among the recurrent components of Uri Aran's low-key, conceptually secretive installations are simple work-tables: standard fixtures of an artist's studio, repurposed as artfully scrappy display structures. Varying in size and style, these utilitarian supports – scored and smeared with traces of agitated creative labour – are laden with meticulously untidy assortments of man-made objects and organic materials. This busily cryptic *bricolage* – that might include broken spectacles, balls of string, cut-up rubber gloves, coffee cups, chocolate-chip cookies, autumn leaves, pears, pool balls and pizza boxes – appears to manifest, in each instance, a distinct moment within an obscure project of analysis, arrangement or assembly.

Although he was born in Jerusalem, Aran is a long-term resident of New York; as such, his work was included in the Whitney Biennial's survey of American art earlier this year. The show included three of his mysterious, messy work stations. Strips of passport snapshots, stuck onto thin plywood cut-offs, kept company with collections of delicate, dried-out sycamore leaves – as if one group of repeating forms was being studied in relation to the other. Panes of glass, little golden rods and cardboard boxes collectively hinted at a desire for structure and containment, despite the general air of mental muddle. In some sections of the coffee-stained and scribbled-on surfaces, there was contrasting evidence of scrupulous care: several of the gathered bits-and-pieces – especially assorted fruits – were neatly packaged-up or very precisely placed. Progress – in whatever strange direction had been planned – seemed more advanced in some parts than others. But without inside information as to what kind of intuitive or strategic exercises had been undertaken, how could we know for sure?

A more expanded, continuous and – tentatively – resolved variation of such calculated 'messthetics' featured as Aran's contribution to 'The Encyclopaedic Palace', a group exhibition concerned with eccentric system-building, at the 2013 Venice Biennale. Here, too, a sense of fiddly, table-top activity was prioritized. But on that occasion it was combined with pronounced associations of museological parsing. A miscellany of humble materials – dog biscuits, wood shavings and bunches of grapes – were selected, compared and carefully positioned. New connections were formed; fresh categorizations were tested. A peculiar, incomprehensible kind of control

was applied to the chaos of ordinary things. Whatever offbeat systems had been implemented, however, the outcomes achieved by Aran were, as always, deliberately provisional – and, as such, purposefully frustrating. His intricate, inconclusive investigations frequently have the look of abandoned experiments; their forlorn contents the confusing leftovers of tasks that, for some reason, have been temporarily stalled. Rather than supporting a satisfying sculptural pose, Aran's work-table pedestals often present moments of uneasy artistic *pause*.

In one way, of course, such a sense of creative hesitation is familiar to anyone with a desk and a deadline. In his brief essay 'Notes Concerning the Objects that Are on my Work-table' (1976), Georges Perec writes of how a 'rearrangement of my territory' tends to take place 'in the middle of those indecisive days when I don't know if I'm going to get started and when I simply cling on to these activities of withdrawal: tidying, sorting, setting in order'. Such periods, for Perec, involved the 'dream of a work surface that is *virgo intacta*: everything in its place, nothing superfluous'. The practical, lived-in reality, nevertheless, is rather different:

'Once my work is advancing or else stalled, my work-table becomes cluttered with objects that have sometimes accumulated there purely by chance (secateurs, folding rule) or else by some temporary necessity (coffee cup). Some will remain for a few minutes, others for a few days, others, which seem to have got there in a somewhat contingent fashion, will take up permanent residence.'

Whatever the reasons for these items' arrival into his working milieu, Perec is eventually quite accepting of things as they are, in all their unmanageable randomness. He delights in the patient endeavour of

Departments, 2014, installation view at Liverpool Biennial

Courtesy the artist, Sadie Coles HQ, London, Gavin Brown's Enterprise, New York, mother's tankstation, Dublin, and the Liverpool Biennial; photograph: Keith Hunter

singling out the details of a given reality, cataloguing the elements of its dizzying, day-to-day heterogeneity. As a reflection on the immediate 'territory' of an artist's work, it's interesting to compare Perec's essay to Elizabeth Bishop's peculiar prose poem '12 o'Clock News' (1973), in which a trusty writing desk is envisioned as a mysterious, newly discovered landscape. Neatly listing the main contents of the desk in one column and using the voice of a fictional foreign correspondent to describe them in another, Bishop surveys the suddenly estranged work surface with bemused wonder, making one surprising imaginative leap after another. Her typewriter becomes an 'escarpment that rises abruptly

from the central plain'. It has 'elaborate terracing' that 'gleams faintly in the dim light, like fish scales'. The ordinary objects making up this desk-landscape lose their customary meanings. Wild speculation begins about their status and purpose within the table-top realm. A typed sheet of paper could be either 'an airstrip' or 'a cemetery'. Two possible destinies, perhaps, for an artist's work: take-off or untimely demise. If, in his notes, Perec seeks to see things exactly as they are, Bishop strives to escape the received definitions of what is objectively right there, formulating substitute meanings for near-to-hand, comfortably knowable things. A commitment to an intensive process of inventory in one

account contrasts with an anxious instinct for invention in the other.

Aran's art labours restlessly in the uncertain space between such divergently attentive positions. His assembled odds-and-ends are mostly recognizable for what they are – but they are on their way to becoming something else. His enigmatic tableaux are transitional arrangements, with transitional meanings. In certain works, a dual sense of setting-out seems to apply: the various stray elements that are placed within loosely designed layouts are, in turn, held within framing structures that seem prepared for imminent moving on, for setting out into the world. So, for example, in addition to work-tables, Aran's installations have featured tailor-made vitrines: formal show cases in which (with a suggestion of preservation) his collected materials come together for inspection. The rudimentary design of such containers, however, also suggests temporary packaging and therefore implies readiness for transportation. The versions included in Aran's solo exhibition, 'Here, Here, Here', at the Kunsthalle Zurich in 2013 are a case in point: constructed from cardboard, they are flimsy, open boxes, precariously held together with packing tape. (And note, too, that repetitive title, with its simultaneous suggestion of dropped-pin mapping and rapid dispersal.)

A similar series of bespoke cases – entitled 'Departments' (2014) – were shown this year at the Liverpool Biennial. Timber-built, they have a more robust materiality, promising greater security and stability. Yet, like the shipping crates that protect artworks as they travel the world, they were made in a way that implies movement. Conservation glass covered the contents in some of these cases but, for the most part, not completely. In one, several small panes rested either on top or at the edges of the box. It was difficult to know if these pieces were in the process of being fitted or removed. As such, we couldn't be sure if this container – neither fully open nor entirely closed – was in a state of arrival or departure.

Two biographical facts are relevant to Aran's enduring fascination with transitional forms. One is that he initially had a career in design, before changing direction towards art: a disciplinary shift that perhaps gave him license for greater imaginative waywardness in his dealings with cultural forms and their meanings. It's worth noting that Aran's tutor for his MFA in visual art (at Columbia in New York) was Liam Gillick – an artist whose work often envisages alternative ways to move between the historically divided fields of art and design. Even if Aran's installations owe very little to the pristine scenarios produced by Gillick, it seems appropriate to register the influence of the 'dynamic contradictions' that characterize the latter's work: a type of art that seeks to complicate customary relations between sculptural objects and their conditions of comprehension, a practice based around presenting ostensibly stable structures that nonetheless enable a new mobility of meaning. Aran, like Gillick, is interested in simultaneously referencing and refusing established organizational patterns of artistic production. This shared aspiration has provided the foundation for some collaborations between them over recent years: such as on the film *1848!!!* (2010), first shown at Esther Schipper, Berlin, and as part of the one-off group project *To The Moon Via the Beach* (2012), staged at the Roman Amphitheatre in Arles. This event (conceived by Gillick and Philippe Parreno) was described as 'an exhibition about work, production and change – ideas in constant motion': principles that are certainly applicable, in broad terms, to Aran's ongoing if unsteady transitional processes.

The second biographical fact of note is Aran's expatriate status. As an Israeli

1
Installation view
at the Whitney Biennial,
2014

2
Untitled,
2013, mixed media,
37 × 28 cm

Courtesy
1 the artist, Sadie Coles HQ,
London, Gavin Brown's Enterprise,
New York, mother's tankstation,
Dublin, and South London Gallery •
2 the artist, Sadie Coles HQ, London,
mother's tankstation, Dublin, Gavin
Brown's Enterprise,
and The Whitney Museum of
American Art, New York; photograph:
Ronald Amstutz

artist based for many years in New York, he is sensitive to the gaps and glitches in meaning that occur through a back-and-forth movement between different cultural contexts, different languages and different landscapes (or between different ideas of landscape). The passport photographs that he often uses in his work are of acute importance in this regard. While Aran considers these images as having principally existential rather than 'émigré' significance, they are inescapably political: concentrating our attention on the procedural processes and categorization systems that either constrain or facilitate movement. They are deceptively simple things – pictures of faces – that become powerfully charged with meaning at borders. They form a decisive part of the often devastating identification process that determines who might be able to proceed with a planned transition from one territory to another. But, endlessly returned to and resituated within Aran's work – pasted and printed onto different types of surface, brought into unanticipated proximity with other images

1

As an Israeli artist based in New York, Uri Aran is sensitive to the glitches in meaning that occur through a back-and-forth movement between different cultural contexts.

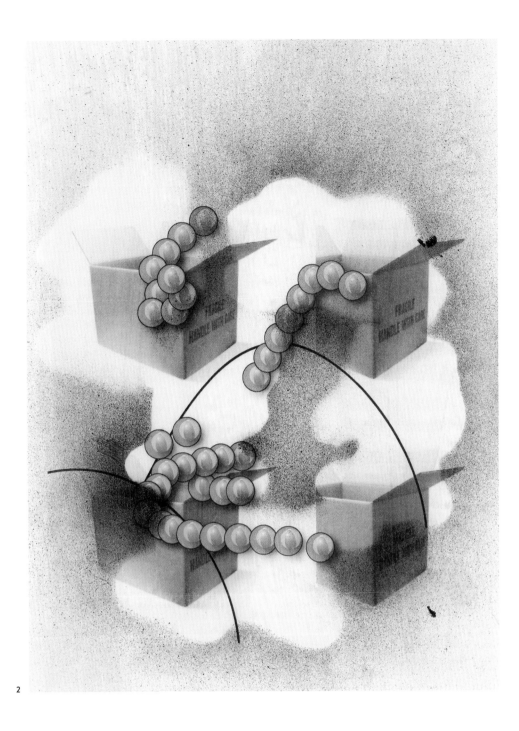

2

and objects – their function and meaning as images becomes unfixed and indeterminate. They become 'images in constant motion', even as they also speak of impediments to motion: closed borders, frustrated progress.

Indeed, what is often most fascinating – and even, in the best possible way, a little maddening – in Aran's art, is the extent to which the forms of 'constant motion' in his work are often impeded or troubled. His work is always, down to the smallest detail, invested in process. The grapes he uses will age and rot. The pool balls he sticks into position are designed for speedy roll and ricochet. Even the ubiquitous chocolate-chip cookies might be thought of as crucial sustaining elements within a working process: treats that help to mark stage-by-stage advances. But Aran is also fixated on the conditions and restrictions of process. All of the items listed above are a type of circle – a shape that occurs a great deal in Aran's art, and which could

be perceived as the basis of an intentionally tail-chasing aesthetic strategy. In some of the video works that are regularly displayed alongside (and often within) Aran's installations, this circularity is especially evident. In *Untitled Chimpanzee* (2013), (also included in the Kunsthalle Zurich show), or *Uncle in Jail* (2012) (shown as part of 'By Foot, By Bus, By Car' at Gavin Brown's Enterprise, New York) we are given behind-the-scenes access to recording processes in which various actors speak directly to camera or into obviously imposing professional microphones. They each tell very short stories or make brief textbook-style statements – and then they return to the beginning, starting again, delivering the script slightly differently for each take. Sometimes, the content of a story transforms entirely. Sometimes, it stays more-or-less the same. On occasion, the process will seem to flow – accompanied in several instances by a soundtrack of

improvisational jazz – or it will be constantly breaking down, as if we are watching a peculiar, melancholy kind of blooper reel. As in all of Aran's work, there is both repetition and release: a continuing attention to the difficulty of creating movement, as well as to the consistent possibility of new departures. ❖❖

Declan Long is a writer and lecturer at the National College of Art & Design, Dublin, Ireland, where he is co-director of the Masters programme, 'Art in the Contemporary World'.

Uri Aran lives in New York, USA. This year, his work was included in the Whitney Biennial, New York, and the Liverpool Biennial, UK, and he had a solo show at Peep Hole, Milan, Italy. In 2013, he had solo shows at South London Gallery, UK, and Kunsthalle Zürich, Switzerland. He will have an exhibition at mother's tankstation in Dublin, Ireland, in January 2015.

HEADS ABOVE WATER

The anarchic 1920s Tokyo art movement **Mavo** and the internationalism of the Japanese Avant-garde
by Andrew Maerkle

In July 1923, a new Dadaist-Constructivist art group debuted in Tokyo. Calling themselves 'Mavoists', and taking the letters MV as their monogram, the five founding members announced the establishment of Mavo in a manifesto published on the occasion of their first group exhibition: 'We are standing at the cutting edge, forever standing at the cutting edge. We have no constraints. We are radical. We will revolt. We will advance. We will create. We ceaselessly affirm and negate. In all senses of the word we are alive – more alive than anything.'

Against the backdrop of an expanded empire and economy post-World War I, and a government that sought to suppress oppositional politics, the Mavoists, whose numbers fluctuated over the course of the group's short life, were inspired by anarchist, nihilist and leftist thought. They practiced what their catalyst, the artist Tomoyoshi Murayama, called 'conscious Constructivism', a dialectical approach to art that rejected universal aesthetic values and challenged the artist to push beyond individual subjectivity. Made with materials including photographs and advertising imagery, samples of Russian texts, concrete, cans and women's shoes, their mixed-media collages, paintings and assemblages reflected the emerging global culture.

The Mavoists also antagonized existing institutions by bringing their art into public spaces. In August 1923, they attempted to mount a roving exhibition of works placed on handcarts and accompanied by a marching band, which was ultimately stopped by the police. The artworks had been rejected by Nika-kai (Second Section Association), a group of painters from the Ministry of Education's academic salon, which was celebrating its tenth annual exhibition with a special display of paintings by artists including Georges Braque and Pablo Picasso. In November, the Mavoists held a dispersed exhibition of works at cafés and restaurants across Tokyo. They also expanded across other fields of expression, engaging with dance and theatre, and starting a limited-run experimental journal called *Mavo*.

On 1 September 1923, just days after the failed exhibition, the Great Kantō earthquake devastated Tokyo, claiming over 100,000 lives. As with other groups involved in what was called the 'New Art' movement, the Mavoists joined efforts to rebuild the city, designing expressionistic facades for shops and restaurants, and submitting Constructivist models to the 'Exhibition of Plans for the Reconstruction of the Imperial Capital' in April 1924. That same year, Murayama designed Japan's first Constructivist stage – a multi-storey structure partitioned into cubicle-like sections – for a production of Georg Kaiser's 1912 play *From Morning to Midnight* at the Avant-garde Tsukiji Little Theatre.

While relatively few of their works survive, Mavo's intellectual dynamism is still felt in the pages of their journal, published for seven issues from 1924 to 1925, and reissued in 1991 in a facsimile edition (itself now out of print) by Nihon Kindai Bungakukan (the Museum of Modern Japanese Literature). From its distinctive cover lettering in both Japanese and English to its bold compositions of reproductions, prints, type and design elements, the journal bristled with provocative content, arranged upside down, right to left and left to right, inverted or stretching across several pages in irregular columns, so that one almost tumbles through it. Contained within it were translations of poems and texts by Wassily Kandinsky and El Lissitzky, commentaries on local and international art, essays on Soviet Avant-garde architecture, as well as scenarios for Dadaist stage productions and poems filled with nonsense words and absurdist imagery by group members and other writers.

For the cover of the third issue of *Mavo*, published in September 1924, artist Michinao Takamizawa created *Portrait of a Foreigner's Mistress*, a collage incorporating strands of hair and firecracker packets. Within the journal, the group staged a kind of conceptual exhibition, with prints and reproductions individually pasted onto sheets of found newsprint integrated into the binding. A text introducing this section compared the journal itself to the explosives on its cover, and asserted: 'We are the basic preparation for the eternal revenge of the proletariat against the bourgeoisie, and we are pushy but frank destroyers.' Cited for the potential public danger of the firecrackers, the issue was censored upon its release.

The history of modern and contemporary art in Japan, filled with odd lacunae and ideological rifts, has proven to be highly malleable. It begins with the institutionalization of

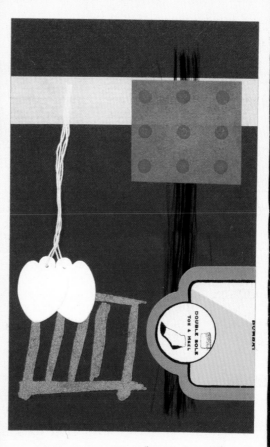

Michinao Takamizawa
Portrait of a Foreigner's Mistress (cover image), *Mavo*, issue 3,
1 September 1924, reissued 1991

1

2

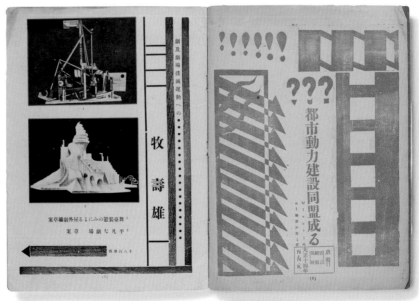

3

4

1
Mavo, issue 6, 18 July 1925,
reissued 1991

2
Masao Kato, *The Delightful Castle
Gate*, *Mavo*, issue 4, 1 October 1924

3
Left: Kyojiro Hagiwara, untitled
collage; right: poems by Kiyoshi
Enomoto, Yoshihisa Torii and Kinichi
Umetsu, *Mavo*, issue 6, 18 July 1925,
reissued 1991

4
Left: illustrations for Toshio Maki's
'Two Theatre Proposals as Part
of a Commonsense Process Toward
a Movement to Eradicate Drama
and Theatres'; right: Urban Power
Construction League announcement;
Mavo, issue 7, 24 August 1925

5
Left: Kimimaro Yabashi, *Portrait of
an Aristocrat*; top right: Seicho
Sawa, *Konstrukcha 13*; bottom right:
Michinao Takamizawa, *Poem*; *Mavo*,
issue 4, 1 October 1924

6
Mavo, issue 7, 24 August 1925

7
Tatsuo Toda, *Prophecy* (cover image),
Mavo, issue 4, 1 October 1924

All images courtesy: Art Library,
Museum of Contemporary Art,
Tokyo; photographs: Kei Okano

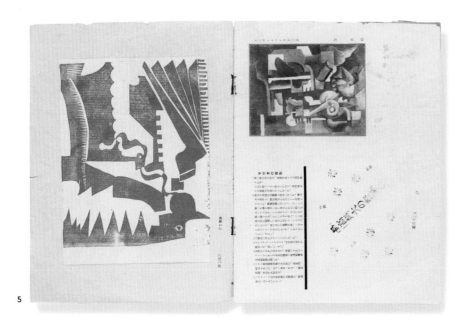

5

6

The Mavoists compared their journal to the explosives stuck to its cover: 'We are the eternal revenge of the proletariat against the bourgeoisie, and we are pushy but frank destroyers.'

7

1

art during the Meiji-era social reform and Westernization campaigns of the latter half of the 19th century, which resulted in a schism between the idea of a nativist Japanese art and an invasive foreign art. This foundational rift has continued to shape art discourse in Japan. Japanese practitioners of Western art forms could either be dismissed as slavishly copying the West, or they could establish credibility by claiming an authentic knowledge of Western trends. Mavo's Murayama, who engaged in the former and benefited from the latter, was a case in point.

In such a climate, 'influence', both from the West and from Japanese forebears, becomes a loaded word. There has been a tendency among successive Japanese art movements to present their work as *sui generis*, only to be rejected by subsequent generations. This situation has contributed to a messianic desire to proclaim the arrival of an authentically 'Japanese' contemporary art. Recent years have seen, for example, Takashi Murakami's attempt to hotwire a lineage connecting Edo-period eccentric painting to his theory of Superflat Japanese contemporary art through *manga* and *anime*. Similarly, in the catalogue for her 2007 survey of recent Japanese art, 'The Door into Summer: The Age of Micropop', the critic Midori Matsui elevated the art of the 1990s – which she says 'responded to the specific problems of the Postmodern age in Japan' – in contrast to the 'artistic models imported from the West' of previous generations.

This rhetoric obfuscates the history of art in Japan, and misrepresents the character of Japanese artists' interactions with Western art.

Disrupting assumptions about an intractable time lag between centre and margin, early-20th-century Japanese art periodicals, and even the mainstream press, provided coverage of new art movements – particularly Futurism – as they emerged in Europe. Information also arrived in the form of visitors from abroad, such as the Russian Futurist David Burliuk, who spent two years in Japan from 1920–22, and the Constructivist Varvara Bubnova, who arrived in 1922 and remained until 1958. Japanese artists were in a position to engage critically with European art and adapt it to their own ends.

There were, by this point, several generations of Japanese artists who had studied in Europe, and returned home with publications, reproductions and actual works. Murayama went to Berlin in January 1922 to study philosophy, but dropped out because he lacked the requisite knowledge of Latin. Introduced to the Berlin art scene by Japanese compatriots, by March of that year he had been invited to participate in the 'Great Futurist Exhibition' at the Neumann Gallery in Berlin, and in May he took part in the 'First International Art Exhibition' and Congress of International Progressive Artists in Dusseldorf, where Lissitzky and Theo van Doesburg declared their plans for an international Constructivist movement. What makes this all the more remarkable is that the then-21-year-old Murayama had not been a practicing artist in Japan. It was only after his return to Tokyo, where in May and June 1923 he held a series of exhibitions of his 'conscious constructivist' works, that he met his peers in the New Art movement.

Against the backdrop of an expanded empire and economy post-World War I, and a government that sought to suppress oppositional politics, the Mavoists were inspired by anarchist, nihilist and leftist thought.

1
Tomoyoshi Murayama
Construction, 1925,
oil, paper, wood, cloth and metal,
84 × 113 cm

2
Iwane Sumitani,
Tatsuo Okada and Michinao
Takamisawa, *Dance*,
performance documentation,
published in *Mavo*, issue 3,
1 September 1924

1 courtesy
Gallery TOM, Tokyo

2

A number of contemporary artists have sought to engage with the legacy of Mavo, perhaps seeing the ability to rethink historical movements as a means for reinventing art's political mission.

Murayama's case might be exceptional, but it suggests two things: at a time when the European Avant-garde was itself being invented on the fly, Japanese artists proactively recognized themselves in these new developments; and European artists, in turn, recognized a shared international sensibility with their Japanese peers. Indeed, the listings of publications such as *De Stijl*, *Der Sturm* and *Merz* in the *Mavo* journal testify to the Japanese Avant-garde's confidence in its place in an international community.

The year 1925 was a high-water mark for the New Art movement, with two exhibitions and a theatre event being held by Sanka (Third Section Association), a super group that included members from Mavo. But internal divisions between the members became untenable and, by the end of the year, Mavo's core had disbanded. A number of Sanka artists, including the Mavoist Masamu Yanase, gravitated to the Proletarian Arts movement. Murayama became a prolific director, playwright and set designer in the Proletarian Theatre movement; his works include 1929's *Bouryokudan ki* (Record of a Gang of Thugs), about the 1923 massacre of labourers working on the Jinghan Railway in China. However, contending with censors who could alter works or ban them outright, the leftist art and culture movement encountered further suppression in advance of war in the Pacific. During periodic government sweeps of Communists and Communist sympathizers, Murayama was arrested in 1930, 1932 and 1940.

Following World War II, the rediscovery and critical appreciation of Mavo was gradual. In 1951, for a special feature on 50 years of Western painting in Japan in the art periodical *Bijutsu Techo*, Murayama wrote a brief article reflecting on Mavo and the Proletarian Art movement and, in December 1957, in the same publication, the critic Yusuke Nakahara grappled with the complex dynamics between Mavo, Proletarian Art and Surrealist painting in the pre-war Avant-garde. A wealth of contemporaneous writings and materials exist about Mavo, and a substantial body of scholarship has since built up around the subject. However, the group is arguably still underappreciated in the contemporary art context, particularly compared to the current re-evaluation of postwar interdisciplinary groups such as Jikken Kobo (Experimental

Workshop) and the Gutai Art Association. The unresolved issues of the war and subsequent US occupation of Japan loom as a subconscious boundary between then and now. Mavo's example shows that it may be time to consider the possibility that internationalism is a precondition for all Japanese art since the Meiji period. Conversely, it also invites doubts about whether – for all our international surveys and biennales, Japan Foundations and Goethe-Instituts, residencies and art fairs – we are, in some way, less international now than before; about whether, through the institutionalization of a global contemporary art, we have become international in spite of ourselves.

Looking at the landscape of Japan today, it is hard to believe that an internationalist, anti-authoritarian movement like Mavo ever existed, just as it is hard to believe that during the postwar protest movement the streets were filled with students battling police. Within art schools, museums and the art market, the institution of visual art in Japan has generally been ambivalent about directly confronting social issues. Particularly among the generation that came of age after the 1980s bubble economy, artists have tended to focus on more diaristic, inward modes of expression. But the March 2011 earthquake, tsunami and nuclear disaster brought questions of art's social responsibility back to the forefront. What can art do in the face of such a crisis?

Responses have varied. In the immediate aftermath, the guerrilla artist group Chim↑Pom challenged media representations of the disaster, infiltrating the exclusion zone around the Fukushima Daiichi Nuclear Plant to raise a flag emblazoned with the international radiation symbol – which, as is made clear in the video documentation, also contains within it a 'rising sun' emblem – on a bluff overlooking the damaged facility. During the height of the anti-nuclear movement in 2012, the artist Yoshitomo Nara uploaded to the internet an image of a work he had made in 1997, depicting a young girl holding a 'No Nukes' sign, for protesters to print out and turn into placards. Other artists have channelled their anger into cogent social critiques, as Tadasu Takamine did in his exhibition 'Cool Japan' in 2012–13, which examined the ideological systems of control surrounding nuclear energy in Japan.

But the question also has an implicit historical dimension: how is art's role in Japanese society defined? Here, a reflexive approach is necessary for rethinking the complex relations between state and culture, institution and practice. Based between

Los Angeles and Tokyo, the multimedia artist Koki Tanaka has made a series of works that deftly explore the latent connections between Japanese art history and social action. For *Painting to the Public (Open-Air)* (2012), Tanaka invited participants to march with their paintings from the Meguro Museum of Art to the Aoyama | Meguro Gallery in Tokyo. Tanaka's event posited links between the early Modernist school of Japanese *plein-air* painters and the 1964 'Promenading-on-the-Street' exhibition, staged by the artists Hiroshi Nakamura and Koichi Tateishi, who paraded their paintings around Tokyo Station. For Tanaka, such precedents allow for the recognition of painting – an activity that can be pursued and appreciated without reliance on nuclear-energy sources – as a political practice, regardless of its content. For another participatory event, Tanaka rephrased Jiro Takamatsu's 1974 instruction piece, *REMARKS 5*, which states, 'Try to repeat the content of a specific consciousness as many times as possible', into the action *Precarious Tasks #7: Try to Keep Conscious about a Specific Social Issue, in this Case 'Anti-Nuke', as Long as Possible while You Are Wearing Yellow Colour* (2013).

As the advances of the anti-nuclear movement in Japan are rolled back by the current prime minister, Shinzō Abe – who is pushing nuclear energy as the engine of his 'Abenomics' agenda – these works shift agency away from institutions and back to individuals. They show us that anyone can organize their own political action at whatever scale is feasible – something that might be obscured in the mainstream media's coverage of the protest movement. The recent railroading through parliament of the controversial State Secrets Law, and the 'reinterpretation' of the pacifist postwar constitution to allow for the right of collective self-defence, are also worrying for the state of democracy in Japan. When the present looks hopeless, art can provide an imaginary horizon for stimulating political consciousness and collective organization, precisely because it speaks across generations.

The ability to rethink historical movements, as Tanaka has done, suggests a means for reinventing art's political mission. A few artists, have, in fact, already revisited the work of Mavo. In 1983, Yoshio Shirakawa organized the exhibition 'Dada in Japan / The Japanese Avant-Garde 1920–1970: Photo-Documentation' at Kunstmuseum Düsseldorf, attempting to synthesize the pre-war and postwar Avant-gardes through the recurrence of anarchic performance in Japanese art. More recently, Ei Arakawa, who learned of Mavo through Shirakawa's writing, has incorporated it into performances such as *M for Mavoists (and so on…)* (2010) and *Joy of Life* (2012), while Miwa Yanagi staged the three-part *Theatre Project: 1924* (2011–13), revisiting key moments in the careers of Murayama and the founders of the Tsukiji Little Theatre.

Shirakawa based his reading of the Japanese Avant-garde on the metaphor of *uneri*, an image that evokes the ouroboros-like motion of waves swallowing other waves and being swallowed in turn. But perhaps a closer analogy can be found in Italo Calvino's *Mr. Palomar* (1983), who sees in the waves the possibility to 'over-turn time, to perceive the true substance of the world beyond sensory and mental habits', only to walk away, 'even more unsure about everything'. What Arakawa identifies – when he has participants in a Japanese art history workshop at Tate Modern mimic poses from Mavo performances, as he did for *Joy of Life* – and what Yanagi shows through her reconstruction of the Tsukiji Little Theatre's 1924 production of Reinhard Goering's *Seeschlacht* (Sea Battle) – with its frenetic action and modular, shifting stage – are the uncanny parallels that arise from a history in which the international and Japanese contexts, past and present, are themselves caught in an ouroboros-like cycle. We recognize correspondences with our own time, but we don't quite know where to place them, or where to place ourselves.

Perhaps the question of how to define art in Japan will remain unresolved, but we might nonetheless see Mavo as a kind of reverse cipher for unlocking history's idiosyncrasies. Rather than showing us the expected alignments between past and present, it reveals the inherent discontinuities. In seeing how Modernism and the Avant-garde, both in Japan and elsewhere, were contingent upon a wide array of systemic and chance factors, we can, paradoxically, find the courage to make the art we need right now. ◆●

Andrew Maerkle is a writer and editor based in Tokyo, Japan.

1

2

1
Tadasu Takamine
The Hyogo Room, 2012, exhibition
view of 'Cool Japan', Art Tower Mito

2
Miwa Yanagi
1924 Human-Machine, 2012,
documentation of performance at National
Museum of Modern Art, Kyoto

Courtesy
1 the artist and Art Tower Mito •
2 the artist and National Museum of
Modern Art, Kyoto

Abandoned cinema
in the Sinai Desert, Egypt

Courtesy
Hotspot Media; photograph:
Kaupo Kikkas

Egyptian Desert Cinema

—

Sukhdev Sandhu

Estonian photographer Kaupo Kikkas gives good origin myth. This image, he claims, is of an abandoned cinema in the Sinai Desert that was dreamt up by a crazy French visionary. On the opening night, the generator broke down, no film was projected and, very quickly, the whole scheme collapsed. It already seems to have joined that pantheon of cinematic follies and hubristic undertakings that will forever be led by Werner Herzog's *Fitzcarraldo* (1981), in which the cast yomped across the Amazon basin, dragging a 320-tonne steamship over a hill.

Everything about Kikkas's picture heaves with mystery. What are those markings on the seats? Some kind of Mayan tattoo? Graffiti from the ancient kingdom of Kush? If they're languages or codes, then they're indecipherable, glamorously opaque. Aerial images from Google Maps have this site resembling the crop-circle-etched landscapes that materialized across rural Britain in the 1990s. From above, the desert looks as if it's been scarified, ritually marked by the members of an extraterrestrial jam band.

It's hard not to see in this glorious project that was not to be a sad echo of the promises and disappointments of the Egyptian Revolution of 2011. But there's a broader allegory, too: across the world, the cartographies of classic cinephilia are becoming ghostscapes.

The cinema cedes cultural gravitas to the art gallery and accessibility to the mobile phone; celluloid gives way to digital; mass audiences fragment into ever-smaller contingents who consume film on HD systems in their own homes.

Ambiguity, I think, is what makes Kikkas's image so eerily compelling: it seems to represent remote times and far-off, fabled lands; but it also summons up the spectres – political, artistic – that may befall us all. ◆●

Sukhdev Sandhu is an associate professor at New York University, USA, where he directs the Colloquium for Unpopular Culture.

Reviews

Gwangju Biennale

VARIOUS VENUES, GWANGJU, SOUTH KOREA

1

It was unfortunate if revealing that, a few weeks before the opening of the 10th Gwangju Biennale, news broke of the censorship of a work included in a show marking the 20th anniversary of the Gwangju Biennale Foundation. Officials from the city government, which provides most of the exhibition's funding, banned a painting by Hong Sung-dam titled *Sewol Owol* (Sewol May, 2014). The satirical work depicts an enraged Park Geun-hye, the current South Korean president, being held back by her late father and former president, Park Chung-hee, and her chief of staff, Kim Ki-choon, from attacking the families of school children who died in the MV Sewol ferry disaster in April. The small-minded ban resulted in the resignation of the Biennale Foundation's president, Lee Yong-woo, as well as the show's chief curator, Yun Beom-mo. This attempt to silence a critical response to the government's handling of the recent Sewol tragedy is particularly pertinent to the Gwangju Biennale's history: it was founded to commemorate the Gwangju massacre of 1980, when peaceful pro-democracy demonstrators were

murdered by military forces. The government's dictat to exclude Hong's artwork's from the Foundation's anniversary show – which is not part of the 10th Biennale – served to justify the public's discontent at the government's perceived failings in its handling of the tragedy. Ultimately, this sad prelude only prompted more questions about how much or little has changed or been learnt in South Korea since the events of 1980.

If this controversy had any impact on curator Jessica Morgan's exhibition, it didn't show. Hers was a tough and testing – at times, even testy – biennale. Not shying away from the show's sombre history, she courageously decided to make Minouk Lim's powerful performance *Navigation ID* (2014) the centrepiece of the show. The work involved the installation of two shipping containers carrying the remains of victims of the nationwide massacres that followed the outbreak of the Korean War in 1950, in which suspected North-Korean sympathizers and political opponents of the government, led by Syngman Rhee, were killed. As well as the

containers, Lim arranged for families of the victims to travel to the biennale and to be greeted by mothers of victims of the Gwangju massacre. This moving ceremony took place in the Biennale Forum during the exhibition's opening.

The laudable geographic diversity of the show spoke to Morgan's former role as a curator of international art at Tate Modern (she has recently been appointed director of New York's Dia Art Foundation) yet coherent thematic threads ran through the exhibition. Contra the titular idea of 'Burning Down the House' (after the 1983 song by Talking Heads), the show was a thoughtful taking stock and setting of one's house in order: focusing equally on rebellion and commemoration, critique and reconciliation. For those wanting to read it, here was a show of Agambian bio-politics writ global. In a number of different national settings, politics of the home were distinguished from those of the polis, with the body enacting the threshold of political interference. The opening room set the tone with a three-channel video and slide installation documenting Lee Bul's early performances from the late 1980s and early '90s. The excruciating *Abortion* (1989) sees the artist, naked, reciting a monologue while suspended painfully by ropes; *Sorry for Suffering – You Think I'm a Puppy on a Picnic?* (1990) shows the artist walking around public places in South Korea and Japan in one of her monstrous, oversized, appendage-laden costumes. (That two female South Korean artists were given prominence in the biennale was a deserved and edifying highlight.)

Uncomfortable body-based work continued in Young Soo Kim's *Torture* (1988), a series of black and white photographs of staged torture scenes, highlighting the all-too-real events that took place under South Korea's military dictatorship throughout the 1970s and '80s. A number of studios refused to print these works, fearing government retaliation. British artist James Richards's four-slide-projector installation *Untitled (The Screens)* (2013) similarly underscored the power of the decontextualized image, showing, for example, flickering, unsteady images of cuts and bruises taken from an instructional book on how to apply theatrical makeup.

Camille Henrot's burnt-looking artefacts, *Augmented Objects* (2010) – household items bought on eBay and caked in clay and tar – were the lynchpin of a rather literal, medium-specific section of the show that enforced themes of burning down and building up: a work from Yves Klein's 'Fire Painting' series (1961) was placed next to Cornelia Parker's installation of carbonized fragments from a Florida forest fire (*Heart of Darkness*, 2004). Anna Maria Maiolino's beautiful Raku ceramic sculpture *More Than 50, from the Prepositions Series* (2008–14) and Rosemarie Trockel's fantastically strange ceramic wall pieces were unfortunately shoved into corners. One of the show's highlights (of which there were several) was the powerful short video *We Are not your Monkeys* (1993) by Anand Patwardhan, which documented the poet Sambhaji Bhagat singing a poem refuting the 'divine' justification for India's caste system. The series 'Prison Paintings' (1972–78) by Turkish artist Gülsün Karamustafa, depicting everyday scenes of imprisoned female political activists, based on her own six-month incarceration for political activism, and Filipino Brenda Fajardo's satirical paintings aping comic strips (*Crossroads*, 2003) – Uncle Sam being spanked like a naughty schoolchild – activated a keen-eyed feminist perspective on political and cultural oppression. Paintings were abundant, among them Xiaodong Liu's *Time* (2014) – a block of 20 canvases showing a group of teenagers in an idyllic site blighted by the Gwangju massacre – and a selection of Apostolos Georgiou's and Tang Dixin's satirical scenes of human futility. Where film appeared, it was effective: Ramallah-based artists Basel Abbas & Ruanne Abou-Rahme's split-screen video *The Incidental Insurgents: The Part about The Bandits* (2013), a dense, immersive layering of searching political storylines and strobing subtitles, took on poignancy in the light of recent events in the Middle East. Akram Zaatari's *Exploded Views* (2014) was a more oblique narrative: a tracking shot showing an eerily quiet site used for the testing of building structures in downtown Beirut.

Anything but quiet was the show-within-a-show: the bombastic one-to-one scale installation of Urs Fischer's New York apartment, *38 E. 1st St.* (2014), the interior papered in photorealist wallpaper, replete with 2D renderings of his own collection of artworks, and containing the 3D work of other artists in the biennale proper. The similarly loud *Name Announcer* (2011) by Pierre Huyghe, a performance by a suited man calling out the names of visitors in the style of a court announcer, helped puncture the decadence of this setting.

Quieter, historical positions ended the show: Ulrike Ottinger's alluring photographs were coupled with

2

1
Carol Christian Poell
Squartter in Urs Fischer, *38 E. 1st St.*,
installation view

2
Liu Xiaodong
Time (detail), 2014, oil on canvas,
20 canvases, each: 60 × 60 cm

3
Minouk Lim
Navigation ID, 2014, performance
documentation

Gavin Kenyon's lumpen curios – sculptures made in dyed plaster and fur. This pair found solace with the coupling of Lionel Wendt's beautiful staged portraiture from 1930s Sri Lanka and the heavy hemp, jute and iron floral sculptures by New Delhi–based Mrinalini Mukherjee. Sharon Hayes's four-channel video *We cannot leave this world to others* (2014), shot in the US and Seoul this summer, rightly brought the exhibition back to the present tense. Hayes's filming of different generations of Korean women wrestling in a public square struck a similar note to the stark publicness of Lim's work. Exiting the final gallery through Carsten Höller's series of mirrored *Sliding Doors* (2003) leading back out to the mezzanine overlooking Lim's containers, and seeing one's reflection vanishing forward and back, proved a fitting end to this show. When faced with the humiliating legacy of past tragedies, remembrance and recollection are only productive when acknowledged and made public.

———————

PAUL TEASDALE

3

Made in LA

HAMMER MUSEUM, LOS ANGELES, USA

1

2

Dorothy Parker once described Los Angeles as 72 suburbs in search of a city. It's that multi-facetedness that makes the idea of a biennial here all the more tricky and presumptuous. As both a premise and title, 'Made in LA' has been critically debated since the exhibition's debut in 2012. Questions were raised as to whether such a localized biennial was needed. Yet this seems the wrong line of inquiry – the meat of the issue is more in why so many artists choose to work here, and how they do so. As one of the many recent New York transplants getting to know the deeper recesses of the city, its tribes and micro-histories, these questions have been on my mind lately. 'Made in LA' is, at the very least, a show in which the many faces of the city can take to the stage in turn.

The biennial took over the entirety of the Hammer Museum's galleries and courtyard, elbowing out its permanent collection. At its helm was the Hammer's Chief Curator, Connie Butler, and writer/curator Michael Ned Holte. In 2012, the exhibition splayed out across three separate venues and included 60 artists.

1
'Made in LA', installation view,
foreground: Gerard & Kelly, *Kiss Solo*,
2012, four-channel video installation;
background: A.L. Steiner, *Accidenthell™*,
2014, photo-installation

2
Made in LA', installation view,
right: Clarissa Tossin, *Brasília, Cars, Pools
& Other Modernities*, 2009–13

3
Samara Golden
Thank You, 2014, installation view

Bold and somewhat unwieldy, that show made an effort to tie down specific themes, or watchwords. In 2014, the 35-artist exhibition was much tighter and more pared-back, but no less ambitious. Notably, it featured more women artists than men. Although officially without a theme, shared sensibilities and a mood emerged; a certain lush sadness punctuated by fanciful moments, a feeling that is not unlike one that comes when exploring the streets of LA.

Collectivity and collaboration too often become catch-all terms for loosely themed exhibitions. In the case of 'Made In LA', it was less curatorial talking point than fact; in Los Angeles, people, and even institutions work together in ways that are rare in other national and international art centres. Perhaps it's a survival strategy. With LA a few degrees to the left of being an art commercial capital, smaller platforms tend to thrive, forever in the shadow of the city's gleaming entertainment industry. Small networks do big things.

'Made In LA' highlighted several 'micro-organizations'. Public Fiction, an exhibition venue and quarterly publication founded in 2010 by Lauren Mackler, was given free reign of a lobby space. Joined by writer Sarah Lehrer-Graiwer, Mackler created a structure of six episodic exhibitions, performances and writing contributions, featuring artists such as Eric Wesley and Darren Bader, and writers including Chris Kraus and Becket Flannery. The curiously complicated and expansive programme unfolded over three months at the Hammer as well as at Public Fiction's home base, a storefront in the Highland Park neighbourhood of east LA.

Not far from their base, in Eagle Rock, sits The Los Angeles Museum of Art, a three-and-a-half by four-metre shed-cum-exhibition space founded, programmed and designed by artist Alice Könitz. LAMOA, which has been showing small exhibitions of LA artists in its driveway venue for the last two years, was transplanted to its own room in the museum. Könitz designed modular hanging and display structures recalling Russian Constructivist exhibition design, only grittier and, for me, more charming. LAMOA's exhibition within an exhibition included work by 23 artists, ranging from Tony Conrad, to Judith Hopf, to a mask used by the Bread and Puppet Theater in 1973.

'Made in LA' was animated by a bevy of performances. The most visible was the *Gold Stage*, a temporary home in the Hammer's inner courtyard given to Jmy James Kidd, the founder of Lincoln Heights dance space, Pieter. In addition to scheduled performances programmed by Kidd, the stage became an open rehearsal space for the larger Pieter community, making dancers stretching in the sunlight of the courtyard a common sight. The performance styles varied but seemed a collective homage to prolific LA-based dancer Simone Forti, with her focus on the physicalization of emotions and the flow from relaxed to ecstatic states.

It is the afterlife of performance, though, which seemed central to many other works, including those by Emily Mast. The choreographer's energetic and absurdist performances as part of *ENDE (Like a New Beginning)* (2014) were spread throughout the museum as installations occasionally activated with unannounced performance and video. Highly scripted and theatrically playful, the performances featured an organized chaos of players, from children to the elderly, repeating simple gestures and manipulating props including baguettes, lemons, buckets and boxes. Stylistically, they echoed another LA artist, Guy de Cointet, and his Structuralist-inspired, prop-strewn stage productions. When they weren't being used as part of the act, Mast's objects operated as sculpture, an interesting solution to showing performance in a gallery.

Performance and humour were at the core of Piero Golia's charming monumental sculpture *The Comedy of Craft (Act 1: Carving George Washington's Nose)* (2014). As the title suggests, each day, a group of workers carved a large block of Styrofoam to produce a scale replica of George Washington's nose as rendered on Mount Rushmore. Though confined to a gallery here, the performance work of Jennifer Moon undoubtedly comprises the artist's entire life. She exhibited work from the series 'Phoenix Rising Saga: Part 2' (2013), which starts with a hallucinatory promise she made with an entity, 'Bob', to give up love for the sake of her career. The works at the Hammer are part of her attempt to nullify that deal; that is, to find the ever-elusive balance between love and work. It's a self-help fantasy in sculpture and text, the works winking hard at kitsch Californian New Age ideology, as with *A Story of a Girl and a Horse: The Search for Courage* (2014), a digital photo of Moon riding a unicorn off into the sky. It is in the work's more down-to-earth moments that the artist reveals some of her vulnerability, however. *The Book of Eros* (2014), for example, is an over-sized book documenting her love affairs, which designed to resemble Dungeons and Dragons score cards for characters. The backstory of her project, as read in the catalogue, describes

how Moon's work was influenced by her time spent incarcerated in a women's correctional facility in California in 2008–09.

Moving-image works in the exhibition were particularly strong. Mariah Garnett's video, *Full Burn* (2014), follows former soldiers turned stuntmen, one of whom specializes in setting fire to himself. His plain-spoken manner in documentary-style interviews about his current job are intercut with his descriptions of active duty tours in Iraq, leading the viewer to the horribly fascinating suggestion that his movie work constitutes some kind of immersion therapy to combat PTSD.

Poet and artist Jibade-Khalil Huffman's room-sized installation *The Parts of Speech* (2014) layered slide projections of garden landscapes and street scenes with short disjointed videos of characters. Brief hints of narrative suggested a story that built only to collapse back in on itself, as if falling into its own visual lushness. *The Parts of Speech* expresses a roundabout quality, balancing mundane familiarity and beauty that seems strangely suited to LA in particular.

Documenting the periphery of a city's culture, Wu Tsang presented an excellent two-channel film, *A day in the life of bliss* (2014); a sci-fi drag story starring the performer boychild, with her highly charged approach to dance. Shown on two screens opposite mirrors, the work surrounded the viewer. I could have seen this mirrored over a whole floor. *Tony Greene: Amid Voluptuous Calm* was an exhibition-within-an-exhibition, curated by David Frantz of LA's ONE National Gay & Lesbian Archives. The work of Greene, who died of AIDS-related complications in 1990, was paired with artworks and activist ephemera of his contemporaries in the 1980s, including extreme performance figures Ron Athey and

Bob Flanagan. Greene's project was a striking and controversial departure from that of his peers as he painted decadent patterning on vintage photographs of male pinups. In the exhibition, Frantz teases out the edges of a turbulent social history that's often only heard of in the contexts of San Francisco and downtown New York.

'Made In LA' was strikingly diverse and its many through-lines and alliances were oblique and difficult to pin down. It seems fitting that these connections should be sketchy and speculative, reflecting something of the city itself. Many of the artists included seem to find inspiration in the city and its discontents; its sprawling and vast anonymity, which is nonetheless more human-scale in its culture and lifestyle than many major cities. For an artist, this is partially because the visual arts are not the main game in town. Living in the shadow of the Hollywood sign can have its advantages, allowing artists the distance to step back and get on with their work. Relatively less pressure and competition of the kind that comes with a bustling commercial gallery system has numerous advantages – as does living in communities forged by the heady idealism of art school. (Numerous artists first move to LA to attend one of its highly rated art schools, with their reputation for building deep mentor-student bonds. For the many that stay on after their studies, being a teacher is synonymous with being a working artist.) Even as the number of galleries keeps growing along with the diversification of sources for art world capital, the LA vernacular remains palpable and the Hammer remains an institution atypically close to the street.

SUMMER GUTHERY

BEN RIVERS
Temporary Gallery, Cologne

Slow Action (2011) – one of two 16mm films comprising Ben Rivers's solo show, 'Fable', at Cologne's Temporary Gallery – sketches out a possible future in which Earth has been flooded and mankind has withdrawn to a few islands where strange and highly distinct cultures have taken shape. Rivers conceived the work in four chapters with a screenplay by sci-fi author Mark von Schlegell. While it is clearly fictional, it is presented as an ethnographical documentary of sorts, in which Rivers 'visits' four of these islands: the dry and desert-like Eleven (filmed on Lanzarote in the Canary Islands); Hiva (actually the Pacific island of Tuvalu); the deserted Kanzennashima, full of industrial ruins (in real life the abandoned Japanese coal-mining island of Gunkanjima); and Somerset, shot in the eponymous British region, where Rivers grew up. A voice-over provides encyclopaedic facts about each locale's geographical features, peoples and tribes, flora and fauna, history and political systems. Over the course of 45 minutes, *Slow Action* unfolds a (post-)apocalyptic panorama of utopic and dystopic endings to history.

Things (2014), Rivers's most recent film, is also a sort of travelogue, albeit a wholly different one. Likewise structured in four parts – winter, summer, spring and autumn – the film's underlying principle is one of a year-long travel through 'one's own room'. The press release references Xavier de Maistre's short travelogue *Voyage autour de ma chambre* (Voyage Around My Room, 1794) as a source of inspiration. Like De Maistre, Rivers remains in his apartment, 'travelling' only by scanning his rooms with his antiquated 16mm camera, filming images and artefacts he collected from various trips and research projects. *Things* reaches its crux with a reading of the first page of Robert Pinget's 1971 novel *Fable* – a strange

surrealistic account of a man on his voyage home through an apocalyptic landscape. Then, a drawing of one of these very scenes from the novel appears in the flickering projection, as well as a drawing of the cover of Pinget's book (the drawings themselves – together with two other 'by-products' of the film – were also on display). Rivers's show seems to collapse different spaces and times: the literature referenced in the film, the images being filmed, the film shown alongside the images.

The final chapter of *Things*, 'Autumn', takes us on a computer-animated walk through the very apartment scrutinized in the three previous segments, with images and details reappearing as posters on the wall. The strangest effect, though, comes from Rivers's use of computer-generated 3D renderings filmed in 16mm – an odd fusion of old and new media. Above all, *Things* is a meditation on the nature of film itself: not so much as a window on to the world (as the travelogue genre usually suggests), but as the creation of a completely new one – a room in its own right.

The atmosphere of the exhibition – and, ultimately, its content – was defined by Rivers's use of the outdated 16mm format. This is 'film' in the most literal sense of the word: a specific (and now historical) medium, rather than an inaccurate substitute name for any moving image work. The fuzzy, crackling analogue material gives Rivers's works a patina of nostalgia. If you want to use a buzzword from a few years ago, you could term Rivers's approach 'hauntological' – a reflexive mourning of utopian dreams; 'ruins of ruins' as the voiceover puts it at one point in *Slow Action*. His films seem to come from a just-passed age: too young to be rediscovered, too old to be trendy, the lee-side of progress. I say this not to criticize 'Fable' for being out of tune with current aesthetics; rather, the contrary. The feeling of the just-passed paradoxically adds to the show's vigour or, to quote *Slow Action*: 'We are our own visitors and ghosts', which is also true, it seems, of Rivers's approach.

DOMINIKUS MÜLLER

LET THE BODY BE ELECTRIC, LET THERE BE WHISTLEBLOWERS
Dan Gunn, Berlin

Only a few years ago, every second contemporary art exhibition seemed to host the clatter and whirr of 16mm projectors, a phase that was quickly superseded by digitized aesthetics and the ubiquity of HD. It was something of a flashback, therefore, to find the entrance of Dan Gunn's gallery blocked by a bulky projector stand, and its darkened rooms illuminated by the flicker of largely black and white projections on suspended screens. For this exhibition, guest curators Heidi Ballet and Anselm Franke selected three artists spanning three generations – veteran American experimental filmmaker Ken Jacobs (born in 1933), Danish artist Joachim Koester (born in 1962) and Allison Gibbs (born in 1978), a recent graduate of Glasgow School of Art.

Opening the show, Jacobs's flickering montage of early-20th-century footage of a steam train (*Let There Be Whistleblowers*, 2005) dispensed with the film projector altogether, and was projected digitally. This was the first of several displacements raising questions about the broader socio-political, perceptual or metaphorical potentials of machinery, rather than seeking its nostalgic resonance. Jacobs uses short sections of footage to hypnotic effect: repeating fragments, enlarging images to unrecognizability, or varying the light to a violently stroboscopic degree. The soundtrack is Steve Reich's *Drumming* (1970–71), in which two drummers play the same rhythmic patterns, slipping in and out of synchronization – the aural equivalent of Jacobs's own experiments in perception-splicing editing. The sound lends the film an almost voodoo-like atmosphere, not to mention accruing sexual overtones, as the locomotive enters and reenters a tunnel, or blurry patches of grey and white turn out to be passengers waving white handkerchiefs from open windows, like some ambiguous ancient ritual. History dissolves and becomes a facet of perception while both railways and film become means of twisting perception, as the subversive double meaning of the title's 'whistleblowers' suggests.

Koester's pair of pendant black and white 16mm films were silent save for the projectors' whirr. In each, the camera lingers almost fetishistically over the contours of a machine: a 16mm film projector in *Body Electric* (2014) and the first sewing machine in *HOWE* (2013), invented and patented by Elias Howe in 1846. Like the steam train, these both had a revolutionary impact on society, but Koester's films focus on their surfaces, suggesting their physical as well as functional similarities (as the show's press release tells us, the 'presser foot' mechanism of the sewing machine was adapted by the Lumière brothers for their early Cinematograph.) The most potent similarity, however – albeit a metaphorical one – is with the human body. Gibbs's *How to wash your hands in molten metal* (2014) seemed to draw this fact forth. In this colour film, a woman's hands perform a series of gestures like a conjuror, appearing in turn from the right or left sides of the otherwise black screen. That these codified gestures actually represent the form of double entry book-keeping, with each side of the screen representing either credit or debit, could not be deduced without prior knowledge, but seen here in relation to Koester's films, the introduction of the hand clearly suggested humanity's relation to civilization, with self-devised systems and mechanic inventions as the fulcrum between the two.

The sexual undercurrents of the man/machine relationship became literal in Koester's *Of Spirits and Empty Spaces* (2012), in which well-paced subtitles on a black screen narrate a fascinating if bizarre event: a séance conducted by mid-19th-century spiritualist John Murray Spear to bypass Howe's patent by accessing information about the sewing machine from the spiritual realm. As the subtitles vividly describe, the séance's participants – the 'Needlist', 'Eyeist' and 'Wheelist' – each act out a machine part in a frenzy of sexualized movements, while the 'Implementer' interprets their movements to aid his design of the machine. The machine itself becomes some kind of metaphysical product, conjured by magic into the material world.

Despite initial appearances, the works here were anything but nostalgic. The questions they raise about the impact that new machines may be having on our bodies, perceptions and on society are as relevant to the present as they were to the past. 'Let the body be electric,' declares Koester's film. Would we now say, 'Let it be digital?'

KIRSTY BELL

4

SOPHIE TAEUBER-ARP
Aargauer Kunsthaus, Aarau

'Heute ist Morgen' (Today is Tomorrow), a glorious retrospective exhibition of Sophie Taeuber-Arp's work, and the most comprehensive to date, encouraged a reconsideration of the Swiss artist's life and *oeuvre*. In particular, it championed the equal evaluation of the many facets of her practice. It has taken some 70 years since Taeuber-Arp's premature death for the brilliance of her output to be recognized. Born in 1889, Taeuber-Arp was in the thick of the Dada movement as it emerged in Zurich in the early 20th century, before her move to France in the late 1920s. Since the artist's death in 1943, her work has generally been corralled with the Dadaists as well as the Zurich Concretist and Constructivist movements. Her widower, the artist Hans Arp, also influenced the reading of her work; however well intentioned, his descriptions of her method as intuitive and dream-led – and his proposal of certain shared interests between them – have been challenged by recent research, a challenge that is sustained by this detailed presentation at Aargauer Kunsthaus.

Around a hundred years ago, Taeuber-Arp wrote to a friend bemoaning the fact that the applied arts were not accorded the same respect as fine arts. Having first studied drawing in Switzerland, then at the School for Applied and Free Art in Munich, she returned to Zurich in 1914 where she attended Laban's School for Expressionist Dance and, soon afterwards, taught textiles at the Trade School. Her textile work was highly regarded, but she did not exhibit artworks until she arrived in Paris in the 1920s. This show opened with a display of some of her finest works across multiple disciplines: centre-stage was a desk designed for gallerist Ernst Rott's private residence around 1930, while textile works and paintings, including the woollen tapestry *Composition* (1918) and the oil-on-canvas *flottant, aligné, oscillant, écartant, soutenant* (floating, aligned, oscillating, distancing, supporting, 1932), hung on surrounding walls. Each piece is testament to Taeuber-Arp's precision; the desk is rigorous and streamlined, the painting demonstrates a masterful sense of equilibrium, while the woven work – its colours referring to the Swiss flag and brown military wool blankets, with a stick figure

held in a stiff salute – combines wit with an adroit graphic style.

Thereafter the exhibition concentrated on Taeuber-Arp's formal and subject-based enquiries sustained over many years, rather than organizing works based on chronology or media. It was a productive strategy: for example, in one gallery you could see the way in which Taeuber-Arp confidently worked out grids of circular and rectangular forms, in two and three dimensions, as sculptural reliefs or beaded bags. Though her contemporaries may not have appreciated the importance of the applied iterations of her ideas, Taeuber-Arp moved between fine art and utilitarian objects without hesitation. Such agility enabled the development of objects like the painted, turned wood 'Dada Heads' (1916–20), which she abstracted from hat stands, as well as costumes for performative art happenings, of which only a few remain.

Taeuber-Arp also shifted continually from the figurative to the abstract. One gallery was devoted to the wooden marionettes she designed for the puppet show *König Hirsch* (King Stag, 1918) – a work in the Commedia dell'Arte tradition updated and adapted by René Morax and Werner Wolff to include references to the rival psychoanalysts Carl Jung and Sigmund Freud. The final galleries highlighted Taeuber-Arp's architectural and interior design projects, including furnishings for the house she designed in Meudon, France, for herself and her husband. If it was frustrating that the exhibition did not include images of this building, it was in keeping with the policy of showing only the artist's primary materials (her visualizations of other architectural projects were displayed). The show closed with her later series of black and white 'Constructions géométriques' of 1942, which are curled up like taut springs, as well as collaborative publishing projects, including the magazine *Plastique*, which ran from 1937–39. It was clear that new, fresh lines of investigation were emerging just as her life was cut short. (Taeuber-Arp died in her sleep in 1943 from carbon monoxide poisoning due to a leaking gas stove.) I would have liked to learn more about the historic and artistic context Taeuber-Arp operated within, as well as the artists that she inspired (Yves Netzhammer, Meret Oppenheim and Mai-Thu Perret come to mind) – but, I am hopeful that there will be an opportunity for more exhibitions to follow, now a solid basis for understanding the artist's impressive work has been established.

AOIFE ROSENMEYER

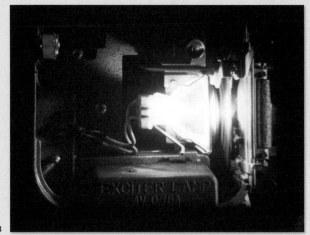

3

3
Joachim Koester
Body Electric, 2014, 16mm
film still

4
Sophie Taeuber-Arp
Entwurf für ein Kostüm (Nr. 60) (Design for a Costume, No. 60), 1922, gouache and pencil on paper, 35 × 50 cm

1

LE MOUVEMENT
Various venues, Biel/Bienne

'As long as I'm walking, I will not repeat. As long as I'm walking, I will not remember.' These last two lines of Francis Alÿs's text *As Long As I'm Walking* (1992), exhibited at Centre PasquArt as part of 'Le Mouvement', the 12th Swiss Sculpture Exhibition, epitomized much of my experience of this year's edition. Over three days of quiet strolls around the French- and German-speaking Swiss town of Biel/ Bienne, I watched some of the 22 performances that, each repeated on a number of occasions, made up the public performance phase of the exhibition, and tried to record the variations between them.

With 'Le Mouvement', curators Gianni Jetzer and Chris Sharp decided to abandon the exhibition's normally fixed format (a temporary display of sculptures in urban space) to instead celebrate 'the body as a living sculpture'. Postmodern dance – with its elegant mix of everyday gestures and fixed postures, made by laboriously trained, muscular bodies – was the most prevalent element. The curators' parallel attempt to 'embody the essence of public space' proved trickier: their argument, made in the exhibition catalogue, that 'Le Mouvement' 'features no activism' doesn't acknowledge the possibilities offered by freedom of movement and expression, nor the implications of their potential suppression. However, these performances – which addressed street actions and protests and the tension between spectacle and invisibility – were nevertheless thought-provoking.

'Le Mouvement' felt refreshing and energetic compared to, for example, the suffocating live performance exhibition '14 Rooms' at Art Basel this summer, with its performances presented in discrete boxes, like sculptures on pedestals, and turned into instant (Instagram) commodities.

The exhibition itself unfolded over several different instalments. The first phase of the show, 'Sculptures on the Move', from June to August, involved four artists (Alex Cecchetti, Christian Jankowski, Marko Lulić and Ariana Reines) 'reanimating' existing sculptures: Lulić, for instance, orchestrated a dance around Franz Eggenschwiler's sculpture *Farbige Baumruine* (1975), which he then documented in an energetic music video entitled *A Proposal for a Workers' Monument* (2014). Jankowski collaborated with professional personal trainers to create *Kunstturnen* (2014), a routine employing public sculptures as exercise machines, with an ironic take on 'fitness' as a socially desirable expression of performativity.

In the last week of August, a cycle of free, open-air performances, called 'Performing the City', was launched, followed by 'The City Performed', an ongoing group show at CentrePasquArt. This documentary exhibition appraises pioneering practices in urban space by the usual suspects (Vito Acconci, Trisha Brown, VALIE EXPORT) as well as by lesser-known artists of older generations, punctuated by the work of contemporary artists, some of whom were included in the 'Performing the City' programme.

The outdoor performances were low-key, attracting small crowds, occasionally interspersed with sneering teenagers, curious children or indifferent passers-by. The curators asked the artists not to use props or costumes and to stage all the works around three busy locations: the train station, the central square and the shopping area of Nidaugasse. Each performance was set to take place at given times every day but at unannounced locations, so that visitors encountered them (or stumbled upon them, or missed them) only by walking around. Appropriately, Biel/Bienne is the birthplace of Robert Walser and the city where he wrote *Der Spaziergang* (The Walk, 1917); it was hard not to feel haunted by his *flâneur*-like ghost during Myriam Lefkowitz's *Walk, Hands, Eyes (Biel/Bienne)* (2014), a one-hour

walking performance that 'viewers' undertook alone, with their eyes shut, guided only by the performer's hands and voice.

Alexandra Pirici's *Tilted Arc* (2014) used a line of standing performers to re-create Richard Serra's infamous 1981 outdoor sculpture, while Pablo Bronstein's *Girl on a Late-19th-Century Swiss Balcony* (2014) blended into the city's architecture to the point of almost vanishing. Germaine Kruip surprised the crowds of travellers exiting the station by exposing them to a Sufi dancer whose traditional attire had been substituted for black trousers and a white shirt (*A Possibility of an Abstraction, Circle Dance*, 2012). No work focused on repetition, trial and error more beautifully than Nina Beier's *The Complete Works* (2009), in which the retired dancer Ellen van Schuylenburch rehearsed, from memory, all the choreographies she has danced during her career. Staged in the quiet Elfenaupark, it provoked a reflection upon memory and muscle memory, as well as upon tolerance and the negotiation of bodily limits with the passing of time.

Endurance and vulnerability were also key to the *tableaux vivants* by Berlin-based duo Prinz Gholam (*Nastagio's Itinerary*, 2014), who re-created scenarios from Old Master paintings. *The Pleasure Project* (2014) by Uruguayan-born New York-based choreographer luciana achugar was one of the few works to explore the terrain of sexuality and the implications of publicly exhibiting 'uncomfortable' bodies (unfit or oversized, according to the prevailing norms) sometimes semi- or entirely naked. The contributions by Swiss-based artists were the most understated, but also the most concerned with the boundaries of the public domain: San Keller tried to convince his fellow citizens to break at least one law, while the Biel/Bienne- and Zurich-based duo Köppl/Začek developed three intersecting circular itineraries (*Drei Kreise*, Three Circles, 2014) for three groups of walkers (artists, sex workers, asylum seekers) with 36-hour shifts paid at different rates. This work, like many of the performances in 'Le Mouvement', was a reminder that decisions about who can 'perform the city' – whether beautifully or in protest, visibly or in private – are ultimately defined by economic conditions.

BARBARA CASAVECCHIA

2

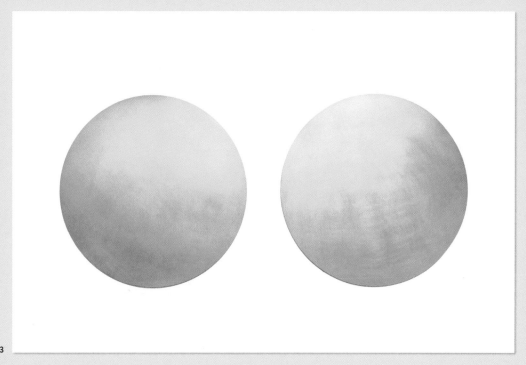

3

LAURENT GRASSO & WIM DELVOYE
Galerie Perrotin, Paris

So tucked away in the top corner of the room that I only noticed it on my second tour of the galleries, hangs a white geodesic dome, 18 centimetres across (*Sphère géodésique*, Geodesic Sphere, 2014). It is a perfect copy, in miniature, of the listening stations employed by the American National Security Agency at Teufelsberg in Berlin, Menwith Hill in Yorkshire, and elsewhere. But suspended from the ceiling and perpetually spinning, it also brings to mind disco balls. Constructed of solid marble, the sphere neither reflects nor surveils: it exists purely as a symbol of two very different kinds of temples to listening; a rare meeting-point for the iconographies of disco and the cold war.

Despite its peripheral position in the room, *Sphère géodésique* is central to Laurent Grasso's concerns and typical of

the propensity each of his works has to open up a portal onto multiple histories of power, knowledge and wonder. Across eight rooms packed with videos, neons, oil paintings, sound works, sculptures and installations, this impressive show, 'Soleil Double' (Double Sun), takes us from the destruction of Pompeii to World War II-era psychoacoustics and the remnants of Benito Mussolini's Italy in a manner at once aesthetically rich and intellectually rewarding. Grasso's work exhibits a knack for finding an idea that crystallizes a certain image of the present in its relationship to the past.

Wim Delvoye, in Perrotin's other space around the corner, is less iconographer than iconoclast – a point made rather forcibly by his *Icon (Self Portrait)* (2013), a colour print of the artist cheerfully flipping us the bird, partially covered over with the distinctive, decoratively embossed metal covering (an 'oklad' or 'riza') commonly used to protect Russian icons. Most of Delvoye's works here are in series, re-imagining everyday objects like car tyres or suitcases as if designed in parallel worlds. 'Untitled (Car Tyre)' (2010–13), for example, comprises seven works, all of which are presented under spotlights in a darkened room like religious artefacts in an ethnographic exhibit. But the original manufacturer of the tyres was Dunlop, upon whose workmanship the artist has engraved complex filigreed patterns gesturing towards a web of art-historical references, from the baroque to art nouveau.

Delvoye's car tyres have something of the cargo cult about them, but in *Double Helix Alternating Current 13cm x 15L* (2009) he has produced an icon that perhaps even Richard Dawkins would approve of, weaving several dozen nickelled bronze crucifixes into the distinctive interlocking curves of a DNA strand. Never mind that the work could be as much a response to the quasi-religious fanaticism of modern biological rationalism as to the mass production of sacred artefacts.

What links Delvoye's work to Grasso's is a kind of folding of the past into the present

– and vice versa. Each finds in anachronism a means of estrangement that could be either satirical or analytical. The former's 'Dunlop Geomax 100' series (2013) imagines the Gothic cathedral builders, beloved of John Ruskin, now working with bicycle wheels, their *trefoils* and *fleurs-de-lys* rendered in steel spokes and twisted rubber. The results are strangely beautiful, almost Ballardian.

Grasso, meanwhile, uses his undated 'Studies into the Past' series to project marvels like eclipses and sun dogs (an atmospheric phenomenon) into Renaissance oils closely modelled on the likes of Paolo Uccello and Fra Angelico with the aid of professional art restorers. It's a project he's been adding to since 2009, but the series remains without a date in his catalogue in order to emphasize this game of travelling through time. Presented here alongside genuinely old books, such as the prophecies of Nostradamus, we are apt to wonder for a moment if Grasso's paintings are the real thing or a modern fabrication.

It becomes a question of how we picture disaster. Several of these 'Studies' present ash clouds and eruptions, encoding them back into an out-of-date mode of representation. Contemporary means of capturing catastrophe is all too recognizable in the film that closes the exhibition, *Soleil Noir* (Black Sun, 2014). Its title a quote from Gérard de Nerval's ode to depression, 'El Desdichado' (The Unfortunate, 1854), the film takes us on a drone's eye-view across the ruins of Pompeii and the caldera of Stromboli. Captured by this cool machine gaze, the former becomes any of a number of modern wreckages (Iraq or Afghanistan post-invasion, for instance), while the latter seems a terrible threat, perhaps even a weapon. Two small white domes on the mountainside (actually there to provide protection for tourists) suggest geodesic domes, recalling the importance of seismological research to the US military since World War II. Delvoye may frequently seem to leap out of his own works but his frame of reference tends to stay within the histories of art. Grasso's work, on the contrary, draws you in, even as it points out, beyond art history to other circuits of force and of memory, both real and imagined.

ROBERT BARRY

1
Pablo Bronstein
Girl on a Late-19th-Century Swiss Balcony, 2014, performance documentation

2
Jiří Kovanda
Kissing Through Glass, 2014, performance documentation

3
Laurent Grasso
Soleil Double, 2014, two brushed brass discs, 90 × 90 cm each

4
Wim Delvoye
Untitled (Truck Tyre), 2013, hand-carved truck tyre, 148 × 60 cm

4

THE PROMISE OF MOVING THINGS

Centre d'art contemporain
d'Ivry – le Crédac,
Ivry-sur-Seine

A series of four exhibitions curated by Chris Sharp, 'The Registry of Promise' explores humankind's changing relationship to the world at a time when impending economic and ecological disaster have, for many, eroded the belief in progress. The first exhibition, titled 'The Promise of Melancholy and Ecology' was held in July at Fondazione Giuliani in Rome, and addressed our problematic relation to nature, while the second, 'The Promise of Multiple Temporalities' (which closed in September), at Parc Saint Léger, Pougues-les-Eaux, questioned the concepts of linear time and progress. 'The Promise of Moving Things' at Crédac is the third chapter in the series. Highlighting the fatal consequences of environmental devastation, it portrays a post-apocalyptic universe devoid of human activity, in which only alien, mutant objects are able to survive.

Reflecting the diverse influences – from Surrealism through Animism to Object-Oriented Ontology – that inform much current object-based art, the exhibition incorporates a number of pieces in which objects seem to take on human traits and emotions. In Michael E. Smith's *Untitled* (2014), the motor of a handheld circular saw has been implanted in the front section of a welding mask. The pairing of these incongruous objects evokes the Comte de Lautréamont's famous description of an encounter between an umbrella and a sewing-machine that so inspired the Surrealists. However, by embedding the saw in the mask, the artist also conflates two conflicting forces, aggression and protection – an allusion, perhaps, to the often fraught relations between individuals or states. Meanwhile, in Mandla Reuter's installation *The Agreement, Vienna* (2011), a wardrobe

unsettles the supposedly secure environment of the exhibition space by hovering in mid-air.

Other works muddle the very definition of the object. Smith's second piece, also *Untitled* (2014), consists of a black wire harness ripped out of a car that snakes and curls like viscous entrails across the ceiling at the entrance to the exhibition. Like Antoine Nessi's *Unknown Organs* (2014) – a collection of grotesque steel, aluminium and brass sculptures evoking mechanized body parts – Smith's harness has more of an affinity with the 'thing' described by W.J.T. Mitchell in his book *What do Pictures Want ?* (2005) than with such discrete, readily identifiable objects as wardrobes. As Mitchell writes: '"Things" are no longer passively waiting for a concept, theory, or sovereign subject to arrange them in ordered ranks of objecthood. "The Thing" rears its head – a rough beast or sci-fi monster, a repressed returnee, an obdurate materiality.' The monstrous hybrid sculptures by Smith and Nessi likewise resist classification.

Most striking of all however, are those works that query anthropocentric thinking. Nina Canell's sculpture *Treetops, Hillsides and Ditches* (2011) consists of four upright shafts of wood, on the upper ends of which the artist has spread lumps of mastic gum that imperceptibly ooze down the logs over the course of the exhibition. The gum forms furrows, grooves and hill-like protuberances, testifying to the artist's interest in processes such as gravity and entropy, which lie beyond human control. Although this exhibition does not focus on a particular philosophical movement, Object-Oriented Ontology has its place here: its emphasis on objects and their interactions with each other seems particularly relevant not only to Canell's piece, but also to Alexander Gutke's film *Auto-scope* (2012). Here, a piece of film embarks on a journey that takes it through the interior of a projector out into the world, over the snowy landscape in which the projector is installed and back again to the point from which it began. As the celluloid interacts with its environment, the viewer looks on, seeing what an object 'perceives'.

Tying together these different approaches to the object, Hans Schabus's *Konstruktion des Himmels* (Celestial Construction, 1994) consists of balls of wax of different colours and sizes scattered around the pool of light cast by an architect's lamp lying on its side. The wax balls are a reference to the constellation *Apparatus Sculptoris* (Sculptor's Studio), identified by the 18th-century astronomer Nicolas Louis de Lacaille. Yet, grouped around the recumbent lamp, the balls also evoke the more prosaic scenario of a game during which the lamp was knocked down. Their positioning is moreover entirely at the discretion of the curator, who thereby superimposes his own vision of the constellation *Apparatus Sculptoris* – and hence of a sculptor's studio – onto that of De Lacaille. The piece formulates the question raised by all the works in the exhibition: are the properties and qualities we attribute to them merely our projections, or are they inherent in the objects themselves?

RAHMA KHAZAM

JENNIFER TEE

Signal – Center for
Contemporary Art, Malmö
at Kunsthal Charlottenborg,
Copenhagen

Since the late 1990s, the independent project space Signal has been a consistent source of energy in Malmö's art scene. Its programme works closely with artists and provides an extended amount of time and support to develop exhibitions. Earlier this year, however, Signal lost its space and has thus far remained nomadic.

This autumn, Signal journeyed across the Øresund Bridge to Copenhagen's Kunsthal Charlottenborg. There – in line with Charlottenborg's recent series of smaller, short-run projects alongside their main exhibition programme – Signal organized a pop-up space wedged into the last two galleries of the Kunsthal's cavernous exhibition floor, and hosted a show of recent work by Jennifer Tee entitled 'Occult Geometry'.

Tee regularly uses ideas rooted in esoteric thought and claims to have 'internalized' Tao magic into her working process – aspects reflected in her ornate titling: *Shuudan Koudou (Collective Action) Ether Plane / Material Plane* or *Talisman To Vitalize The Kidneys / Two Female Dancers With Yin Receptacles* (both 2014) and so on. Her titles might sound ponderous but they're lightened by the crafty, shabby-chic qualities of her sculptures. *Crystalline Floor Piece / Nona 1+2* (2013–14) is one of a pair of hand-dyed and woven wool carpets. Placed near the entrance, coloured stripes ran laterally across seven roughly woven and connected triangles that radiated out in winged vectors from the centre of the nearly touching textiles. Two sleek ceramic pods glazed with speckled colour gradations (*Oval Spheres*, 2014) were placed on each wing, as if pinning down a strange, giant bird.

The exhibition's most charged works were three floor-standing assemblages: *Subtle Planes~Spirit Matter* (2013), *Primordial Chaos~Selfhood Meltdown* (2014) and *Ether*

1
Nina Canell
Treetops, Hillsides and Ditches,
2011, mastic gum and logs,
dimensions variable

2
Jennifer Tee
Occult Geometry, from the series
'The Movement of the Triangle /
The Pyramid', 2014, mixed media,
50 × 35 cm

3
Matias Faldbakken
foreground: *Gas Sculpture*;
background: *Four Flat Boxes*, both
2014, installation view

1

3

Plane~Material Plane (2014). All consist of a basic stone pillar: one with a bending bamboo pole resting on top, two balancing archery bows that echo the wing-like carpets. Some of the pieces have colourful ceramic cones attached to their ends like dumbbells. At the base of each cone are stamped letters spelling out phrases like 'Primordial Chaos' and 'Melt Selfhood'. Each rod is looped on both ends by a pair of glowing fluorescent tube halos, accentuating their fragility. Tee sometimes incorporates dance in her work, and her sense for tension, weight and balance instilled an acute awareness of your own movement through the exhibition. There was a palpable risk that if you made the wrong move, you'd easily knock the bows off their pedestals or dirty the carpets with your footprints.

The walls of the second room contained a number of colourful prints resembling aleatoric or channelled drawing. In the centre of the room hung *Bit By Bit / Woman Holding Her Balance* (2009), a mobile made of a curved piece of wood lined with moulds of human teeth. From each end dangled birds made of unfired clay, and below their drooping bodies hung two large crystals – the type used by New Age healers to harmonize the unstable self with the cosmos.

Tee cites artist-mystics like Wassily Kandinsky and Hilma af Klint as influences. Both were active during a revival of occultism at the end of the 19th century prompted by the divinations of spiritualists like Madame Blavatsky and Georges Gurdjieff, gurus who were voracious cultural hybridizers. Their impulses hinted toward the rise of the New Age movement from the 1960s and its focus on individualism and cosmic relativism, all delivered with a pop-cultural twist. Indeed, 'Occult Geometry' was more invested in taking a light-hearted romp through esoterica and New Age geometry than in the perpetuation of 'occultural' traditions. Tee may borrow her ideas from obscure sources, but her work unmistakably plays with, and implicitly critiques, a mainstream culture and a contemporary art world that are saturated with magical thinking and constructed through leaps of faith.

NATHANIEL BUDZINSKI

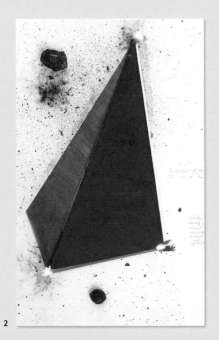

2

MATIAS FALDBAKKEN
STANDARD (OSLO)

To call Matias Faldbakken a bad artist is not necessarily to berate him. The intelligence of slackerdom lies in its shrugging self-protection: you can't judge that which never really tried in the first place. Or can you? The laziness, non-commitment and disavowal that can be read into the Norwegian sculptor's works are less remnants of actual disaffection than representations of contempt. They show how the agency in any act of making, when actualized, can splinter into debris. And representations, unlike intentions, are not judgement-proof.

The distressed or broken industrial sculptures (sawed-open propane tanks, plastic containers filled with cement) and framed two-dimensional works Faldbakken presented at STANDARD (OSLO) may have been formally opposed (damaged vs. polished, floor vs. wall), but both were two sides of the same trash aesthetic that Faldbakken has fruitfully propagated for the past decade. To turn detritus into treasure – as the artist does in his four, framed cardboard boxes (*Four Flat Boxes*) and trash bags and sacks [*Untitled (Burlap & Plastic)*] (both 2014), might suggest a boastfulness that anything – even a disposable container – can pass as art. Reciprocally, such disavowal may seek to comment upon and eventually sink that whole, broken plane of valuation, holding itself to higher, if invisible, standards. Resignation and idealism are often closely aligned.

Faldbakken's demolished car, *Untitled (The Wheel)*, displayed in the entrance of the gallery, is a perfect Ballardian emblem, sexualizing technical destruction in the form of the car collision. The work is a partly dismantled Rover 75 from which a triangular structure of bars, a platform and scaffolding extend. Beneath the machismo of the raw, prostrate metal (dis)assemblage lies, I think, a tidy, if somewhat desperate, metaphor of the art object as a vehicle (for meaning and exchange), presented in the gallery (itself a former repair shop), for viewers or collectors (the aluminium film panel which might hold

a film operator and camera) by gallerists/assistants (scaffolding). The installation suggests the masculinity of an artist holding power – if destructive – over his own objects; but it's in such loaded acts of pathos that self-hatred reveals itself, in the guise of institutional critique. In the same room hung collages made of arranged, illegible newspaper strips while in actual news, an Oslo newspaper reported Faldbakken's car as the most expensive for sale in the city (no small feat).

There's an unexpected emotionality to works like *Gas Sculpture* (2014), sawed-open gas tanks of different colours, arranged in a line: they literally take the steam out of the artist's own process, equating art with its own (also procedural) failure. The quasi-performative sculpture *Untitled (Wall Drag)* was a groping, dramatic tangle of welded automobile tailpipes and mufflers, which Faldbakken hauled into the gallery space, leaving a 'drawing' on the (scratched) wall.

Faldkbakken's is not the grand tragic failure of the unresolved masterpiece, but the banal botch of a lost parking ticket or a joke falling flat. I do like the sly, conscious oscillation between humour and failure in his art, which plays performatively off the bathos of ruin. Less justifiable, though, is the artist's defence of his perhaps feigned naiveté, which is always a recourse to outside context, as if to say, 'it's not me, it's the culture.' This is the 'liberation' claimed in the show's press release as the flip side to failures of agency (or the 'catastrophe' of making): the negative freedom of non-accountability.

If the art world is prepared to allow half-heartedness and stupidity into its roster, then it's to blame for its own low standards. This reasoning – Faldbakken's own, I think – can be seen not only in terms of its causes (an 'anything goes' context), but also its effects (exclusion, repetition). After all, even the hyped, hyper-contextualized object (ultimately, the artist Faldbakken) has generative power: as subject, maker, meme or hero. By this logic, are we not also to judge Faldbakken for the student-level works of his considerable imitators?

PABLO LARIOS

KEVIN COSGROVE
mother's tankstation, Dublin

In certain quarters, that art world desire for the eternally new seems, thank goodness, to be getting tired and old. In the contemporary Irish context, you can see the hunger for something other than faux innovation in the critical and popular reception of such artists as Mairead O'hEocha and Kevin Cosgrove.

Since his highly acclaimed degree show at Dublin's National College of Art and Design in 2007, Cosgrove has been mining the same realistic seam in his detailed paintings of places of work. These are not offices or grand spaces but the often dirty, though usually highly ordered, workshops where physical labour happens.

Cosgrove is aware of the fluctuating trends around which his work is received, joking that he is 'so old fashioned that he's almost cool'. He's similarly arch about the title of his current exhibition, 'Remake', which alludes both to his love of film and his continuing focus on concerns that on the surface, are all about the grit and reality of making, doing and repairing.

But there is something about these too-painterly-to-be-photorealistic images that allows them to transcend genre painting. First, there's the complete lack of irony, but there are other strands and stories at play that add both intellectually and visually satisfying complexity to Cosgrove's workshop scenes.

The centrepiece of the tightly curated exhibition, just seven works in all, is *Remake* (2014). Here, an old Austin A35 car is parked in a workshop, awaiting repair. The oil-on-linen work contains many of Cosgrove's motifs: the ranks of tools on hooks, the chaos of compressors, sanders and other blue collar paraphernalia, all meticulously worked, and the total absence of people. It also foregrounds his homage to Diego Velázquez and, more particularly, to Johannes Vermeer, in the light that

floods in from an open metal door to the right of the car.

Through this doorway, in a less layered, less worked section of the painting, is the outline of a wall and another door, yellow in the sunshine. Seen sideways, it is also a small piece of geometric abstraction, nudging up against Cosgrove's cluttered realism. Two schools of art, side by side, the Modernism possibly fading: Is Cosgrove saying that, ultimately, the older tradition will triumph?

Light spills into all save one of the works on show, *Museum workshop with coats* (2014) being more completely enclosed than its companion pieces. The gridded and barred windows in *Radiator repair workshop* (2014) and the heavy metal door a little ajar in *Workshop with unlocked door* (2014) offer a sense of a wider world, paradoxically intensifying the focus of Cosgrove's little spheres of work. These paintings carry nostalgia for a world fading away. Does anyone really repair radiators any more? It seems particularly pertinent that Cosgrove's work deals with redundancy, given the art world's periodic dismissal of painting as irrelevant.

This is part of Cosgrove's brilliance: he reaches back in subtle ways while also commenting on the here and now. *Stone workshop* (2014) echoes the Dutch Golden Age, its deft use of perspective drawing you in until you're standing exactly where the craftsperson would have been standing. A frame above the hanging tools takes the gaze even further down the rabbit hole – to the extent that you feel you could really lose yourself.

Just as the Dutch painters of the 17th century proclaimed the morals and messages of a newly Protestant society and represented subjects from the emerging mercantile classes, Cosgrove's suite of works celebrate the presence and power of craft and labour. In this way, they act as a counterpoint to the glibness of so much contemporary consumerism, and, in the process, produce a powerful thesis for the enduring value of painting itself.

—————————

GEMMA TIPTON

1

26TH INTERNATIONAL BIENNIAL OF GRAPHIC DESIGN
Various venues, Brno

Biennials proliferate. Old ones survive; new ones spring up. Recent biennials like Massimiliano Gioni's 2013 Venice Biennale, 'The Encyclopedic Palace', and Rem Koolhaas's 2014 Architecture Biennale, 'Elements of Architecture', eschewed gathering the new in favour of casting fresh light on the old. Such shows concentrate less on illustrating the current state of play and more on demonstrating curatorial theses. In line with this trend, the 26th International Biennial of Graphic Design Brno, with its subtitle 'Graphic Design, Education & Schools', rather than providing a snapshot of contemporary graphic design activity, reflected on the education of graphic designers.

Since its first edition in 1963, the greater part of the Brno Biennial has traditionally comprised work by professional designers chosen through an international competition. The three Czech designers who curated this outing – Tomáš Celizna, Adam Macháček and Radim Peško – were all educated abroad and now work respectively in Amsterdam, Berkeley and London. Instead of judging the work of fellow professionals, the trio took the controversial decision to hold a student competition. The successful entries were displayed on the ground floor of Brno's Museum of Applied Arts, some of them on furniture that was originally conceived for graphic design schools and had been remade in the museum's workshops for this exhibition. While the winning works – mostly books and posters, with surprisingly few films and websites – had a sense of highly produced gloss, the furniture, designed by, among others, Max Bill, Karel Martens and Wolfgang Weingart, was strikingly simple. The display created an interesting contrast between the style of the graphic pieces and the stark environments in which they were likely produced.

Pursuing the schools theme, the curators invited designer and teacher Nina Paim to stage an exhibition about the assignments given in graphic design courses. Titled 'Taking a Line for a Walk' (after Paul Klee's famous dictum), this show within a show explored historical and contemporary assignments and displayed a selection of objects used as educational prompts – such as a set of shapes that could be explored in two or three dimensions, or plaster casts of body parts. Graphic design is ostensibly a practical discipline, yet schools offer a chance to work speculatively and educational briefs have to imagine a conduit between the applied and the theoretical.

Other educational elements of the biennial included a reflection on 'The Study Room', which comprised publications selected by a group of designers displayed on Enzo Mari's Autoprogettazione furniture and held vertical by broken-brick book ends. This was shown in tandem with a meditation on St Jerome's study that was assembled by the curators but referred to a project by Céline Condorelli (*Revision*, 2009–ongoing). Between them, the two parts of the display prompted analogies between the layout of two- and three-dimensional space, and the structure of thought. Like the art school furniture, it suggested that the shape of things and the shape of ideas are inextricably bound. Picking up on a related theme, a large-scale blackboard illustration by Rudy Guedj, summarizing the evolution of the art school from the Academy through Bauhaus to the contemporary, used a series of simple forms to represent complex educational philosophies.

The two non-educational elements of the biennial were monographic shows of the work of veteran Czech designer Rostistlav Vaněk and the esteemed Dutch design team Mevis & Van Deursen. Both were prompted by previous honours – Vaněk was given a lifetime contribution award at the 2010 biennial and Mevis & Van Deursen were the winners of the Grand Prix in the professional competition of 2012. While Vaněk played it straight, showing a career's worth of well-crafted identities, publications and typefaces, Mevis & Van Deursen fooled with the format by exhibiting only a handful of pieces and overwhelming each of them with outsized, overly detailed captions. The shows were an effective pair, allowing comparisons of not only the designs produced by the respective studios, but also the designers' sense of their own roles. Vaněk posed as a creator of order, Mevis & Van Deursen as generators of disturbance.

The biennial occupied parts of Brno's Museum of Applied Arts and the Moravian Gallery as well as the ground floor of a third building, the Governor's Palace, which was given over to an 'Off Program' – a revolving selection of workshops, presentations and exhibitions, largely staged by students. The last element of the biennial proper was a statistical study of the genders, nationalities and ages of the winners of the last ten Brno competitions, presented in a book titled Off-White Paper. Although its authors, the Korean designers Sulki & Min Choi, claim an interest in 'quantities, not qualities', their title suggests otherwise. The figures reveal a disconcerting consistency in the biennial's previous few outings, most of the winners being men from Europe. Although it could be argued that the 26th edition didn't venture into dramatically new geographical territory, it made a significant step simply by breaking the cycle of professional self-congratulation.

EMILY KING

3

ADRIAN PACI
Kaufmann Repetto, Milan

Adrian Paci described this exhibition as a return to a more intimate and handcrafted practice. Its title, 'La gloria vostra fu sole' (Thou glory was made of sun), comes from a verse by 19th-century poet Gavril Dara Junior, who wrote in Arberesh, the language of Albanian communities in Italy. Paci planned the show a year ago, after months spent editing his last video, The Column (2013), for his retrospective 'Lives in Transit' (which toured from Jeu de Paume in Paris to Musée d'art contemporain de Montréal and Padiglione d'Arte Contemporanea in Milan). He felt the urge to grant a weightier physicality to the fleeting images from his huge archive, which ranges from obsolete VHS tapes to photographs found online. Trained as a realist painter in the Albanian capital, Tirana, Paci started to shoot photos and moving images only in the late 1990s, when the county underwent a dramatic phase of political turmoil and he fled to Milan.

For 'La gloria vostra fu sole', Paci chose an unequivocally heavy material – marble – working with it in mosaic, a traditional technique that the artist first explored a few years ago and has since developed with the help of an assistant. In comparison to the two mosaics, which cover a wall in each of Kaufmann Repetto's two rooms, a series of small paintings – acrylics on wood and watercolours on paper in delicate colours – sparsely hung at eye level on the other gallery walls, appears very light, almost as if the works were floating. The contrast is intentional.

One of the mosaics, Il salto (The Jump, all works 2014), in black and white, depicts a soldier climbing over an obstacle; Facciata (Facade), in full colour, shows a Romanesque church, with five men on the roof and a white-clad figure standing next to the portal. Both images are hard to decipher and appear slightly blurred, as if frozen in the middle of something, or affected by a loss of definition having being translated from one medium to another. This is, in fact, exactly what has happened, as originally they came from video and film stills: Il salto is based on a 1970s documentary on military training

found on YouTube, and Facciata on Armenian director Sergei Paradjanov's extraordinary 1968 film The Colour of Pomegranates, which was censored in the Soviet Union because of its unorthodox religious imagery. According to Paci, however, specific sources are less important than the ambiguity of the images per se, which is emphasized by their uncertain provenance and visual 'noise'.

The act of abstracting images from their time and context in order to open them up to new readings is a recurring feature in Paci's work. In the past, the artist has sourced footage from Pier Paolo Pasolini's films, private wedding tapes, newsreels, soft porn, documentaries and family photographs. Up close, the irregular tesserae of the mosaic are akin to pixels, but, from afar, the images they form are interrupted by glitches, so that the viewer goes back and forth without being able to focus; only once you see the image reproduced on a smaller scale does the picture finally look coherent.

From the small paintings, other hazy figures emerge: soldiers with outstretched arms, in the manner of a routine at the gym or an act of surrender: A braccia aperte (Arms Wide Open); a group of swimmers: Nuotatori (Swimmers); an acrobat attached to a rope: L'appesa (The Hanged Woman); young street fighters: I rivoltosi (The Rioters); a young man's head, eyes shut, enclosed by hands: Il riposo (The Rest). The painting is sketchy, the brushstrokes fluid, but otherwise the only link between the works is the presence of figures in a state of suspension between movement and stasis, relaxation and violence. The group of swimmers, in fact, are migrants who, almost two decades ago, crossed the Mediterranean to reach Italian shores – like so many who are still trying, despite the daily shipwrecks and unthinkable body counts. Yet, here, Paci refuses to adopt the clichéd iconography of desperation and grief and, instead, frames his subjects as seemingly normal bathers. 'The body is what we are left with, after all the journeys, the experiences and the wars', Paci told me. In times when we are exposed to instant circulation of brutal imagery of savaged bodies, of soldiers and refugees, kidnappers and hostages, executioners and victims, Paci's approach to figuration and human scale asks for detachment, and reflection.

BARBARA CASAVECCHIA

2

1
Kevin Cosgrove
Remake, 2014, oil on linen,
1.1 × 1.4 m

2
'Taking a Line for a Walk.
An exhibition about design school
assignments', 2014, installation view
at 26th Brno Biennial

3
Adrian Paci
Facciata (Facade), 2014, marble
mosaic, 2 × 2.6 m

DAVID FERRANDO GIRAUT
LABoral Centro de Arte y Creación Industrial, Gijón

'In the end, there is no control of the unconstitutionality or irrationality of the law beyond the ballot boxes or social movements', says a voice-over at the start of *Speech Prosthesis (an Alchemical Conversation)* (2014), the latest work by Spanish artist David Ferrando Giraut, which was staged as a solo show at LABoral. The four-channel video installation explores how irrationality, triggered by greed and fear, runs rife in current processes of political decision-making. Ferrando Giraut's 'case study' is the Spanish government's controversial revision of the energy laws last year, which resulted in penalizing the renewable-energies sector, whereas only a year earlier it had been incentivized.

Ferrando Giraut's immersive work was shaped as a conversation between the four natural elements – wind, water, earth and fire – which assumed several guises across the different components of the installation: as voices, as colours, as objects and as sounds. Each channel of the video featured a specific background colour (yellow, blue, green or red) and two digitally animated, rotating objects, each signifying the ways in which human beings have harnessed these natural elements throughout history. Earth, for example, was represented by three prehistoric stones and a hydraulic hammer; water by a Greek amphora and a water cooler. Wind took the form of bellows and an artificial-respiration machine. Finally, fire was embodied by a tinderbox and a camping stove. The use of this genealogical set of objects is a recurrent strategy in the recent work of the London-based artist, one that allows him to impress upon the viewer the sense of a historical continuum, which he sees as having been supplanted by the rhetoric of rupture, of relentless 'life-changing technological revolutions'.

In front of the panoramic widescreen projection at LABoral, four speakers, in the triangular forms of the alchemical symbols of the four elements, were placed on top of metallic poles. The speakers were positioned in a square formation, creating a space that you had to enter in order to hear the different parts of the quadraphonic soundtrack. The audio featured fragments from interviews that Ferrando Giraut had conducted with a local group of experts, including an environmental activist, a lawyer, an economist, a geologist, a climate-change specialist and a philosopher of science. In a clear nod to Bruno Latour's concept of the 'Parliament of Things' – a rejection of Modernity's dualistic distinction between nature and society, which was first mentioned in his oft-quoted book *We Have Never Been Modern* (1991) – the artist employed the experts' testimonies as if to give a voice to the objects. These voice-overs offered varied insights into the energy problem in Spain, emphasizing not only the political and economic motivations behind the recent revision of government energy legislation, but also the impact that traditional methods of energy extraction are having on the environment.

Despite the local nature of its source material, *Speech Prosthesis* tackles universal issues, particularly the widely discussed question of whether to endorse 'Anthropocene', a recently popularized term coined to designate a new geological era marked by the deep transformations caused by humankind. But it is the work's critique of the irrationalism of much contemporary politics – expressed mainly through the experts' voice-overs – that makes this piece so timely.

While it clearly belongs to the tradition of research-based art, *Speech Prosthesis* doesn't avoid formal experimentation. Crucially, and despite the seriousness of its claims, it's a sensuous and enthralling work. The objects mentioned above rotate mid-air on the screens for the duration of the piece (24 minutes) and the voices – carefully treated with sound effects that evoke the four elements – become haunting cyphers for our mistreated ecosystem: they're like voices of conscience that stubbornly emerge from near-obliteration. Ferrando Giraut's installation is not just an illustration of a critical creed or a documentary-style piece about a political situation, it endeavours to tell us about something we might already know, but in a way that we've never been told it before.

LORENA MUÑOZ-ALONSO

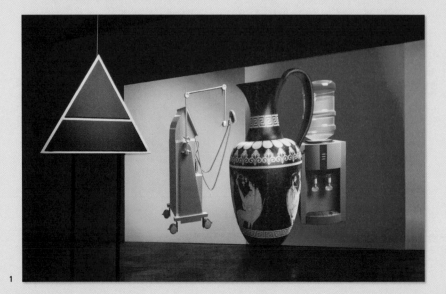

THIS IS NOT MY BEAUTIFUL HOUSE
Kunsthalle Athena

Rarely has a show been so aptly titled. In a magnificent wreck of a building, in a magnificent wreck of a city, the non-profit art space Kunsthalle Athena hosted the show 'This Is not my Beautiful House'. The line is from the Talking Heads' track, 'Once in a Lifetime' (1981), which is one of the few pop songs that manages to be as uplifting as it is bleak. I'm sure it's no coincidence that it also includes the words: 'into the blue again, after the money's gone', which pretty much describes the situation the Greek capital has found itself in after years of crippling economic crisis. There may be no government funding in Athens right now but, thanks to a rare mix of philanthropy, private initiative and cheap rent, the art scene is, on many levels, thriving.

The Kuntshalle Athena was set up in 2010 by the dynamic curator and writer (and occasional *frieze* contributor) Marina Fokidis, in a semi-derelict 19th-century building in Metaxourgeio, a once-affluent neighbourhood of Athens that fell on hard times and is now experiencing the first buds of gentrification (The Breeder and Rebecca Camhi Gallery are also in the area). The Kunsthalle – which is run by volunteers, survives on donations and hosts a lively talks programme as well as exhibitions – states that it wishes to learn 'through the experiences and insights of others' and 'through mistakes – not least its own'. It's also wonderfully self-reliant: in a country battered with gloom and humiliation, the gallery declares that it 'will be what we make of it for as long as we want to make it'.

Sensitively curated by Klea Charitou, Marina Fokidis, Eleanna Papathanasiadi and Apostolos Vassilopoulos, 'This Is not my Beautiful House' included the work of four Greek artists, Anastasia Ax, Apostolos Georgiou, Socratis Socratous and Kostis Velonis. Meaning emerged through a mix of suggestion and imagination via installation, photography, sculpture and painting, all of which inhabited different rooms in this deeply atmospheric mansion with a sense of both possibility and despair. Dislocation was the

order of the day; remnants from previous shows haunted the once-grand rooms like welcome ghosts taking stock of the present.

Ax's installation, *Exile* (2014), evoked a sort of 21st century Pompeii. Large, whitewashed triangular shapes, some collapsed, some loosely strung together, filled the space. The work seemed to be in a state of flux; it had been smashed up, walked over and then categorized by an archaeologist, the results of which were displayed in a vitrine. Ax seems to be asking: 'How we do make sense of history as we are living it?'

Georgiou's large untitled painting from 2012 depicts a man and a woman falling over two chairs, their faces obscured. Are they fighting, having fun, drunk? Who knows? But then, what do we ever know of other people's motivations, despite the fact that we're all the same species? What I do know is that this powerfully ambiguous painting, rendered in the artist's trademark dusty lilac, brown and eucalyptus-green palette, stayed with me long after I had left the gallery.

Gardens – sites of solace – often feature in Socratous's finely wrought sculptures. For *Stolen Garden* (2014) he cast branches, leaves, flowers and fruit from the National Garden of Athens in bronze: some are national symbols of Greece, while others are weeds. Delicate, despite the toughness of their materials, these melancholy objects seemed to have grown through the ancient floorboards and been rendered immobile at their moment of flowering.

Fascinated by 'failed builders', Avant-garde theatre and working class history, Velonis's sculptures combine both personal and histori-cal references. *Tribune Leading to the Ramp and Ramp Leading to the Tribune* (2014) is an enigmatic Minimalist structure that evokes both stairs and anvils; it was paired with a black and white photograph of a man slumped on a wall next to an empty pram. It's a desolate, mysterious pairing; a private moment juxta-posed with a Modernist shape. A deceptively simple video by Velonis from 2010 was also on show: it's a single shot of a photograph of classical ruins attached to a wall with a bull-dog clip, fluttering in the breeze. Titled *How One Can Think Freely in the Shadow of a Temple*, it's a question as a statement of fact, and one that is still as achingly relevant – in the words of Talking Heads – as it ever was.

JENNIFER HIGGIE

1
David Ferrando Giraut
Speech Prosthesis (An Alchemical Conversation),
2014, installation view at LABoral Centro de
Arte y Creación Industrial

2
Foreground: Socratis Socratous
Stolen Garden, 2014; background: Anastasia
Ax, *EXILE*, 2014, installation view

3
Ash Kilmartin
OHN, 2014, neon sign operated by resident
studio artists

OCTOPUS 14: NOTHING BESIDE REMAINS
Gertrude Contemporary, Melbourne

Gertrude Contemporary has a special place in the hearts of the many who have passed through its doors. Since its inception in 1985, the gallery, project space and studio complex has fostered and supported artists, curators, independent publishers, writers and academics. For Melbourne's arts community, it's the next step up from the rich array of artist-run initiatives for which the city has become known.

Gertrude Contemporary originally occupied a former home-ware factory and emporium, Johnston's, which opened in 1889. The model for the gallery was New York's PS1, which repurposed a school as artists' studios and exhibition spaces. But Gertrude is now at the next stage of its institutional career. Though well funded by state and federal government, the gentrification of the surrounding inner-city suburb of Fitzroy has caused rents to soar and Gertrude must now find another home.

Gertrude's history is the focus of the 14th edition of its annual 'Octopus' exhibition, for which it invites a curator to develop an idea for a show. Tara McDowell, who recently arrived in Melbourne as the inaugural associate professor and director of the Curatorial Practice PhD programme at Monash University Art Design and Architecture (MADA), curated 'Nothing Beside Remains'.

One of McDowell's innovations was to stage the exhibition throughout Gertrude Contemporary's rabbit-warren of corridors, storage spaces, stair-wells and staircases, as well as in the gallery. Visitors accessed the show through the usually private studio entrance, walked up a steep flight of stairs and then percolated throughout the building. Artists Saskia Schut and Scott Mitchell programmed a series of readings by local writers, publishers and designers, which took place in the gallery's shop-front entrance. That McDowell is a newcomer to Melbourne led her to examine the traces of the gallery's history that many locals have, perhaps, overlooked simply because they are so familiar.

The histories revealed by the exhibition have curiously universal echoes. Lining the entrance stairway was an untitled series of photographs from 2010–12 by Georgian artist Otar Karalashvili, which document the hand-made notes that people looking for work attach to Tbilisi's buildings and street lamps. Other pieces in the show also explored forms of labour. Allan Sekula's *Untitled Slide Sequence* (1972/2011) is a series of 1970s black and white slides of employees ending their shift in an aero-space factory, while Harun Farocki's film *Workers Leaving the Factory* (1995) interweaves footage from the first film by the Lumière brothers with other clips of workers exiting factory gates.

3

A number of past and present Gertrude artists engaged directly with the building's inhabitants. At the top of the stairs, Agatha Gothe-Snape created a cosy den with comfortable chair, reading light and crocheted rug, where she and gallery invigilators read from texts that former studio artists nominated as having been influential during their residencies (*An Uncertain Reader*, 2014). Ash Kilmartin's neon sign spells out *OHN* (2014) – the only remaining letters of the building's original sign. It was illuminated as the last studio artist to leave the building turned it on, and then turned off by the first to arrive the next day.

Other works also drew attention to the fabric of the building. Nicholas Mangan's *A Division of time that neither begins nor ends here ...* (2014) is the finest of geologi-cal cores, drilled from the gallery and studios' timber-and-masonite surfaces, and presented in a glass-fronted display case embedded into a corridor wall. Zarouhie Abdalian's *Simple Machines* (2014), a series of small black lacquered wooden wedges, were placed on the floor, in ceiling cavities and in other unexpected spaces. Susan Jacobs re-assembled the vast conveyor belt that had lain untouched in storage at the rear of the building in the downstairs gallery: *Conveyor (George Watts is a traitor)* (2014) was a monument to redundant industry.

The exhibition's apt title, 'Nothing Beside Remains', is a quote from Percy Bysshe Shelley's sonnet 'Ozymandias' (1817), an ode to the ravages of time. Gertrude Contemporary will move to a new, as yet undecided, venue in 2016, in a location that hopefully is not too far from its original roots.

REBECCA COATES

AROUND TOWN
Gallery EXIT
Pearl Lam Galleries
Oi!, Hong Kong

With 95 percent humidity, Hong Kong's air can already make you feel like you're walking underwater, but Trevor Yeung's 'That Dog at That Party' at Gallery EXIT attempted to create an effect of total submersion. In *Silver Duckweed* (2014), three sets of helium-filled Mylar balloons rose to the gallery ceiling, trailing white ribbons and long, blonde horsehairs. If these silver orbs were floating against an imagined watery surface, we were trawling slowly underneath. A faded blue-grey carpet in the middle of the floor (*The stone garden in your fish tank*, 2014) inferred the gravel on the bottom of an aquarium. Several irregular shapes indented in its weave suggested large rocks that may once have sat on top, but the only objects that remained were a comb covered by a small stone. With a few scant props, Yeung's sculptural installation trapped us in an evocative aquarium, but he insisted on piling in several more inert sculptures. In *I am fine, but please don't disturb me* (2014) an air pump sent ripples through a spot-lit cube of water, making shadowy traces on the walls. The dense formal presence of *Black Triangle* (2014) – three panels covered with black aquarium sand – filled one corner. As if all these aqueous nods weren't enough, two *Volcanic Lovers* (2014) sat on plinths – craggy rocks with deep red coral growing in their crevices. Yeung could have achieved the same effect with less: his suggestive titles, mixed metaphors and sense of melodrama perhaps led not so much to intricate fables than to, as the title of the show suggests, the random, failed connections of half-remembered anecdotes.

The three-person group show 'After Time', curated by David Ho Yeung Chan at Pearl Lam's Hong Kong space, similarly cast the viewer in an abandoned setting. Upon entering the gallery, the viewer was provided a view of Morgan Wong's *Untitled (DVD Burning)* (2014), a mock-studio set up with a desk covered in discs and chairs scattered on the floor, via a transparent wall. This show didn't seem to imagine a point 'after time' so much as a point after humans, or after humans cease toiling in the ways they currently do. Erica Lai's staid photos depicted dark, overgrown gardens and empty observation towers and platforms. The only bodies visible here were on video; in Chung Seo Yung's *2013 4 O'Clock* (2013), a woman doggedly traces a path through the concrete shell of an unfinished building using black duct tape. Wong's video *Frustration of Having more than Two Choices to Make in Life* (2013) features the artist, dressed in white in a white room, like a psychiatric patient, staring motionless at a large steel bar and file lying on the floor beside him. Both Chung's and Wong's works seem like self-imposed purgatories, where the artists are immersed in determinedly pointless activities. Each participating artist's work was installed in a separate area of the gallery and, likewise, their three approaches never quite met. While

1

Chung's actions and remade objects, like the ink-stained grid etched into the wooden table of *Place* (2013), have an air of performative masochism, Lai's serene images seem comparatively aloof. Wong's studio set-up manages to suggest a Samuel Beckett-like burrowing through time with repetitive mundane gestures. The desktop computer incessantly creates DVDs with nothing on them and his *Study of Eventfulness and Durationality* (2014) is a video loop showing him moving a set of stools in varying stacks and arrangements, before deciding, as the physical artefacts displayed in the gallery attest, to cast their legs in a cylinder of concrete. If we can't stop time, we can at least celebrate the illusion of capturing it.

The theatrical sets suggested by these two exhibitions were made manifest in 'Zoo as Metaphor' at Oi!, an arts complex in the former Royal Hong Kong Yacht Club. Perhaps the most notable thing about this controlled, immersive exhibition was its structure: guest curator Orlean Lai invited five artists (Au Wah-yan, Steve Hui, Vee Leong, Kingsley Ng and Wong Hung-fei) to participate, but their work (left uncredited) was dissolved into a wider performative fiction. Visitors were given supervised access to three sets: the study, storeroom and seemingly forgotten back room belonging to a character simply known as The Collector. What he collects seems arbitrary: leaves preserved in bell jars, boxes of matches, old records, stereoscopes with unknown family portraits, old-fashioned radios and small plastic animal figurines.

On the walls next to old film posters, black and white drawings depicted unlikely diagrams, such as the ways in which a jockey can fall off a horse. As I flipped through Cantonese comics and eyed the range of tree branches lining one wall, a watchful actor-chaperone explained that The Collector tries to preserve what he considers to be a disappearing Hong Kong; the branches were from plants in his neighbourhood, which has been undergoing urban redevelopment. So this was primarily a doe-eyed eulogy to the casualties of the rapidly changing megalopolis. The real puzzle was the title itself: zoo as metaphor for what? The Collector's hoarding certainly spoke of a desire for preservation and, at points, I also felt slightly like a caged animal as I was led around the rooms. But the zoo trope seemed to point mainly to the show's use of taxonomies and archetypal roles; casting the curator as theatre director and the artists as both set designers and the expressions of different aspects of the 'Collector' character. The audience, however, played the same role that it always does. Imposing a narrative on a setting, it seems, only limits our capacity to imagine its histories and possible trajectories.

CHRIS FITE-WASSILAK

2

3

4

5TH FUKUOKA ASIAN ART TRIENNALE & YOKOHAMA TRIENNALE 2014
Various venues

This summer saw a bounty of international exhibitions in Japan, with the return of the Fukuoka Asian Art Triennale and the Yokohama Triennale, as well as the recently inaugurated Sapporo International Art Festival. Hosted by the city's Asian Art Museum, the Fukuoka Triennale showed work by 46 artists from 21 countries and regions in Asia. Much of the work in 'Panorama of the Nextworld – Breaking out into the Future' addressed social inequality or government repression in the artists' home countries. The prevalence of moving-image and lens-based art illustrated the disparity in technical sophistication and access between countries like China and less developed regions like Bhutan or Nepal. Chinese artist Lu Yang's ambitious, elaborate project *UterusMan* (2013–ongoing), for example, which imagines an asexual superhero, spreads across several analogue and digital platforms including *manga*, digital video and gaming.

More subtle works demonstrated how photographic imagery can be used to rattle the political status quo. In Vietnamese artist Nguyen Trinh Thi's *Landscape Series #1* (2013), for instance, 35mm slides and prints showed people pointing at something in the rural landscape, but the pictures remained mute as to what the meaning of this gesture might be. Nguyen sourced the images from online articles about social problems in Vietnam. Their enigmatic quality indicates that, in a region where government censors must approve exhibited artworks, it is still safer to show rather than tell.

The spectre of government censorship also haunted *Myohyangsangwan* (2014), a video by Korean artists Moon Kyungwon and Jeon Joonho. It tells the tale of the doomed love between a South Korean artist and a North Korean woman who works in a Shanghai restaurant – one of the 100 or so establishments that are remotely operated by the North Korean government in 12 countries. A note at the end of the video explained

that, in these outposts, visitors can eat North Korean food and see traditional songs and dances performed by North Korean women. For Koreans on both sides of the border, they are 'the only places to openly meet without restriction from their respective governments'. Told through realistic and oneiric scenes, this love story hints at a yearning for a united Korean peninsula.

As the earthquake, tsunami and nuclear disaster of 3 March 2011 are still at the fore-front of the Japanese collective conscience, works addressing disasters in other countries brought to mind the tragedies of 3/11. The most moving was Philippine artist Kiri Dalena's three-channel video *Tungkung Langit* (Skywards, 2013), which told the story of the Philippine floods in 2011 through the conversations, drawings and games of two children who survived the deluge by clinging onto logs. The video's aesthetic is murky, with some shots filmed in dark, rushing water. When one of the children asks the other, 'How do you feel now they are gone?' she replies, 'I cry, I regret, I worry'. It is a heartbreakingly beautiful work. If only it need never have been made.

Dalena's videos also appeared in the Yokohama Triennale in a small section devoted to her work. Under the artistic direction of Japanese artist Yasumasa Morimura, the title of Yokohama's Triennale, 'ART Fahrenheit 451: Sailing into the sea

5

of oblivion', paid homage to Ray Bradbury's eponymous dystopian novel. Work was installed across the Yokohama Museum of Art and the Shinko Pier Exhibition Hall. As its fatalistic title prophesied, the Triennale took visitors on a journey through a string of rooms with carefully curated groupings of works connected to the idea of oblivion, although the use of that term did stretch the limits of poetic licence. The heart of the exhibition began around the halfway mark of the route through the Yokohama Museum, introduced by four chapters of Taryn Simon's *A Living Man Declared Dead and Other Chapters I–XVIII* (2008–11), including a section devoted to the kidnapping of a South Korean fisherman that was censored when Simon showed the work in China. In Yokohama, Simon chose to absent this chapter by painting the wall with black redaction bands, as had been done in China. The room also included sculptures by Michael Rakowitz made out of Bamiyan stone, seven television sculptures made by Ed Kienholz and Nancy Reddin between the late 1960s and early '90s, and Dora García's *Fahrenheit 451 (1957)* (2002), a trestle table heaving with copies of Bradbury's novel printed in mirror-image type. Books from the Yoshihisa Otani Collection of jingoist pre-World War II Japanese novels were displayed beside exquisite photographs from the 1950s by Ikko Narahara depicting life in a Trappist monastery in Hokkaido and a women's prison in Wakayama. This selection of works – addressing the power of the media and its abuse by generations of political bullies – made a forceful argument about the capacity of artists to resist oppression.

In the centre of this room, people joined a short queue to climb three steps to a small white stage, resembling a pulpit, which held a large book. *Moe Nai Ko To Ba* (The Only Book in the World, 2014) was created by Morimura as a tribute to Bradbury's novel and included sections by Austrian novelist Elfriede Jelinek, Russian poet Anna Akhmatova and filmmaker and former Japanese Red Army member Masao Adachi. The tome was a crucible of acts of resistance through creation, intended for destruction at the end of the show in a suitably dramatic-sounding *Annihilation Performance*, when it would be given over to the 'sea of oblivion'.

ELLEN MARA DE WACHTER

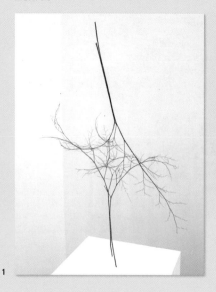

1

DANIEL STEEGMANN MANGRANÉ
Proyectos Monclova, Mexico City

Stepping into Daniel Steegmann Mangrané's elegant exhibition '_/____/_/__/_____' at Proyectos Monclova, visitors left behind the hustle and bustle of the city streets and entered an oasis of calm. A delicate black skeleton formed by two intertwined, leafless branches of a fern (*Rama de avenca*, Avenca Branch, 2014) welcomed viewers to the space. Beyond this, the gallery was almost empty, save for an arrangement of neatly cut steel sheets resembling a giant Modernist children's puzzle on the floor (*Systemic Grid*, 2014).

Manipulating space to alter perception is something Steegmann Mangrané knows how to do well. This was effectively demonstrated here with *Fólego* (2014), made in collaboration with Joana Saraiva. A composition for seven flutes, the piece was played by musicians throughout the exhibition space, resonating within the near-empty gallery and contrasting with the clang made by footsteps against the steel sheets of *Systemic Grid*. This

contrast was echoed in the tension between the clean-cut Modernity of the steel and the organic structure of the ferns in *Rama de avenca*.

For the first few minutes of the 16mm film *Phasmidea* (2013), you see nothing but a branch, which, as you look closely, forms a pattern resembling the geometric cutouts of *Systemic Grid*. Then, you notice an inanimate object coming to life. As the title suggests, the film depicts a phasmid – or stick insect – the name of which derives from the Greek *phasma*, or 'phantasm', presumably on account of the insect's ability to disappear into its surroundings, or to resemble an inanimate stick.

The insect slowly creeps from a branch, through the artist's studio and into a origami-like white paper structure, which recalls the neat geometries of some barely-there pencil-and-watercolour drawings on the walls nearby. Both contrast with the organic lines of the insect's body. The film works to highlight the moment at which we begin to discern movement from stasis, the visible from the invisible. This play with perception was also continued in the artist's collages, *Simetrías* (Symmetries, 2014), in which photographs of natural forms, such as leaves, were cut into geometric shapes and recombined in assemblages that play with the perception of spatial depth on the flat surface of the image.

The show, whose title could be written but not spoken, articulated a gap between nature and culture. Steegmann Mangrané's titles, the show's musical accompaniment and the film *Phasmidea* made me think of Jean Painlevé, whose videos of underwater fauna crossed nature documentary with Surrealism (an element which is not foreign to Steegmann Mangrané's work, either). Painlevé might well have enjoyed *Phasmidea*. As he wrote in his 1931 essay 'Mystères et miracles de la nature' (Mysteries and Miracles of Nature): 'Nothing is so strangely splendid as the most static life forms, which leave us to freely dream each instant without imposing upon us what happens next.'

GABRIELA JAUREGUI

2

THE THEATER OF THE WORLD
Museo Tomayo, Mexico City

The metaphor of the world as a theatre goes a long way back. Greek philosophers first conceived of life as being directed by master puppeteers (God, Fortune and Fate) centuries before it was most famously articulated in William Shakespeare's *As You Like It* (c. 1600). Yet, the premise that 'all the world's a stage / and all the men and women merely players' has, for the most part, focused on the players. The exhibition 'El Teatro del Mundo' (The Theatre of the World) – the title echoing Pedro Calderón de la Barca's 1655 play *El Gran Teatro del Mundo* – instead drew attention to the theatre set. More specifically, it aimed to show how monuments, urban planning and architecture have been used as a means of fictional construction by nation states and their leaders – the puppeteer turned stage designer. The show attempted to weave together many lines of inquiry that weren't always clearly defined. The catalogue text, by curator Andrea Torreblanca, was more successful in doing so. It began by citing the late-18th-century tale of Grigory Potemkin and Queen Catherine II's tour of the Crimea, when Potemkin temporarily constructed whole villages, complete with hired local inhabitants, to show the regions' prosperity, before dismantling and reconstructing it further down the road. Whilst the story of the Potemkin village was not directly referenced in the exhibition, the inclusion in the first of the two main galleries of Yto Barrada's *A Guide to Trees for Governors and Gardeners* (2014) – a series of prints that serve as a manual to prepare for the visit of official dignitaries by planting trees – shows how the spirit of Potemkin is alive and well today. The prints were exhibited alongside a rudimentary model train set that featured a limousine driving through a barren landscape with trees rising as it passed. How the veneer of a city is used as a political and propagandistic device appeared later in the exhibition with the film *Give Me the Colours* (2003) by Anri Sala, in which he interviews his friend Edi Rama, then Mayor of Tirana (currently the prime minister of Albania), who initiated a set of urban development pro-grammes including, most famously, working with inhabitants to paint the city's public buildings and housing blocks in garish colours or clad them in geometric forms.

By the mid-19th-century, as Torreblanca tells us, the introduction of the World's Fair ramped up architectural theatrics to new levels, allowing nation states to flex their ideology to millions of visitors. David Maljkovic's *Lost Cabinet* (2008) – a large, free-standing cabinet based on those built by Exat 51, a group of designers, architects and artists who produced Yugoslavia's pavilions in the mid-20th-century – contained newspaper clippings related to World's Fairs and the role they played in the country's own Modernist history. The legacy of the World's Fair was referenced more directly in Olivia Plender's *Empire City – The World on One Street* (2009), a scale model reconstruction of the bombastic, neo-classical British Empire Exhibition held at Wembley in 1924. World fairs are an important point of

3

reference but using two works as a means of addressing this history felt slight. A whole exhibition could have been given over to the history of World Fairs and the role they played in the development of the image of the nation state. And here was a more general problem with the show; there was little or no supplementary material, leaving 'Theater of the World' to feel more like a survey of recent artistic practices about architecture, rather than playing with different registers of artifice and documentation the title suggested.

The third strand of Torreblanca's show, urban planning, was most clearly articulated through Livia Corona Benjamin's series of photographs 'Two Million Homes for Mexico', (2007–14), which documented the extraordinary social housing initiative by former Mexican president Vicente Fox Quesada. The photos depict endless rows of housing, what Benjamin describes as 'ubiquitous grids of ecological and social intervention on a scale and of a consequence that are difficult to grasp'. Indeed, the exhibition was at its sharpest when focused on its own Mexican context. In the light-filled spaces of the Modernist Museo Tomayo, neighbouring the Museum of Modern Art and the Anthropological Museum, both built in the 1960s as a result of the 'Mexican miracle' of economic growth that began in the 1940s, and as bold statements of a nation increasingly sure of itself, I felt as if I had finally entered a stage. It is a shame this heightened sense of awareness was not played out on a more ambitious scale throughout the show.

NICK AIKENS

DAVID HAMMONS / YVES KLEIN
Aspen Art Museum

The exhibition 'David Hammons Yves Klein / Yves Klein David Hammons' is one of eight shows that this past summer inaugurated the beautiful new Shigeru Ban-designed home of the Aspen Art Museum. Behind Ban's woven 'basketwork' facade – an extraordinary frontage made from treated paper – were solo exhibitions of drawings by Tomma Abts and ceramics by Rosemarie Trockel, alongside an installation by Cai Guo-Chiang (*Moving Ghost Town*, 2014) that makes controversial use of African Sulcata tortoises with iPads affixed to their backs. (The instrumentalization of another species with consciousness – one that humans have no access to – for the purposes of art always makes me feel deeply uncomfortable, no matter how well it's claimed they are treated.) The museum also includes a baffling but beguiling display of local Coloradan minerals, an outdoor sculpture project in front of the museum by Jim Hodges (*With Liberty and Justice for All [A Work in Progress]*, 2014) and an informative exhibition about Ban's work designing architectural structures for humanitarian crises.

The centrepiece exhibition was, arguably, the double-header 'David Hammons Yves Klein / Yves Klein David Hammons', its title suggesting some sort of easy interchangeability between the work of the two artists. Curated by Aspen Art Museum director Heidi Zuckerman Jacobson, the exhibition of 49 works features a number of Klein's famous 'Anthropometries' – made using naked women covered in blue paint and pressing their bodies against the canvas – alongside a powerful selection of body prints and 'basketball' prints by Hammons, their grey surfaces contrasting with the International Klein Blue monochromes dotted around the exhibition. Zuckerman Jacobson assembled an impressive number of Klein works for the show. Also included were Klein's 'fire paintings', his iconic *Le Saut dans le vide* (Leap Into the Void, 1960) and the 1962 alchemical transformation piece, the *Zones of Immaterial Pictorial Sensibility* – which involved the sale of empty space to a collector, the transfer of ownership made during a complex ritual involving throwing gold into the Seine in Paris and the collector burning his cheque. This was presented alongside Hammons's *Blizaard Ball Sale* from 1983, in which the artist sold snowballs on the street, during a snowy

New York winter. Transubstantiation of matter, ephemerality and a complex relationship to the body were the threads that connected this exhibition together, underwritten by cults of personality of extremely different stripes; Klein the publicity-seeking showman and Hammons the elusive phantom, refusing to dance with the professionalized white art system.

A criticism that any half-sensitive visitor might level at the show is that of pseudomorphism; just because two art works look similar, it doesn't follow that they mean the same. It's almost too obvious to have to state that an African-American man using his own body to produce an image means something very different to a white European man using white European women to create his canvases. Throwing gold into the Seine in glamorous 1960s Paris is scarcely a comparable context to selling snowballs on the street in run-down 1980s Manhattan. Looking around the show, there are a surprising number of mark-making and methodological echoes of Klein found in Hammons's art – and both share a trickster's sensibility. It's easy to see why similarities between these would be attractive territory to explore. But there are many more differences. With allusions including the US flag, the hoodie, basketball and so on, Hammons's work is far more deeply political and class conscious than Klein's, which – for all his innovation, spiritual interests, art-historical significance, not to mention up-and-down relationship with the art world – comes off as a little macho and reactionary (making art with flamethrowers, for instance, or wearing a tuxedo and choreographing naked women covered in paint whilst a chamber orchestra plays in the background). But it's hard not to believe that by giving permission to be paired with Klein, Hammons is asserting a degree of control. An artist of his intellect and acuity must know full well that this pairing would create an exhibition about difference rather than similarity, and if the exhibition had any power, it lay in this uneasy friction. Two cooks given the same set of ingredients aren't necessarily going to make the same dish.

'David Hammons Yves Klein / Yves Klein David Hammons': these names can't be swapped in and out with each other that easily. However, as the tragic and racially charged events of this past year in the US have proved, conversations about difference – especially in the art world – are the ones that need to be aired right now, not glossed over with assumptions about happy similarities.

DAN FOX

4

ALEX BECERRA
ltd los angeles

Alex Becerra is a young painter who seems to value freedom over pretty much everything else, even at the expense of such musty old notions as moral responsibility or restraint. Left to its own devices, his mind goes, most often, to the naked human form: to pictures of fulsome ladies in compromising positions, up-skirt shots caught in mirrors, women with legs akimbo, examining themselves. In this exhibition, Pablo Picasso's *Les Demoiselles d'Avignon* (1907) is evoked more than once. Becerra makes unapologetically reckless pictures that are, at their best, thrilling to look at and, at their worst, vexing to think about. In this exhibition, there is never a dull moment.

Becerra paints fast and loose, leaving background areas of his canvas raw (and dirty) while other parts of the picture are so thickly and urgently caked with paint that he squeezes it straight from the tube. Colours are unmixed, or get mixed directly on the canvas. An untitled installation in the back room of the gallery illustrates his working methods: pizza boxes, repurposed as grimy portfolios, explode with marker-pen drawings on mismatched sheets of paper spread out across the floor. A free 'massage guide' newspaper, featuring a buxom babe on its front page, gives an indication of Becerra's high-low source materials.

In a speech at the opening of 'Entartete Kunst' (Degenerate Art, 1937) in Munich, the artist-curator Adolf Ziegler voiced his outrage at the way artists in his exhibition insulted 'the German mother' as 'a sort of whorish female archetype, or give her a facial expression of utter imbecility'. Ziegler was responding, though he didn't acknowledge it, to the non-judgmental realism of artists whose models, in many cases, also moonlighted as prostitutes.

Is such realism feasible in figure painting today? Or, for that matter, such outrage? Becerra's exhibition's title, 'Las Putas Problematicas', roughly translates as 'The Problematic Bitches' or 'Whores' – which looks, in print, flatly misogynistic but which spoken in Chicano slang comes off merely as cheeky, even affectionate, and not necessarily gender-specific. ('Wassup, bitches?') Becerra, who is Mexican-American, refuses to take a moralistic position on the vernacular that shapes his aesthetic sensibility. Partly what is at stake here, as it was for Picasso in 1907, is the privilege of cultural representation: what deserves to be pictured in oil paint on large canvases?

There is a sense, in many paintings, that Becerra is mocking his own coarseness. The self-portrait *Chach (Half Gone)* reportedly refers to Becerra's nickname; it shows him in a hick cowboy hat and Hawaiian shirt slumped drunkenly over a barrel, a green hosepipe in one hand. The best paintings in the exhibition, such as a diptych titled *Living in the Suburbs can be so Depressing* (all works 2014), are touchingly humane. A large naked woman squats near

two agave plants, lost in thought, and in two puddles, her face and her genitals are reflected back at the viewer. As with the nastier *Strictly for CADDY Lovers*, which features a nude woman standing on a mirror, the undignified self-exposure in these pictures is far from erotic.

The grotesque in art is usually understood as arising from the contravention of borders between the body's insides and outside and, by extension, themes such as sexuality, gender roles or race. But who gets to contravene whose boundaries? *Rex Goliath* depicts a black male Olympia, reclining on a shag rug in nothing but a tiger-print coat and a leopard-print pimp hat, grinning maniacally. As a fantasy or a racial caricature, it is an objectionable image; but it is also so ridiculous and horrible that it is funny. I will not pretend to be offended on anyone else's behalf, but I marvel at the self-granted freedom that allows Becerra to paint a picture that no white artist would dare put his name to. He clearly feels no pressure to self-censor, which is a rare thing today, not just amongst artists.

JONATHAN GRIFFIN

1

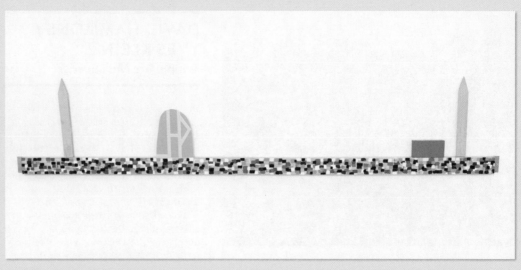

2

CHUCK NANNEY
Jenny's, Los Angeles

Los Angeles: overlooking the dry, late-summer scrub of a lot adjacent to Sunset Boulevard is a nondescript open-air corridor, which leads past a custom sign shop to the back tenants of Suite B. The small, freshly painted studio/office/spare room found here is the recently established gallery, Jenny's, which devoted its second show to a new body of work by American artist Chuck Nanney – his first solo presentation since 2003.

Active in New York and then Paris through the mid-1980s and '90s, Nanney may be best remembered as one of only a handful of male artists included in the 1994 feminist exhibition 'Bad Girls', staged by Marcia Tucker at New York's New Museum. The series of Nanney's photographs included in that show, entitled 'Dress Code' (1994), portray the artist in various poses and positions as dictated by his selection of attire – ranging from the schoolmarm's below-the-knee pleated khaki frock to the trim tailoring of that era's Calvin Klein Collection suit. Nanney's stylish genderbending might well have reflected the limited market for menswear at the time, although the strictly codified differences among his collection of looks casually annotates the cultural identity politics that were then at a height. That the series was accompanied by a cage-like plywood sculpture containing the various outfits modelled by the artist alludes to a more precise act of queering evident in the photographs themselves. In whatever garb, Nanney's long chestnut locks, broad shoulders, unwavering gaze and goatee remain unmistakable: a testament to the unruly boundlessness of socially constructed identity.

This tension between surface and imperfect underlying structure informed a series of Nanney's monochrome paintings on canvas produced around the same time as 'Dress Code'. Made with industrial paints, each of these works is considered by Nanney to be a 'psychologically digested landscape, one perceived peripherally from the perspective of the driver's seat of a car' – an activation of the muddy theatricality of daily life in suburban America, after Tony Smith. Towards the end of the 1990s, Nanney applied unstretched canvases directly to walls or pierced and hung them by means of paper-clip chains, pushpins, staples and binder rings – a nimble, economic method for fastening these swatches to the gallery's clinical contours that also playfully alluded to the sadomasochism of organizational stationery. Yet with titles such as *hot wired heart/appendage* (1999), *reticent infection* (1998) and *colostomy* (1998), the contradiction of depleted bone density and loose flesh that is wasted, though ultimately kept alive by, the scientific introduction of a 'triple cocktail' of AIDS drugs (first made available in 1996) at once comes into sharp focus. (Nanney is HIV positive.)

His pop-savvy installation at Jenny's – a series of painted pine and plywood sculptures – jumped across and along all four walls (and the ceiling) while sensuously attending to, or rhyming with, the room's extruding beams, electrical sockets and cable raceways. The fasteners here are steel brackets and zinc or brass hinges; layered and scraped acrylics are psychedelic in their near-fluorescent hues. Nanney's pastiche of recognizable historical forms is joyously (because anthropometrically) scaled, and also catalogues a certain phallocentric fixation: in the repetition of El Lissitzky's upward-thrusting 'proun' (*multi color composition proun*, *pink corner composition proun* and *phantom composition proun*, all 2014), Constantin Brâncuși's infinite vertical (*truncated endless column viewer*, 2014) and an Anthony Caro-esque splay of nubs and pointed spikes (*telepath*, 2014). This energetic potential is affirmed by the kineticism of works on wheels (*mobile brain in a box*, 2014) or hinges that invite a pinch, push, stroke or other light touch. One might imagine the gentle swinging gesture needed to part the door-like wings of *mobile secret love spell corner* (2014) to be almost prayerful in concentrated motion – a sort of cheeky liberation from such architectonic acts of bunging up as Kazimir Malevich's *Black Quadrilateral*, Carl Andre's copper floor plates or Robert Morris's grey corners.

This encouragement towards the open also resonated through symphonic vibrations collaged together by Nanney from sci-fi film soliloquies, Memphis field recordings and flashes of cut-up poetry or experimental pop that pulse in the airy, ten-hour-long drone accompanying his visual display (*Untitled*, 2003–14). Embedded in the exhibition's restrained sunnyness is a lived, devotional quality – the complex response of a survivor, which rebuffs the entrepreneurial edge of 21st-century wellbeing industries. Because flesh – the 'body parts' examined here – endures despite the holy moral compass of the iPhone and other oracles.

KARI RITTENBACH

3

SARAH CHARLESWORTH
The Art Institute of Chicago

They say that those who survive attempted suicide often recount the overwhelming regret that they experienced the second they jumped – precisely at the point of no going back. Sarah Charlesworth's series 'Stills' (1980/2012), on view for the first time in its entirety at the Art Institute of Chicago, reproduces and magnifies photographs of people – both named and anonymous – attempting to jump to their deaths. Caught between living and dying, the subjects confront that quintessential moment of self-affirmation and self-destruction. We cannot know if there were survivors amongst those depicted; thus we long for a chance to intervene, to reverse time and to reject the documentary function of the photograph. This desire is perhaps especially pertinent considering Charlesworth's passing last year; a well-respected teacher and friend, she imprinted her spirit on the hearts of many. Like Roland Barthes's 'winter garden photograph' – a picture of his mother discussed at length in *Camera Lucida* (1980) – 'Stills' is between this world and the next, an illustration of the photograph's ability to instigate our will to existence and remembrance.

The in-between status of the suspended jump also has parallels in Charlesworth's treatment of her materials: she was among the first artists to print life-size photographs on cheap supports, a direct insult to the prevailing idea of the precious unique print. As a result of Charlesworth's particular process, and demonstrating her love for newspaper and stock photographs, the 'Stills' images fall apart into stacks of horizontals and dots, hovering somewhere between clarity and disintegration. Despite their unsympathetic,

deadpan and tabloid-like appearance, there is nevertheless something beautiful about these appropriated acts of desperation, not only for their balletic associations, but also for the understated formal virtuosity of every print. Each of the 14 stills has its own character because of Charlesworth's careful cropping and tearing, the signs of which she leaves visible. Unlike the people they represent, who are often left unnamed, every print has a distinct personality. Portraying people at the precise moment they have lost all control, the artist's own rigour is asserted, leaving us with a simultaneously critical and intensely emotional image.

These are not didactic images and you would be hard-pressed to find a simple illustration of mass media's callous relationship to human life. Charlesworth instead evokes a transitional psychic space and prompts the question: 'What could they be thinking about right now?'. She attempts to make visible the exact moment in which bodies face the possibility of destruction, translated, in the photographic medium, as the point at which forms disentegrate into lines and dots. As a result, we find ourselves in a world marked by inspiring contrasts – beauty and ugliness, anonymity and identification, bodies and pure forms.

Perhaps longing for the past, for a time when choices could yet be amended, the individuals in 'Stills' come to represent an embodied netherworld – a darkroom wherein bodies constantly emerge and are dispersed. We do not know these figures, but there is nevertheless something perversely brave about their acceptance of the unknown. As Kate Linker noted in the panel discussion that accompanied the opening of the exhibition, Charlesworth's 'toughest, strongest images had a kind of seduction'. She invited her viewers to come with her to the darkest places – darkness and light, after all, are the foundations of photographic practice. This first major museum show of the artist's work since her death is exemplary of her radical charge into the unknown.

WILLIAM J. SIMMONS

1
Alex Becerra
Fresa, 2014, oil on canvas,
1.8 × 1.6 m

2
Chuck Nanney
telepath, 2014, acrylic on plywood
and pine, 36 × 189 × 2 cm

3
Sarah Charlesworth
*Unidentified Man, Ontani Hotel,
Los Angeles*, 1980/2012,
from the series 'Stills', photograph

JIM SHAW
Metro Pictures, New York

Populated by Superman/chicken hybrids and human corn-cobs, comic book characters and candles in the shape of Richard Wagner's effigy, Jim Shaw's latest group of paintings, 'I Only Wanted You to Love Me,' inflate their mix of philistine Pop and highbrow allusion to a grand, sweeping scale. These are hybrid images containing strange physical admixtures and synthesizing various myths, contemporary and ancient. 'YOU ARE ALL WHORES AND BLASPHEMERS' reads the textual screed of *The Flood* (2014), its receding, cartoony letters set off against streaks of water, awash in some modern riff on Biblical wrath. In what might be considered the show's central piece, *The Deluge* (2014), a buff and shirtless Cary Grant whisks Eva Marie Saint to safety in the wake of a stylized wave, which – along with the steam from a tug boat – appears to form part of the damsel's body, metamorphosing in turn into an outsized hand, alighting before an outsized nose carved out of a cliff face.

As even these brief descriptions suggest, Shaw's images appear steeped in an outlandish and droll imagination. A lightning rod of America's proto-punk culture, Shaw has left his mark on everything from assemblage and drawing to conceptual interventions (for instance, his celebrated collection of paintings gathered from second-hand shops, 'Thrift Store Paintings', 2000–ongoing) and covers for imaginary paperback novels. Having invented and developed his own religion, Oism – the principles of which he continues to shape in word and image – Shaw walks a fine, spirited line between empiricism and esotericism, earnestness and irony.

The artist's has worked on an increasingly large scale since 2006. The present paintings continue in that vein. Hung unstretched, these sprawling canvases accommodate an enormous amount of detail, notwithstanding their dimensions; the fine weft of the muslin on which Shaw paints affords detailed applications of acrylic. In several instances (*The Rhinegold's Curse*, 2014, *Judges 19*, 2014, and *The Deluge*, for example), the paintings' backgrounds appear faint, slightly washed-out, while foreground imagery appears crisp and brightly coloured. The effect is almost as if Shaw has painted over banal, saccharine landscapes *à la* Asger Jorn or Enrico Baj. Only his scenes do anything but recoil from kitsch. They elaborate its textures and guilty pleasures with MacDonald's signs and Land O'Lakes iconography. Even his characteristically literary titles offer a decidedly tongue-in-cheek gloss on their imagery; *Wedding of the Ear* (2013), plays upon an anthropomorphized ear of corn, while *Whistle While you Work* (2014) conjures up the theme from Walt Disney's *Snow White* (1937), duly matched by a procession of labouring dwarves.

Garish hues and droll citation often appear alongside more refined, even recondite, allusions. *Wedding of the Ear* crosses The Flash (of comic book fame) with Gothic architecture worthy of some pre-Raphaelite fantasy, while the dwarves that animate the foreground of the three-panelled *The Rhinegold's Curse* effortlessly inhabit Icelandic and Wagnerian epic, alongside mystical runes and a lyre-strumming mermaid.

Trains A Comin' Through (2014), updates St. Sebastian's martyrdom with locomotives rather than arrows, while *Judges 19* (2014), conjures up a gruesome verse from *Genesis* – entailing gang rape and the dismemberment of a concubine – in the form of a supine, fractured female body, with the ground splintering into glimpses of hellfire below.

The disembodied wig perched upon an errant tank, bursting from some ancient near Eastern citadel in *Delilah* (2014) evokes something of René Magritte's Surrealism, in which incongruous objects appear reconciled with aplomb. That Shaw has turned explicitly to Magritte's work in the past (in his painting *Bonne idée,* Good Idea, 1989) comes as no surprise. Yet it is also perhaps in light of 1980s figuration that we might consider Shaw's imagery, its juxtapositions at once absurd and phlegmatic. The Italian 'Anacronisti' painters Stefano Di Stasio and Paola Gandolfi leap to mind, as does David Salle, who similarly layers swathes of imagery in separate planes while managing to link them in a chain of vague association.

Shaw's paintings perform a more seamless conciliation between their objects and spaces, however, as in *Delilah* (which, by the artist's own account, features Farrah Fawcett's famous mane, as it came to him in a vision). Upon closer inspection, in any case, the citadel in the background of the image derives from a latter-day architectural pastiche, as indicated by the signage barely visible at right: 'Citadel Outlet,' from the Samson Tire Factory, a California Art Deco landmark. Not only, then, do seemingly irreconcilable images inhabit the same space, but a near Eastern desert (the site of ongoing American military intervention) is, in fact, revealed to be a landscape much closer to home. Shaw's images repay deeper looking for, as much as their fun-house amusements seem to indulge in mere wit, their figuration conceals various, coy literary insinuations and puns that open onto more serious considerations, from Biblical interpretation to consumer culture to foreign policy.

ARA H. MERJIAN

1

ALLORA & CALZADILLA
Gladstone Gallery, New York

In the 1980s, it was common to speak positively about 'bad painting'. The term was first coined in 1978 by New Museum director Marcia Tucker and later embraced by Albert Oehlen and others who made discourses of quality or rightness visible on canvas, or else instantiated through paint the disappearance of exclusionary aesthetic judgement after decades of Avant-garde prescriptivism. Could we today speak about bad performance or bad installations in a similarly approving way? Jennifer Allora and Guillermo Calzadilla, based in San Juan, Puerto Rico, brought to the American Pavilion of the 2011 Venice Biennale an exhibition that met with a strong critical backlash in some quarters ('angry, sophomoric Conceptualism that borders on the tyrannical', as Roberta Smith of the *New York Times* had it), but it was so openly two-dimensional that you had to start thinking it was intentional. The show featured an ATM hooked up to a church organ (*Algorithm*, 2011): the equation of money and the divine is surely too straightforward? In front of the pavilion was an upturned tank with a working treadmill on top (*Track and Field*, 2011): the equivalence of warfare and athletics is so basic that the ploddingness of the equation must be the point?

For their recent exhibition in New York, 'Fault Lines', the pair filled the gallery with ten massive two-step risers made from a variety of metamorphic and igneous rocks. Throughout the day, pairs of boy sopranos would use the steps in a performance of a 10-minute duet, written by the composer Guarionex Morales-Matos, the lyrics of which consisted entirely of insults. 'Talking to you makes me think that man's descent from the apes hasn't even started yet!' one treble sang. 'You must be the reason for contraception!' trilled the other. The singers were on the cusp of puberty, their voices approaching a breaking point just like the geographical fault lines from which the stones are said to come (according to the press release) – and, hey presto, insults are fault lines too! Surely the obviousness is the beginning and not the end of the matter? Surely?

This is not the first time Allora & Calzadilla have turned to music. In a 2008 work entitled *Stop, Repair, Prepare: Variations on 'Ode to Joy' for a Prepared Piano*, the duo placed a grand piano punctured by a gaping hole in the atrium of New York's Museum of Modern Art and hired performers to step into the gap and play Beethoven from inside the instrument. The hole eliminated two entire octaves from the piano, and the performers had to play the bass notes with their right hand and treble with their left, generating mistake-filled 'variations' on *Ode to Joy* (1823), the anthem of the European Union. *Fault Lines*, like that earlier work, used music not as its own end, but only as a means to enact a collision between two elements in the most crushingly evident way. It is as if the artists read Jasper Johns's dictum to 'take an object, do something to it, do something else to it,' but then resolved always to stop halfway.

2

Artists who seek to create a 'good' performance might see in music a way to subordinate their own totalizing scenarios to chance, or a terrain to explore the possibilities of difference in repetition, or an opportunity to play the force of classical virtuosity against a deskilled art system. Allora & Calzadilla's performances, by contrast, recognized that music – sung by adorable children – is primarily a seduction, creating light entertainment whose obviousness and emptiness is precisely the point.

There is one critical difference between Allora & Calzadilla's 'bad' performance and, say, the bad painting of someone like Oehlen, who quite publicly discussed his ambitions to paint badly. Allora & Calzadilla, on the other hand, have played it straight, speaking about the shallow surface of *Fault Lines* as if it were profound. ('When we found the word "fault lines", it was a moment when we could link geology with speaking,' Calzadilla told the *Wall Street Journal* in September.) It would be safer for the artists to explain ahead of time what they were playing at, but we must assume that their silence about strategically embracing badness is a deviously cunning part of their artistic conceit, a means to incorporate the flatness of art discourse within their intentionally flat exhibition. We really must.

JASON FARAGO

SOPHIA AL-MARIA
Cornerhouse, Manchester

This first major solo show by Qatari-American artist and writer Sophia Al-Maria, curated by Omar Kholeif, sees her working outside the 'Gulf Futurism' context with which she is most commonly identified. This label, coined by Al-Maria and fellow GCC collective member Fatima Al-Qadiri, has lately been adopted to describe work emerging from, and reflecting on, the unique conditions of the Persian Gulf, defined by Al-Maria in her project *Gaze of Sci-Fi Wahabi* (2007–08) as a 'flat desert plateau at the edge of a vast simulacra-sea' which will soon be 'completely immersed'. This year has already seen Al-Qadiri, also a musician and DJ, take a sideways step into Chinese futurist signifiers with her album *Asiatisch*; in this exhibition, Al-Maria in turn moved away from the skyscrapers and supercars of the Gulf and towards the distinctly old-world location of Cairo.

The exhibition centred upon Al-Maria's rape revenge thriller *Beretta*, still unrealized after over three years in the making; the film's arrested development, it seems, is down to artistic differences between Al-Maria and her producers. All the works arranged throughout the gallery space related in some more-or-less clearly defined way to *Beretta*. The most tenuous connection was to the video *Your Sister* (2014), which, with its montage of found online footage of M'alayah dancers, calls to mind Al-Maria's music video for Al-Qadiri's track *How Can I Resist U* (2012).

Taking loose cues from the artist's experiences in Cairo as a student in the early 2000s, the script of *Beretta* pays homage to Abel Ferrera's 1981 exploitation film *Ms. 45*: at the climax, Al Maria's heroine, Suad, embarks on a spree of killings in response to the pervasive sexual harassment she experiences on Cairo's streets. The show included a vitrine of documents related to the film's production, a brace of pre-production trailers (the artist's cut and the producer's cut, both 2014, viewed on separate small monitors with headphones), and the only rushes that were ever shot for the unrealized film compiled into the video work *Slaughter* (2013). A more compelling picture of the details of both *Beretta*'s content and

the reasons behind the project's failure, however, can be gleaned from the book *Virgin With A Memory: The Exhibition Tie-in*, also edited by Kholeif. This brings together script extracts, email exchanges and entries from Al-Maria's diary throughout the relevant period, along with passages from her 'novelization' of the film.

Within these pages we glimpse Al-Maria's frustration at the limitations of the female vigilante genre: 'Aside from *Kill Bill*,' she asks, 'has this been done in a non-exploitative, phallic-replacement, wet-dream way?' *Beretta*, the book makes clear, is intended as an intervention concerning the 'vanishingly rare' presence of women's anger and entitlement to justice in mainstream media culture. It is also envisaged as an activist work, with one of the emails reproduced in *Virgin with a Memory* testifying to Al-Maria's attempts to channel quantities of pre-production funding into the Egyptian anti-harassment intiative HarassMap. The book speaks more of the conflicts between Al-Maria and the antagonist referred to as 'Producer One' than do the various discrepancies between the artist's and producer's trailer cuts, the latter featuring the cringeworthy strapline: 'Meet the baddest ass Egyptian since Cleopatra.' It also offers a generous glimpse at a more ambiguous critical context for *Beretta*, as the 'Gulfie' Al-Maria is occasionally accused of misunderstanding and orientalizing the Egyptian social context. *Slaughter*'s brutal documentary depiction of open-air halal sacrifices could, one senses, be examined in light of this charge.

The Cornerhouse exhibition hinged on the monumental five-channel video installation *The Watchers No. 1–5* (2014), shown on larger-than-lifesize floating screens, each of which frames a predatory, staring male figure (a sixth *Watcher* appears on an LCD screen hung outside the exhibition's entrance). Virtuosically lit, employing strobes and offset colour channels to weird effect, the work fixes you at the centre of its collective gaze, crowding out the other, smaller videos installed in the space. Seemingly based on a proposed nightmare scene from *Beretta*, *The Watchers* renders palpable the threatening atmosphere of highly-charged male attention that is the film's animus. While this exhibition perhaps offered scant consolation for the opportunity to assess *Beretta* as a completed feature-film, it at least stands as an accomplished addition to Al-Maria's body of work.

LUKE HEALEY

3

STUART BRISLEY
Modern Art Oxford

Celebrated as one of Britain's most compelling post-war performance artists, Stuart Brisley had, by the early 1980s, begun to suspect performance's limitations, seeking to expand it by incorporating sculpture, photography, film and painting. At the turn of the millennium, Brisley instituted the Museum of Ordure – ordure: shit, trash, dirt, entropy – to build a collection of scatological objects. Its mission statement: firstly, to examine 'the cultural value of ordure, shit, rubbish' and, secondly, 'the waste of human resources through various ownership, production and management regimes'. 'What is shit for some,' the Museum reminds us, 'has value for others.'

'State of Denmark', a selected survey of Brisley's work, which includes a new, eponymously titled installation, is a collaboration between independent curator David Thorp (Modern Art Oxford's interim director before Paul Hobson) and the Museum of Ordure. The partnership thematizes (and puns on) the relationship between ordure and curating as a form of order and evaluation. Brisley's 2003 novel *Beyond Reason: Ordure*, published by Bookworks, tells the story of the Museum of Ordure's establishment, which is at once a rumination on ordure's intimations. According to the narrator, ordure has its own organic continuum, primitive and humbling. The body's processes of ordure enable life but are also symptomatic of its passage. The body is nourished; shit is flushed away. Bodies age. 'State of Denmark' reflects on the degradation of the ageing performer's body, and the more impersonal forces of history that bear upon it.

The earliest work on display here, *Hille Fellowship Poly Wheel* (1970/2014), was produced by Brisley while contracted, via the Artist Placement Group, to work at the Hille furniture factory at Haverhill in Suffolk. In line with his left-leaning politics, Brisley joined the shop floor, befriending workers in the metal-polishing room – a method Claire Bishop has suggested anticipated many subsequent approaches to site-specific art. Brisley painted the polishing machinery in the colours of the workers' football teams and introduced mobile noticeboards by means of which colleagues could communicate openly with one another. Finally, he produced *Poly Wheel*, a four-metre-diametre sculpture consisting of 212 Robin Day chair bases stacked to form a closed circular structure. Originally displayed vertically for a temporary period outside the factory, for Brisley *Poly Wheel* symbolized closed labour, work without end. At MAO – toppled, laid horizontally, abstracted from its original site – it had a commanding sculptural presence in the upper gallery. The date '1970/2014' bequests the work to today, making it a live proposal and an ambiguous symbol for the workforce for our times. Brisley's work at Hille, he believed, confused his identity as an artist, shifting him away from art 'more into a kind of potentially collective situation'.

Artist Project Peterlee/History Within Living Memory 1976–1977, displayed in the middle galleries, represents an early attempt to expand performance into the social through a continuous engagement with the everyday. With Peterlee inhabitants, who populated the new town from surrounding mining communities, Brisley built an archive of historical photographs and oral testimony over a period of 18 months. The intention was to create a sense of shared working-class identity that would cohere a community and nurture agency and participation amongst its members. It is impossible to know the legacy of Brisley's activities – allegedly the project was curtailed because it was considered too radical – but a digitized archive is now preserved at the Durham County Record Office. At MAO the bureaucratic display of these type-written documents and photographs in vitrines – an 'aesthetic of administration' – is somehow antithetical to the dynamic aspirations of the project. Nevertheless, it remains fascinating for its relation to pioneers of post-war oral history, in particular George Ewart Evans and subsequent archival artistic practices.

By *Poly Wheel* in the upper gallery was the exhibition's titular piece, *State of Denmark*. An iron crown was suspended above a partially clad lumber structure of perpendicular joining walls on a low platform. Each wall was partially covered by removable panels, one side demarcated as open/republican, the other closed/monarchic. Inside was a portrait of a boy prince, apparently caught between these two contradictory systems of governance. Yet the simplistic oppositions set up by the installation seem deceptive: if the structure is open and moveable, might it not also be reconstructed, reconsolidated?

In the basement was undoubtedly the highlight of this exhibition: a four-hour loop of Brisley's films, including *Incidents in Transit* (1992–2014), *Black Red and White* (1997–2009) and his remarkable collaboration with Ken McMullen on the preindustrial origins of performance, titled *Being and Doing* (1984). Many of these durational pieces, including *10 Days* (1978) and *Before The Mast* (2013) are utterly beguiling, foregrounding the body, Brisley's enduring medium. It gives us what is strangely absent upstairs: a harrowing sense of the corporeal. In both of these films, two obdurate concerns of ordure arise: the body's shit and the body's entropy. In the former, Brisley starves himself for ten days; in the latter, Brisley is an elderly man, rolling in waste.

JONATHAN P. WATTS

2

1

JACK BILBO
David Zwirner Gallery, London

Greeting you at the door of this modest, courageously strange and heartening exhibition of Jack Bilbo's drawings, illustrations and paintings was a self-portrait of the artist from 1948. Like an emissary for all the curious creatures to come, Bilbo appears as a spooky faun, bearded and cheerful as a vagabond from a folktale but a far more girlish proposition than he might first appear: magpie eyes circled by starlet lashes and matched with the dark mouth of a young witch. This was but one of the transformations to be seen, with Bilbo elsewhere assuming such forms as a hulking sea-monster with a beard of weeds, a furious captain stuck on a storm-tossed ship and a dopey, blushing devil.

How this shape-shifting artist has stayed hidden for so long is baffling, not least because the chequered tale of his life should have assured him a certain shadowy reputation, even if his work were half as brave and crazed as it is. A fearsome autodidact and wild storyteller who cultivated a rich personal mythology, Bilbo was born under the name Hugo Baruch into a German Jewish family of renowned theatrical costumiers in 1907. (Sinister masks are everywhere in his work and seem to have remained a lifelong fascination.) Fleeing to Spain upon Hitler's ascent to power in 1933, he became a legendarily intemperate publican, subsequently high-tailing it for New York where he supposedly served as Al Capone's henchman before drifting to Britain and starting to paint and sculpt. Following a spell of internment as an 'enemy alien' on the Isle of Man during World War II, he reached London, exhibiting Pablo Picasso and Kurt Schwitters at the gallery he founded during the darkest years of World War II. He carved looming concrete mermaids in the wilderness surrounding his Surrey home, then returned to Berlin where he died in 1967.

Only in the small assortment of his paintings, such as *Island of Rainbow Light* (1944), where things turn Technicolor, kitsch and clumsy is there any sense of his manic energies slackening. Whatever his medium, he maintained what mock psychoanalysis would call a serious 'thing' – a shameless fetish – for the electric unruliness of human hair. It grows over everything in a frenzy of ink or pencil scratches – including the moon, which appears crooked and cool, its surface etched with the drowsy face of a silent film minx, in the sketch *Moon Flapper*. (Like much else on show, this piece is undated, but it presumably emerged from Bilbo's prolific output of the 1940s.) The fact that this fuzzy compulsion isn't his work's most peculiar feature is a testament to its heroic eccentricity.

His freakish daydream *Woman Expecting Triplets Returning Home From The Cinema* (c. 1948) contains the leering faces of conjoined twins, mangled Constructivist graphics, an erumpent breast and what might be a debonair salamander playing a piano, which distends into a trumpet and concludes as a collection of pulsating radio waves. Every frantic little page brims with disquieting excitement, suggesting some apocalyptic version of the crowded cabin sketch from the Marx Brothers' comedy *A Night at the Opera* (1935). Some of them show unreadable symbols dancing around the heads of lost girls from 19th-century fairytale illustrations, others reveal animals hiding in scribbled undergrowth or looking skywards to find plump erotic apparitions. (Few artists are as happily perverted as Bilbo – even his trees are ribald.) Captions explain these cryptic contents with sly one-liners or degenerate into screeds concealing rage in caustic irony: *The Hangman is a Respectable Citizen ...*

Bilbo's spleen against capitalist society courses through plenty of these scenes, though they're not as obviously war-haunted as you might think, scrolling out the vision of a more mysterious and dreamily allegorical combat against state repression with a cast of orphans, cackling, rubber-nosed men and a mighty lion, its paws exchanged for horse hooves.

The exhibition smartly rejected the urge to cast Bilbo as a 'lost' outsider artist, capturing instead how canny and versatile he was. But something about Bilbo conspires to resist even the delirious sweep of his biography – a *sui generis* loner, he often seems to have climbed out of a murky region of his own imagination, emerging as equal parts seafaring rascal and wild-eyed visionary, a man animated by innermost obsessions who filled his work with anarchic life. He belongs in the company of figures like Leonora Carrington and Unica Zürn, enigmatic misfits who maintained a similar belief in drawing as the medium for a private mission, a route into (out of?) the deepest recesses of the mind, which is at once playful and macabre, thorny and haunting. His return should be celebrated with all the wicked glee of the works themselves.

CHARLIE FOX

3

OREET ASHERY
Waterside Contemporary, London

At the back of an anonymous garden, a woman lies on a pile of planks, silver foil on her feet and hands, an apple stuffed in her mouth, the hand of a man with prehistoric features resting proprietorially on her shoulder. A voice-over commences in reassuringly patrician tone: 'Anybody can own a pig.' Over the few minutes of Oreet Ashery's *How to Kill a Pig* (2013–14), an expanding pink and red vortex is imposed over the figures, digitally mincing them. The language of the voice-over – which summarises the artist's research into the legal conditions for sacrificing a pig during a performance – strays from bureaucratic specificity towards a more nameless menace. 'Once your pig is dead, you can do what you want with it.' At Waterside Contemporary, the video screen was suspended from ropes, to be watched from a narrow fabric *Womb Hammock* (2014); beside it, a plaster cast of a pig is wedged mid-air in a crevice, weightless but constrained. Across the gallery, a large black and white print of an image pulled from Google curled into a standing cone depicts a person cuffed into a 'hog-tie': variously used for handling livestock, torture and sexual fetish.

Sex lingers in this show like a bad aftertaste. A seemingly banal photograph, *Untitled (Lollipop)* (2014), of a man's lips puckering around a multi-coloured ice-lolly hangs adjacent to one documenting a 'tea-bagging' from Ashery's performance series 'Party for Freedom' (2013–ongoing). Sturtevant once described pornography as having a 'funny-fun' quality. Ashery seems judiciously suspicious of fun – here, as in previous works, she explores the ambivalent values of

gratification, release, license. ('Party for Freedom' borrowed its title from that of anti-Islamic Dutch politician Geert Wilder's Partij voor de Vrijheid.) The voice-over of *How to Kill a Pig* reports that an animal cannot be privately slaughtered in a state of undue stress, pain or excitement. If excitement, then, is a kind of cruelty, where does that leave the liberatory potential of pleasure? The title of one work on show – *The World Doesn't Have to Be How You Want It To Be* – offers a blunt answer.

Whilst the exhibition hints at what Carol J. Adams's 1990 book called *The Sexual Politics of Meat*, Ashery's primary interest in livestock is as a broader metaphor for stigmatized social groups. Such communities were directly addressed by a grouping of ten sculptural assemblages, 'The Un/Clean' series (2014), which dominated the space. Constructed from cleaning materials, a typical work consisted of a metal mop stood atop a bucket, rolls of blue, industrial kitchen-roll piled up for a head, dressed in a kind of poncho made from orange toxic waste disposal bags and a necklace of rubber gloves. The costumes had been made and worn by members of Freedom from Torture, UK Lesbian & Gay Immigration Group and the charity Portugal Prints whilst participating in Ashery's previous performances, including *The World is Flooding* (2014) at Tate Modern in July – a frenetic musical adaptation of Vladimir Mayakovsky's *Mystery-Bouffe* (1918–21) describing the struggle for dominance of groups of Clean and Unclean after a flood. A certain shift of energy is sometimes unavoidable in the transition from theatrics to objects (the poncho draped mops almost resembled puppets, waiting to be played with) and without the supporting narrative of the Tate performance 'The Un/Clean' series appears more simply as a carnival of corporate cleaners. Nevertheless, the figure of the cleaner – low-paid, low-visibility, frequently migrant and implicated in the symbolic exchange between purity and danger – is an effective stand-in for Ashery's sometime collaborators.

Conceptually, then, a pretty neat trope. But these works possessed a visual neatness too, which did little to convey viscerally the experience of the labour of cleaning, let alone the experience of social degradation or exclusion. The press release's insistence (via Mayakovsky) that 'The Unclean Are Rising Again! They Exist!' was hard to square with the sterile prettiness of the pastel dust cloths, glittering metallic pan scourers, gleaming chrome handles and pristine patterned J-cloths.

What seemd at first like a misstep came to look, however, like an intentional wrong-footing; the astringent quality of the harshly lit installation and its odd lack of mess a rebuff to a lazy cliché of what art made about and by 'The Un/Clean' should look like. Maybe it is impossible to fully appraise these works beyond the meaning they hold to Ashery's collaborators – no less urgent, I suppose, for not being obviously accessible to the outside viewer. Another video, *Winking Series I* (2014), installed discreetly in the surface of a plinth, documented Ashery's collaborators winking in succession at the camera, communicating their mutual identification within a bonded group. At a push, we're all animals with a language: this show was a reminder that, even so, we don't all always necessarily speak the same one.

MATTHEW MCLEAN

1
Stuart Brisley
Before the Mast, 10 day performance,
2013, ten photographs, each
38 × 38 cm

2
Jack Bilbo
Woman Expecting Triplets Returning Home from the Cinema, c. 1948, ink on paper, 36 × 25 cm

3
Oreet Ashery, 'Animal with a Language', 2014, installation view

LISA BRICE
French Riviera, London

The proverb 'cut your coat according to your cloth' is a reminder of the need for humility – to make what you can with the means at hand. It seems apt that the saying was partially appropriated as the title of South African artist Lisa Brice's solo show at French Riviera, her first in the UK, though her work has been exhibited widely across Europe and South Africa for a number of years. The installation was simply threaded together, modest in its materials and the domestic focus of the works, which were hung, draped and pinned to the walls and window of the pocket-sized shop floor that houses the artist-run space.

'Cut Your Coat' comprises eight works on paper that take as their preface the space's former identity as a poodle grooming parlour in the 1970s. On the threshold of the gallery, hovering in its window, the inky outlines of four women (all works *Untitled*, 2014) as primly coifed as their poodles, are positioned as bystanders to microcosms of drama unfolding within the paintings inside. Brice's protagonists are all women – with the exception of the poodles, the star of which is surely a majestic snow-white specimen, poised regally mid-groom in the show's most prominent work. Variants of the same scene, each work opens a portal to the female universe of familiar objects and everyday rituals, steeped in the quiet hush of shared intimacy. Cobalt blue inks trace the forms of a mother kneeling with baby; black Toulouse-Lautrec-like silhouettes of legs slipped into hosiery; a snipped curl of poodle coat.

In spite of the assured draughtsmanship that underpins Brice's *oeuvre*, the artist repeatedly returns to familiar motifs and poses. Take, for example, a pair of ink-on-paper drawings tacked alongside one another to the right of the space, forming a kind of before and after. The before: a drawing, light in touch, that sketches the rough details of a room in which a girl stands before a mirror. The after: another female figure, who seems to float in space, glimpsing her solitude in a mirror, which is all that remains to suggest the domestic interior. In their style and illustrative quality, the drawings have the almost cinematic air of the storyboard. However, there are other influences at play. The flash of a torso in a mirror, a passageway of light that tilts our imagination to the outer reaches of the scene and a dog that has sneaked under a table recall the late paintings of Pierre Bonnard, which were almost exclusively devoted to the interiors of his home – domestic reveries, which resonate in the painterly conversations that Brice imagines in response to the former shop space.

It would be fair to say that Brice's approach to painting since her early days in South Africa (she has now settled in London after a brief interlude in Trinidad) has been restless; tossing and turning between the figurative and abstract, or otherwise segueing between the two. A case in hand is the artist's 2013 monochromatic paintings in which a single motif of a lone figure draped across a bed is repeated, becoming increasingly shrouded in a reverie of masking brushstrokes, as Brice gradually relinquishes the sturdier marks of inks, oils and acrylics to the pallid wash of *Reclining Figure (White and Pink)*, in which the person's outline is replaced by a cloud of pale colour, hanging isolated in a sky of thin light.

In his text accompanying exhibition, writer Sean O'Toole draws on Nikolai Gogol's 1842 short story *The Overcoat*, about a reclusive St Petersburg copy clerk who scrimps and saves to own a new coat. The reference gets to the heart of Brice's show: the antiquated nature of its title; the bygone days of dressmaking; a domesticity void of laptops, TVs or iPhones. Lingering at French Riviera was the subdued resonance of past tenants, made tangible by the artist's indelible lines and fleetingly caught silhouettes.

JOSEPHINE NEW

1
Lisa Brice
'Cut Your Coat', 2014,
installation view

2
Michele Abeles
Watches #85, 2014, archival pigment
print, 110 × 74 cm

3
Ed Fornieles
'Modern Family', 2014,
installation view

MICHELE ABELES
Sadie Coles HQ, London

In the airy street-level space of Sadie Coles HQ in Mayfair, a few steps south of Mount Street, London's HQ of luxury fashion, adornments dangled conspicuously from closely cropped fragments of women's tanned, toned bodies. Watches glistened, diamonds sparkled and shampoo-commercial-quality manes shone. Manicured fingers dripping with glossy candy colours gripped shopping bags and iPhones, rays of sun glinting dramatically off every surface. The proximity of the gallery to the purveyors and patrons of haute couture is unlikely to have eluded the American artist Michele Abeles, whose photographs chronicle the urban catwalk of upmarket shoppers.

Abeles – probably best known for her Pop-ish collaged still lives featuring the male nude, which were included in MoMA's 2012 'New Photography' exhibition – here pitches slick production values against the tense energy of a moving metropolis. One of three new series of work on view in her first solo show with Sadie Coles, 'Watches' (2014) alludes, variously, to the expensive timepieces pictured, to the kind of astute, even obsessive, looking that went into their making and to an internal alertness to being observed that casts a darker note over otherwise bright pictures. Though they share something of the aesthetic of the earlier collage constructions – flattened layers, geometric forms of vivid patterns and colours, frenetic energy – they also have a sense of arrested time. If these images were moving, they'd be moving in the seductive slow motion of advertising, the kind that allows a fantasy of perfection to float through the outstretched moment. In these anonymous, mostly headless shots, clothes and accessories are our only clues to the identities and realities of the women they decorate. Like uniforms, or perhaps armour, these are all they have to distinguish themselves for, or deflect from, the constant audiences of the street.

Each photograph is subtly compounded by the backdrop that frames it – a generic computer-generated motif of watery grey dots in a nondescript swirl, incongruously cheap and banal. This type of impervious digitally rendered imagery moves from background to foreground in a second series of works in the downstairs gallery, where human presence, light and colour are overridden by technological order. Here, large scale and slightly out of focus black and white grids stand in for the motifs of figure or object, like giant, useless versions of the QR codes we're increasingly implored to zap with our smartphones. To make these (all titled *B&W*, 2014), Abeles collaborated with her brother, a military engineer, to process a photograph through an algorithm and then find visual form for the mathematical operations. In some, colour transparencies cling precariously to the edges, messy reminders of their origins. But the mystification of the original source material and the complicated technique makes them as frustrating as they are compelling.

2

Another play on forms of visual information is taken up in *Jungle* (2014), a series of images hung as an installation in the gallery's project space around the corner. Here, photographs of dense foliage, all cropped from a single found stock image, are overlaid with strategically positioned lines of industrial white bathroom tiles, like fragments of code or redactions. The tiles directly reference Marcel Broodthaers's homage to Stéphane Mallarmé, *Un coup de dés jamais n'abolira le hazard (a throw of the dice will never abolish chance)* (1969), in which lines of the eponymous 1897 poem were blocked out with black bars. These are the heaviest and most obtuse of the works on view, though perhaps purposefully so. The scenes of lush green seem to offer an escape beyond reach, half bricked-over by layers of signification – art-historical, economic, technological – that we can't quite grasp.

The title of the exhibition, 'Find Out What Happens When People Start Getting Real', is a reference to a less erudite cultural creation: the long-running MTV reality show, 'The Real World'. And the construction of reality through the codes of images is the binding theme of the show. Abeles's well-known stunt – sending a famous actress-model in her stead to an arts awards ceremony – still confuses the link between the artist's own image and identity; an online search yields photographs of her stand-in, years after the event. Abeles's work similarly scrutinizes the ways in which photographic conventions conform to, or confound, the sense of the real we perpetually contrive. The act of deciphering who we are and what we know through the complicated codes of visual cues – through images we make, consume or project – is increasingly difficult. As Abeles playfully reminds us: images are slippery things.

SARA KNELMAN

ED FORNIELES
Chisenhale Gallery, London

The work of the young London and L.A.-based artist Ed Fornieles explores the interpenetration of URL and IRL in a socially networked world. His performances, staged events and 'Facebook sitcoms' enthusiastically embrace the dissembling aspects of online identity-management – selfies, avatars, twitterbots, Gchat melodrama – and walk a fine line between art-world satire and blatant self-promotion. In *New York New York Happy Happy (NY NY HP HP)* (2013), staged at the New Museum in New York, he orchestrated a semi-fictional charity gala in aid of the online journal *Rhizome,* which operated as a psychological version of fancy dress: rather than wear costumes, guests were invited to adopt new egos. The ambiguous extroversion of such performances, where fake people are encouraged to have authentic encounters, is thematic to Fornieles's work as a whole.

In 'Modern Family' at Chisenhale Gallery, the artist attempted to map and measure the ways in which the internet has infiltrated the family, both as a unit of bourgeois societal stability and as a pop-cultural trope. Rather than present his subject in its traditional and more complex guise, as the Freudian location of sexual trauma, Fornieles was interested in the flat-pack family peddled by mainstream American TV: affluent yet anodyne, 'wholesome' and white – a blatant ideological vehicle and an easy target for satire.

The installation was arranged like a suburban L.A. garden. A few scattered sheets of AstroTurf hinted at a lawn, while an ash-filled barbecue and a long picnic table, littered with bread rolls and hay, implied a recent cookout. The artist's use of breakfast cereal made a familiar comparison between mass culture and junk food, while over-earnest mottoes ('WE ARE ONE'; 'BE YOURSELF') suggests that the old paradox of growing up – craving individuality while aching for acceptance – persists in the second families we find online. Crammed with large sculptural works – from a dancing Lego-like man, an oversize pair of brown trousers and a Pop art apple – the room felt closer to a motley assemblage of isolated works than a convincing installation.

A series of flatscreen monitors mounted on the gallery walls displayed shifting collages of jpegs and gifs, extracted in real-time from the 'back end' of various websites. Sushi, stock photography and hardcore pornography were recurring motifs – the data trails and search criteria left behind by Fornieles's 'family members'. Rather than re-frame or actively criticize, these hypnotically vapid works reiterated online culture as it already exists – an endless procession of ephemeral readymades – without attempting new forms of reception and exchange that might interrogate that image economy.

Theatrical lighting, DIY surfaces and a booming soundtrack provided 'Modern Family' with an array of sensory textures, but it was strangely bereft of affect. Fornieles is avowedly more inspired by sitcoms than art history, yet his installation suffered from

comparison to earlier family-focused works. Paul McCarthy's videos *Family Tyranny* and *Cultural Soup* (both 1987), for example, marshal extraordinary levels of symbolic violence (like forcing mayonnaise down the 'mouth' of a polystyrene ball) to dramatize the malignant psychosexual forces that families can incubate. '[America is] where everything emanates from,' Fornieles remarked about 'Modern Family' in a recent interview. 'Everything' might have included the work of the country's iconoclastic artists, many of whom addressed the same subject decades ago.

But 'Modern Family' was more concerned with striking poses than exploring deeper histories. A performer was present at the exhibition, 'activating' its various zones with somnambulistic understatement. As Marshal McLuhan observed in his prescient book *Understanding Media* (1964), narcissism has a numbing effect, and can turn us into the 'servomechanism of [our] own extended or repeated image'. Placing both hands on the barbecue, the performer stared into its ashy depths, like Narcissus into his lake, as if drugged by the surfeit of information surrounding her.

Social networks comprise their users, yet the profit-focused corporations that facilitate those interactions tend to operate with a shadowy disregard for the ethical boundaries of privacy. Over the course of 2012, Facebook manipulated users' news feeds (without their consent) to track the changes in their emotional state; in August the following year, in the wake of Edward Snowden's leaks, researchers at the University of Michigan found that 'Facebook use predicts declines in subjective well-being in young adults'. 'Modern Family' captured a sense of the numbing effects of online life, but it failed (or refused) to mount a convincing critique of that increasingly sinister status quo, in which users of social media unwittingly become workers on the factory floor of the information economy.

PATRICK LANGLEY

3